Engraved by John Sartain, Phil.ª

FRANCIS ASBURY,

SECOND BISHOP OF THE METHODIST EPISCOPAL CHURCH IN AMERICA.

ENGRAVED EXPRESSLY FOR THE 'HISTORY OF METHODISM IN KENTUCKY' FROM AN [illegible]
PAINTING PRESENTED BY THE LATE BISHOP SOULE, TO THE [illegible]

THE HISTORY

OF

METHODISM IN KENTUCKY.

BY THE REV. A. H. REDFORD, D.D.

VOLUME I.

FROM THE LANDING OF JAMES M'BRIDE IN THE DISTRICT, IN 1754, TO THE CONFERENCE OF 1808.

Nashville, Tenn.:
SOUTHERN METHODIST PUBLISHING HOUSE.
1870.

STEREOTYPED AT THE SOUTHERN METHODIST PUBLISHING HOUSE,
NASHVILLE, TENNESSEE.

TO THE

MEMBERS AND FRIENDS

OF THE

Methodist Episcopal Church, South, in Kentucky,

THIS HISTORY

IS RESPECTFULLY DEDICATED BY

The Author.

CONTENTS.

CHAPTER I.

FROM THE SETTLEMENT OF KENTUCKY TO THE CONFERENCE OF 1787.

CHAPTER II.

FROM THE CONFERENCE OF 1787 TO THE CONFERENCE OF 1789.

CHAPTER III.

FROM THE CONFERENCE OF 1789 TO THE CONFERENCE OF 1790.

CHAPTER IV.

FROM THE FIRST CONFERENCE HELD IN KENTUCKY, IN 1790, TO THE CONFERENCE OF 1792.

CHAPTER V.

FROM THE CONFERENCE OF 1792 TO THE CONFERENCE OF 1793.

CHAPTER VI.

FROM THE CONFERENCE OF 1793 TO THE CONFERENCE OF 1794.

CHAPTER VII.

FROM THE CONFERENCE OF 1794 TO THE CONFERENCE OF 1796.

CHAPTER VIII.

FROM THE CONFERENCE OF 1796 TO THE CONFERENCE OF 1797.

CHAPTER IX.

FROM THE CONFERENCE OF 1797 TO THE CONFERENCE OF 1799.

CHAPTER X.

FROM THE CONFERENCE OF 1799 TO THE CONFERENCE HELD IN APRIL, 1800.

CHAPTER XI.

FROM THE CONFERENCE OF 1800, HELD AT DUNWORTH, ON HOLSTON, ON THE FIRST FRIDAY IN APRIL, TO THE CONFERENCE HELD AT BETHEL ACADEMY, KENTUCKY, COMMENCING ON THE SIXTH DAY OF THE FOLLOWING OCTOBER.

CHAPTER XII.

FROM THE CONFERENCE HELD AT BETHEL ACADEMY, OCTOBER 6, 1800, TO THE CONFERENCE OF 1801.

CHAPTER XIII.

FROM THE CONFERENCE OF 1801 TO THE CONFERENCE OF 1803.

CHAPTER XIV.

FROM THE CONFERENCE OF 1803 TO THE CONFERENCE OF 1808.

PREFACE.

THE History of Methodism in Kentucky cannot be otherwise than interesting, if faithfully delineated. Organized in the District when there was scarcely a cabin outside of the forts in all its broad domain—its standard-bearers exposed to privations, sufferings, and dangers, the recital of which seem more like romantic stories, selected from the legends of fable, than the sober realities of history—planted and nourished amid opposition and difficulties that brave hearts only could surmount, the extraordinary success that has attended it, growing up in eighty years from a single society of only a few members to a membership of nearly fifty thousand, with more than five hundred ministers, (traveling and local,) church-edifices in every community, schools and seminaries of learning in different portions of the State — its truths proclaimed in every neighborhood, and its vital energies and hallowed influence imparting life to other Christian communions, it is invested with an importance at once attractive and commanding. While the rich have sought its temples, and worshiped at its altars, its peculiar glory has been that it searched for the poor, and carried the tidings of a Redeemer's love to the homes of sorrow and of want.

Not seeking controversies with other denominations of Christians, but desirous to live on terms of amity and in Christian fellowship with all who love the Lord Jesus, its ministers have everywhere preached the doctrines of the Bible, as contained in our Articles of Religion; while they have not at any time shrunk from the vindication of its teachings and truths, by whomsoever assailed.

Anxious for the success of Christianity, and the extension of the Redeemer's kingdom, it cheerfully bids God speed to all who love the Saviour, and rejoices in the prosperity of Zion, whether in its own or in other branches of the Church of Christ.

The biographical sketches to be found in these pages are simply sketches. They claim to be nothing more. The limits of our work, when we take into consideration the number of the ministers who have occupied this field, and have been called "from labor to reward," forbid our indulging in detailed historical narrative. In many instances we desired to give more lengthened accounts of the lives and labors of the noble men who laid the foundations of Methodism in these western wilds, but we dared not gratify our own wishes. We have allowed all the space which might be considered expedient.

We regret that in many instances our information has been so meager. To ascertain all that we could, we have spared neither pains, expense, nor labor, in our efforts to become possessed of all the information to be obtained. We have searched the records of the Church, and availed ourselves of a close and faithful examination of the General Minutes, the Methodist Magazine, Quarterly Reviews, and the weekly journals of the Church, together with several volumes of Church-history, biographical sketches, autobiographies, unpublished manuscripts of pioneer preachers, and extensive private correspondence, that we might elicit every thing yet remaining that connects the present with the past.

That many facts, incidents, and matters of importance, in reference to Methodism in Kentucky, are lost to us for ever, we cannot doubt. Many of the most reliable sources of information are closed. Only one of the noble men identified with the fortunes of the Church in Kentucky, previous to the period at which this volume closes, yet remains. Bending beneath the weight of eighty-three years, he is still able to preach the gospel. We are, however, happy to believe that much may hereafter be discovered, that may invest a future edition with greater interest.

It has been for many years our anxious desire that some one would rescue from oblivion the names and the memories of the pioneer preachers of Kentucky, and place their lives and labors in a permanent and enduring form. The fact that no one else has accepted the task, is our apology for having undertaken it. For several years we have been collecting materials for this work, and amid the arduous duties of the Book Agency, we have prepared this volume for the press, and now submit it to the members of the Methodist Church.

If in these pages we have contributed any thing toward the advancement of religious truth—if in recounting the difficulties under which Methodism was planted in Kentucky, its principles shall be rendered dearer to the Church — and if we have recovered the memory of any of those worthies to whom, under God, we are so greatly indebted for the rich inheritance they have bequeathed us, we shall feel that our labor has not been in vain.

A. H. REDFORD.

NASHVILLE, TENN., May 1, 1868.

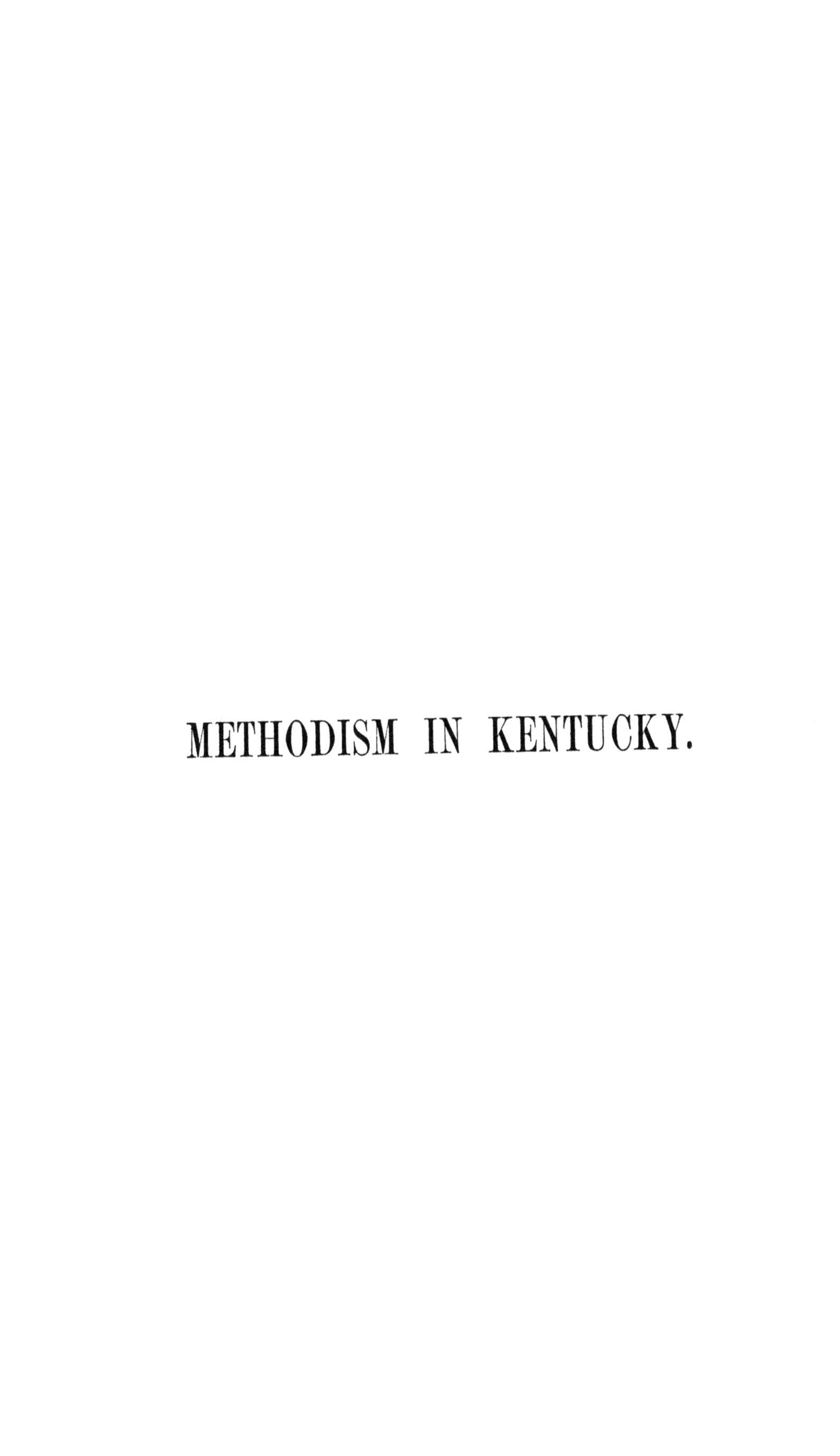

METHODISM IN KENTUCKY.

HISTORY

OF

METHODISM IN KENTUCKY.

CHAPTER I.

FROM THE SETTLEMENT OF KENTUCKY TO THE CONFERENCE OF 1787.

Daniel Boone—James McBride—Dr. Walker—John Finley—The early emigrants—Kentucky formed into a county—Indian cruelties—James Haw, Benjamin Ogden, the first Methodist missionaries to Kentucky—William Hickman—James Smith—Elijah, Lewis, and Joseph Craig—Tanner—Bailey—Bledsoe—Baptist Church organized—The Presbyterian Church—David Rice—Blythe—Lyle—Welch—McNamar—Stone—Reynolds—Stewart—First Presbytery formed—Bishop Asbury—Benjamin Ogden, a revolutionary soldier—Francis Clark—William J. Thompson—Nathanael Harris—Gabriel and Daniel Woodfield—Philip Taylor—Joseph Ferguson—Methodism planted in Kentucky by Francis Clark, a local preacher—John Durham—Thomas Stevenson—Mrs. Sarah Stevenson—The character of the early preachers—Mrs. Jane Stamper.

THE early history of Kentucky presents a record of savage cruelties, of extreme suffering, and of heroic endurance. The name of Daniel Boone, the first white settler who sought a home amid its dark and almost impenetrable forests, and whose dust now slumbers beneath its soil, will always be held in kind remembrance. The first discovery of Kentucky, however, was made by James McBride, who as early as 1754 "passed down the Ohio River, with some others, in canoes, landed at the mouth of the Kentucky River, and marked the initials of his name and date upon a tree."* Four years later, Dr. Walker, led by curiosity, or by the spirit of adventure, made a brief trip to the north-eastern portion of the District.† Nine years afterward, and only two years previous to the date of Boone's first entrance into Kentucky, John Finley, with some other Indian-traders from North Carolina, made a considerable tour through it.‡ The stay, however, of McBride, Walker, and Finley, was short, and to Daniel Boone belongs the honor of being the first pioneer.

The first emigrants to the District of Kentucky were chiefly composed of men who were "rough, independent, and simple in their habits, careless and improvident in their dealings, frank of speech, and unguarded in their intercourse with each other and with strangers, friendly, hospitable, and generous." Deprived of educational advantages, they were generally their own school-masters, and their book the volume of nature. It was not the dull, the unaspiring, the idle, but the bold, the resolute,

---

* Methodist Magazine, Vol. III., p. 386.

† Collins's Kentucky, p. 18.

‡ Methodist Magazine, Vol. III., p. 386.

the ambitious, who came to carve out their homes from the kingly forests of the fresh and untouched wilderness.

The settlement of Kentucky by the Anglo-American pioneer was no easy task. The fierce and merciless savage stubbornly disputed the right to the soil. The attempt to locate upon these rich and fertile lands was a proclamation of war—of war whose conflict should be more cruel than had been known in all the bloody pages of the past. On his captive the Indian inflicted the most relentless torture. Neither the innocence of infancy, the tears of beauty, nor the decrepitude of age, could awaken his sympathy or touch his heart. The tomahawk and the stake were the instruments of his cruelty. But notwithstanding the dangers that constantly imperiled the settlers, attracted by the glowing accounts of the beauty of the country and the fertility of the soil, brave hearts were found that were willing to leave their patrimonial homes in Carolina and Virginia, and hazard their lives amid the frowning forests of the West. Thus valuable accessions were continually received by the first emigrants.

In the winter of 1776, Kentucky was formed into a county. Although this act invested the people with the right to a separate county court, to justices of the peace, a sheriff, constable, coroner, and militia officers, but few instances occurred in which it was necessary for the law to assert its supremacy. Banded together by the ties of a common interest, and alike exposed to suffering and to peril, it was but seldom that any disposition was evinced to encroach upon the rights of another. For mutual comfort, as well as for mutual protection, the people dwelt principally in forts, by which means they were the better prepared for a defense from the frequent attacks of the Indians.

It would be impossible to describe the sufferings of the first settlers in Kentucky—they are beyond description; yet we may imagine the anguish of heart endured by the husband and father, whose wife and children had become a prey to savage vigilance and cruelty, or to the tortures, worse than death, inflicted upon the Indian's helpless captive; or we may attempt to realize the grief, whose deepest shades had fallen upon the breaking heart of the wife and mother, as the shadows of the evening gather around her lonely home, and she listens in vain for the familiar footstep of him on whose strong arm she had trusted for protection, or for the return of those little ones that had been the light of her home and the joy of her heart. Words cannot express, nor mind can scarce conceive, the pain that hardy race endured. A lifetime of suffering is sometimes crowded into a single hour. It was so with them. The hostility of the Indian never slumbered; and during this period, capture, torture, and death inflicted in the most cruel manner that savage malignity could invent, were of common occurrence. On one hand were instances of shocking barbarities; and on the other of long captivities, of untold sufferings, of deeds of daring, and of heroic achievements, which seem more like romance than reality. These noble men, so patient under all the pangs of war, and want, and wretchedness, were the benefactors of the West; and though no marble pillar may mark the spot where many of them rest, yet they live embalmed in the affections of a grateful people—a monument far more enduring.

It was during this period and amid these dangers that James Haw and Benjamin Ogden were appointed missionaries to the District of Kentucky. Previous to this time Methodism had been established in the States of New York, New Jersey, Pennsylvania, Maryland, Virginia, North Carolina, and in portions of South Carolina and Georgia; but up to this date the General Minutes report no Church under its auspices in Kentucky. Baptist ministers were the first to proclaim the truths of Christianity here. As early as 1776, the Rev. William Hickman, a man of piety, came from Virginia on a tour of observation, and during his stay devoted much of his time to preaching the gospel. He was perhaps the first preacher of any denomination who lifted the standard of the cross on "the dark and bloody ground." Other Baptist ministers soon followed, among whom were James Smith, Elijah, Lewis, and Joseph Craig, and Messrs. Tanner, Bailey, and Bledsoe. The Baptist Church, however, was not organized until the year 1781. Their first organization was known as the Gilbert's Creek Church, located on Gilbert's Creek, a few miles from where the town of Lancaster now stands.*

* When Lewis Craig left Spottsylvania county, Virginia, most of his large Church there came with him. They were constituted when

The Presbyterian Church was organized at a later period. The first Presbyterian preacher who came to Kentucky was the Rev. David Rice. He immigrated to Kentucky from Virginia in 1783, and settled in Mercer county. Previous to this date small bodies of Presbyterians had settled in the neighborhoods of Danville, Cane Run, and the forks of Dick's River.

These were gathered into regular congregations by Mr. Rice, and as he had opportunity "he ministered to them in holy things." In the meantime other Presbyterian ministers followed Mr. Rice, among whom were Messrs. James Blythe, John Lyle,* Welch, McNamar, Stone, Reynolds, and Stewart; and in the year 1786, the first Presbytery was organized, under the name of the Presbytery of Transylvania.†

It was in this year that, at the hands of Bishop Asbury, James Haw and Benjamin Ogden received their appointment to Kentucky. The Conference from whence they were sent was held in the city of Baltimore. A long and perilous journey through a pathless and untrodden wilderness lay before them, and at the termination a dense forest, inhabited by savage beasts and the no less savage Indian; while

---

they started, and were an organized Church on the road. Wherever they stopped they could transact Church-business. They settled at Craig's Station, on Gilbert's Creek, a few miles east of where the town of Lancaster, Garrard county, is now situated.—*History of Ten Churches*, p. 42.

* Bishop Kavanaugh lived several years, when a youth, with Mr. Lyle, and was traveling with him when converted.

† Collins's Kentucky, p. 132.

no official board to hold out the generous hand of welcome, no church-edifice, no comfortable home, awaited their arrival. James Haw first appears in the Minutes for 1781, on Isle of Wight Circuit. In 1782 he is reported "admitted into connection." He then traveled successively the South Branch, Amelia, Bedford, and Brunswick Circuits, all lying in the State of Virginia. Mr. Haw was familiar with the sacrifices incident to the life of an itinerant Methodist preacher in his day. He was inured to hardship. Kentucky was Mr. Ogden's first appointment, yet he was no stranger to privations. Though only twenty-two years of age when he came to Kentucky, he had participated in the American struggle for independence. He had followed the fortunes of the American arms when only a youth, during the years of the Revolution, amid assault, pursuit, and slaughter. He knew what privations meant. In his soldier-life he had pitched his tent on the cold, damp ground, and slept beneath the moonlit sky. He had passed days together without sufficient food; had breasted the storm of battle, and stood undaunted and unmoved amid its leaden hail. The quick, discerning eye of Bishop Asbury detected in these men the qualifications requisite for a life of toil, of sacrifice, of suffering; and their deep devotion to their Heavenly Master's cause eminently fitted them to become pioneer preachers in this far-off Western country. Theirs was a noble design. It was not to engage in speculation, or to seek for worldly opulence. No; they were impelled by higher motives. Men were perishing, and they came to snatch them from ruin. They came to establish a system whose purpose it is to recover man from sin; to elevate him, morally and socially; and when dying, to kneel beside his pillow, and point his fading eyes to the "land afar off."

Messrs. Haw and Ogden were preceded by the Rev. Francis Clark, a local preacher from Virginia. He emigrated to Kentucky in 1783, and settled in the neighborhood of Danville.* "He was a man of sound judgment, and well instructed in the doctrines of the Methodist Church. As a preacher he was successful, and was made the instrument of forming several societies, and lived many years to rejoice in the success of the cause that he had been the instrument, under God, of commencing in the wilderness. He died at his own domicile in the fall of 1799, in great peace, and in hope of a blessed immortality. Rev. William J. Thompson also emigrated at an early day from Stokes county, North Carolina, and settled in the same neighborhood. He became also a useful auxiliary, and preached with acceptance and success. He afterward joined the traveling connection in the Western Conference; and when he moved to the State of Ohio, became connected with the Ohio Conference, where his labors and usefulness are held in remembrance by many. The next preachers that came to the country were Nathanael Harris, from Virginia; Gabriel and Daniel Woodfield, from the Redstone country. Harris settled in

---

*Recollections of the West, p. 10.

Jessamine county, and the Woodfields in Fayette county; and, not long after, Philip Taylor, from Virginia, settled in Jessamine county. These were considered a great acquisition to the infant societies. Nathanael Harris and Gabriel Woodfield were among the first order of local preachers, and they were highly esteemed and labored with success. They have been connected with the itinerancy, and labored in that relation with acceptance. Gabriel Woodfield afterward settled in Henry county, but, before his death, removed to Indiana, in the neighborhood of Madison, where he lived to a good old age, and died in peace among his friends and connections. Nathanael Harris still lives,* at the age of nearly fourscore years. Joseph Ferguson, a local preacher from Fairfax county, Virginia, moved to Kentucky at an early time, and settled in Nelson county, and was among the first preachers that settled in that section of the country. He was an amiable man, possessed of good preaching talents, and was rendered very useful. He was highly esteemed, blessed with an amiable family; and his house was a home for the traveling preachers, who were at all times welcome guests. Brother Ferguson was subject at times to great depression of mind; but when in the company of the traveling preachers he was always cheerful and happy. He lived to a good old age at the place where he first settled, and died in peace and in the triumphs of that gospel which he had proclaimed for many years. Ferguson's Meeting-

---

* He died August 12, 1849.

house was one of the first that was built in that part of the country, and at one time there was a large society at that meeting-house; and when I was last in the neighborhood, in the fall of 1811, they still maintained a respectable standing."*

Among the local preachers whose names we have mentioned, that of Francis Clark stands preëminent as the founder of Methodism in Kentucky. As early as 1783,† accompanied by John Durham, a class-leader, and others of his neighbors, with their families, he left Virginia, and settled in Mercer county. He immediately organized a class, the first in the far West, about six miles west from where Danville now stands.‡ An impression has obtained that the first Methodist organization in the District was at the house of Thomas Stevenson, in Mason

---

*The Rev. Wm. Burke, in Sketches of Western Methodism, pp. 62, 63.—The following letter from the Rev. T. F. Vanmeter will explain the present condition of this society:

"In answer to your inquiry, I would state that 'Ferguson's Chapel' was originally built in the Poplar Flat neighborhood, about six miles east of Bardstown, Nelson county, Kentucky. The first building was a round-log, with clapboard roof. I cannot ascertain the date when this building was erected. It remained a long time, and became so much dilapidated that it could not be used, and was displaced by a hewed-log building in 1822, about fifty yards west of the former building. In 1844, a handsome brick was erected about fifty yards farther west, where the society now worship, making about one hundred yards from where the Poplar Flat Church now stands to the original Ferguson's Chapel. The society now numbers about seventy members—a thriving, spiritual Church, in the bounds of the Bloomfield Circuit, Kentucky Conference."

†Recollections of the West, p. 10.

‡Rev. J. F. Wright, Western Christian Advocate, March 7, 1866. Mr. Wright fixes the date, however, one year later.

county, under the supervision of Benjamin Ogden.* The emigration of Mr. Clark, as previously stated, was three years in advance of the appointment of Mr. Ogden to the District. It is also an interesting fact that the society formed by Mr. Clark dates one year prior to the Christmas Conference, when the organization of the Methodist Episcopal Church in America took place. As early as 1784, Mrs. Mary Davis joined this society, under Francis Clark; and in 1859, at the advanced age of ninety-seven, sweetly fell asleep, full of faith and of hope, at the residence of her son-in-law, Lazarus Powell, senior, in Henderson county, Kentucky, having been for seventy-five years a member of the Methodist Church.†

Previous to the appointment of Messrs. Haw and Ogden, several families who had been members of the Methodist Church in Maryland and Virginia, "tired of cultivating the flinty fields and unproductive soil of their native States, where, under the most favorable circumstances, the utmost that could be hoped for, as the result of the most energetic and unremitted attentions, was a bare subsistence, determined to wend their way to the 'far-off West,' concerning which they had heard so many glowing descriptions and thrilling accounts." Among these early Methodist pioneers, were Mr. Thomas Stevenson and his wife, from the State of Maryland, who were among the first converts to Methodism on the American Continent. They settled two and a half

*Collins's Kentucky, p. 124.

† Mrs. Davis was the paternal grandmother of the wife of the author.

miles south-west of Washington, in the county of Mason.*

It was in the latter part of the summer of 1786 when Messrs. Haw and Ogden arrived in the District of Kentucky. One of the first families that bade them welcome to their cottage home was that of Thomas Stevenson. At Mr. Ogden's first visit to the house, immediately on his reaching Kentucky, "he remained for several days, preaching to the people by night, and visiting and praying with the families by day, while his labors were duly appreciated by all in the garrison." From this date to the time of his death, which occurred in 1829, the house of Mr. Stevenson was "a regular preaching-place," as well as "a constant home for the traveling ministry of the Methodist Connection."

The Rev. Dr. Stevenson, in his "Fragments from the Sketch-book of an Itinerant," published in the Christian Advocate (Nashville), October 30, 1856, says: "Mr. Collins, in his deservedly popular and well-written History of Kentucky, has represented, on the authority of some one, that the first Methodist society or Church was organized in my father's house. I am not prepared to endorse the entire correctness of this statement. That such a class was associated together in his little apartment, while living in Kenton's Station, in 1786, by Mr. Ogden, is certain; but whether this was the first he formed

---

* They were the parents of the Rev. Dr. Stevenson, who recently died, a member of the Louisville Conference. Mrs. Stevenson joined the Methodists, under Robert Strawbridge, in 1768; Thomas Stevenson about ten years later.

in the country, I have no data on which to affirm or deny. It may not, however, be improper to remark that the first prayer that was ever presented to the throne of the heavenly grace, at a family altar in the District of Kentucky, by a Methodist preacher, was in my father's cottage, in the station above named, Benjamin Ogden officiating." When the author of the History of Kentucky says, "The first Methodist Episcopal Church organized in Kentucky was in the cabin of Thomas Stevenson, in Mason county, by Benjamin Ogden, some time during the year 1786," he can only mean that no organization previous to this year was recognized in the printed Minutes of the Church. And when Dr. Stevenson affirms that the first prayer ever presented to the throne of the heavenly grace, at a family altar in the District of Kentucky, by a Methodist preacher, was in his father's cottage, Benjamin Ogden officiating, he only refers to the prayers offered by the missionaries. Three years before, we have seen a local preacher leaving Virginia, and not only as a settler of the soil, but as a pioneer of his faith, seeking a home in the wilderness of Kentucky. In his house he erects an altar to God, and in early morn and at close of day he offers prayers to the Most High, commending his household to Heaven.

A writer* familiar with the times and the labors of these men, says, "They came fired with holy zeal and deeply imbued with the spirit of their mission. They commenced their labors in earnest and with

* Rev. Lewis Garrett.

good effect. Soon it was rumored the false prophets are come, and some were ready to say, 'they that turn the world upside down are come hither also.' But these alarms and prejudices, the effects of bigotry, were soon overcome by the influence of ardent piety and holy zeal. A mighty revival of religion commenced, and the flame spread like 'fire in dry stubble!' These missionaries were in quest of souls, and were never out of their way where souls and families were to be found. Vivid in my recollections are their first visits to the dwelling of my widowed mother. A word of pathetic exhortation was addressed to each individual, an ardent prayer, whether they tarried all night or made a call in the day-time. Their preaching was characterized by simplicity and earnestness. Ardent in their devotions, and with a zeal commensurate with the importance of their mission, they carried with them the unction of the Holy One. They had but few books, but these they studied thoroughly. They were Bible students, and being 'not conformed to this world' in their dress, they had room in their pockets for a small Bible, which they often consulted, and sought carefully to bring out of that treasury 'things new and old.' Here they found true philosophy and the wisdom that speaks to the heart. To tickle the ear or delight the fancy with fine-spun theories or the flowers of rhetoric, was foreign to their purpose. They were indeed eloquent in the most essential sense, in virtue of the inspiration of that gospel which they preached, 'not in the words which man's wisdom teacheth, but which the Holy Ghost teacheth, in demonstration of the Spirit and with power.'"

A later writer says: "They were men of great piety and zeal, and God owned their labors."* Sometimes guarded by friends as they traveled from fort to fort, but oftener alone, continually exposed to danger, "they counted not their lives dear," if they could only win souls to Christ.

Such is the testimony concerning these men. Familiar with the Bible, they understood the duties it inculcates; its doctrines; its "exceeding great and precious promises," as well as its threatenings against sin; and, "like a workman that needeth not to be ashamed," whenever they hurled the javelin of truth it reached the object and "accomplished the purpose whereunto it was sent." It is said that Mr. Haw "was a man of much zeal, bordering on enthusiasm," and that "he devoted his whole soul to the work."

Dr. Bascom, afterward Bishop Bascom, in a private letter to a friend,† referring to the early Methodist preachers of Kentucky, said "they labored, suffered, triumphed, in obscurity and want. No admiring populace to cheer them on; no feverish community gazetted them into fame. Principle alone sustained them, and their glory was that of action."

It is to be regretted that the records of the Church for this period are so defective, and that we are enabled to learn so little of their labors. And

---

* Rev. Jonathan Stamper. † Rev. Lewis Garrett.

yet it is a cause for gratitude that enough is left us, by which we may form a proper estimate of their characters, their worth, their sacrifices, and their spirit of adventure.

At the ensuing Conference, the printed Minutes show a membership of *ninety* in Kentucky. When we consider the sparseness of the population, the character of the people, and the opposition with which Methodism has everywhere met, in its introduction into any new section, their success was truly remarkable. It was not, however, the immediate results of their labors, as they appear in the Minutes, that chiefly claim our gratitude. True, in this is cause for much thanksgiving to God. In addition to this, here was the incipiency of a system whose developments were to be seen in coming time. They were laying the foundations of an edifice within whose holy courts thousands should in after ages kneel and worship God. They were sowing seeds whose fruitage should be abundant when "they had slept with the fathers." Hence their labors were constant, and owned and blessed of God. Among the first-fruits of their labors was Mrs. Jane Stamper, afterward the mother of the Rev. Jonathan Stamper, who, in later times, by his eloquence, his power, and his untiring devotion to the work of the ministry, contributed so largely to the promotion of Methodism in Kentucky. He was "a burning and a shining light." Mrs. Stamper* had been a member of the Presbyterian Church, but

* Home Circle, Vol. I., p. 108.

a stranger to the doctrine of the new birth. Messrs. Haw and Ogden visited the neighborhood, in Madison county, in which she resided. She waited upon their ministry, and, under the first sermon she heard, she was awakened, and immediately sought and found Christ in the forgiveness of her sins. She joined the Methodist Church, and, after a pilgrimage of forty years, she passed away in Christian triumph, exchanging the sorrows of earth for the joys of heaven.

CHAPTER II.

FROM THE CONFERENCE OF 1787 TO THE CONFERENCE OF 1789.

Kentucky Circuit — James Haw — Cumberland Circuit — Benjamin Ogden — Wilson Lee — Thomas Williamson — Kentucky Circuit divided — Francis Poythress — Devereaux Jarrat — Peter Massie — Benjamin Snelling — Local preachers.

IN 1787, the work in the West was divided into two circuits, one of which still bore the name of Kentucky, and to which James Haw was returned. Thomas Williamson and Wilson Lee were appointed his colleagues. The other was called Cumberland, to which Benjamin Ogden was appointed, where, after laboring one year, he located. The Cumberland Circuit embraced the country now known as Middle Tennessee, and a small portion of Southern Kentucky. The Kentucky Circuit included the whole of the District of Kentucky, except that part embraced in the Cumberland. In that early day it was not common to continue the same preacher for more than one year in the same territory. It was, however, proper, in an eminent degree, to return to this Western field the noble men who had first planted Methodism upon its soil. They had learned the habits of its rude population; had slept beneath its skies, on the cold, damp ground; had become familiar with its dim and unfrequented paths; they enjoyed the confidence of the people, and had achieved success in their ministry; yet the growing interest of the Church demanded an accession to the ministerial strength.

Thomas Williamson was admitted on trial in 1785, and had traveled successively the Yadkin and Salisbury Circuits, in North Carolina. Wilson Lee preceded him in the work of the ministry one year, and had traveled on the Alleghany Circuit, in Virginia; the Redstone, in Pennsylvania; and the Talbot, in Maryland. For piety, zeal, and devotion to the cause of Christ, these men enjoyed an enviable reputation. In the fields of labor they had previously occupied, they were eminently successful. Wilson Lee, the former year, had been assistant to Richard Whatcoat, afterward Bishop Whatcoat, and enjoyed to the fullest extent the confidence of that great man. He was twenty-six years of age, in the prime of life, and the strength of manhood, when he came to Kentucky. His early advantages were of a superior character. Reared in the midst of refinement, and surrounded with the luxuries of life, his manners polished, and possessing talents of a high order, he might have achieved eminence in any profession. But God had called him to the work of the ministry, and, following the voice of duty, he cheerfully obeyed the summons. At seventeen years of age, he embraced religion, and, in the morning of life, entered the ministry. Familiar with the teachings of Christianity, his address handsome, a well-trained and pleasant voice, and with a zeal commensurate with the importance of the work to which he had been called—added to all this, he was truly devout, and an excellent singer—his preaching was "with the demonstration of the Spirit and with power." Whether in his vindication of the great truths of Christianity, or in the tremendous appeals he made to the conscience, the effect was overwhelming. Success crowned his labors, and through his instrumentality many were converted to God.

Thomas Williamson was also a young man of superior talents, as well as of prepossessing manners. He was an excellent preacher. In the pulpit he commanded not only the respect, but the admiration of his hearers, and in the social circle he was remarkably popular. Such were the men who were appointed assistants to James Haw.

Notwithstanding the depredations that were so frequently committed by the Indians, the District of Kentucky, at this time, was populating with astonishing rapidity. The want of the ordinary comforts of life, and the dreadful massacres perpetrated on the frontier, were sufficient to have arrested the tide of immigration; yet from Virginia, as well as from other sections of the country, families came in until the settlements, in some parts, were becoming dense. Undaunted by danger, these devoted missionaries went from fort to fort in the accomplishment of their great work. They "counted not their lives dear," but risked all for Christ and the Church. Men were perishing, and they desired to save them. They had left the comforts of home with no other purpose but to preach the gospel of Christ, and with commendable zeal they prosecuted their calling, and were successful. At the close of the year, they returned *four hundred and eighty* members.*

The Conference of 1788 was held in Baltimore, September 10th, at which time the Kentucky Circuit was divided, and from it were formed the Lexington and Danville Circuits. Six preachers were sent to cultivate these fields. The appointments were: Francis Poythress and James Haw, Presiding Elders;† Lexington—Thomas Williamson, Peter Massie, Benjamin Snelling; Danville—Wilson Lee.‡

The name of Francis Poythress appears for the first time in the Minutes of 1776. His first appointment was to Caroline Circuit. In 1777, his name does not appear in the Minutes. Whether he had been compelled to desist from traveling in consequence of feeble health, or whether his name is omitted by mistake, we have no means of ascertaining.§ In 1778, his name reäppears, and he is appointed to Hanover Circuit, in Virginia, and then successively filled the Sussex Circuit, in Virginia; the New Hope, in North Carolina; the Fairfax, in Virginia; the Talbot, in Maryland; the Alleghany, in Virginia; and the Calvert and Baltimore, in

* Cumberland Circuit not included in these figures.

† The term "Presiding" does not occur in the Minutes until 1789, and is again dropped until 1797.

‡ Poythress presided over Lexington and Danville, and Haw over Cumberland.

§ The early Minutes abound in errors and omissions.

Maryland. In 1786, he was appointed Presiding Elder over Brunswick, Sussex, and Amelia Circuits, in Virginia; and in 1787, over Guilford, Halifax, New Hope, and Caswell Circuits, in North Carolina. The important fields he had occupied evinced the high regard in which he was held by the Church, and the extraordinary success that had attended his labors was, under the blessing of God, the result of that zeal and devotion that ever afterward distinguished him, so long as he was able to lift the ensign of the cross. When appointed to Kentucky, he had reached the meridian of life. He was in the forty-fourth year of his age. "He was a Virginian of large estate, but of dissipated habits in his youth. The conversations and rebukes of a lady in high social position arrested him in his perilous course. He returned from her house confounded, penitent, and determined to reform his morals. He betook himself to his neglected Bible, and soon saw that his only effectual reformation could be by a religious life. He searched for a competent living guide, but such was the condition of the English Church around him that he could find none. Hearing at last of the devoted Jarrat,* he hastened to his parish, and was entertained some time under his hospitable roof for instruction. There he found purification and peace about the year 1772. It was not long before he began to coöperate with Jarrat in his public labors amid the extraordinary scenes of religious interest which prevailed through all

* Jarrat was a clergyman of the Church of England.

that region. Thus, before the arrival of the Methodist itinerants in Virginia, he had become an evangelist: when they appeared, he learned with delight their doctrines and methods of labor, and, joining them, became a giant in their ranks. In 1775, he began his travels, under the authority of a Quarterly Meeting of Brunswick Circuit, and, the present year, appears for the first time on the roll of the Conference.* Henceforth, in North Carolina, Virginia, Maryland, and Kentucky, he was to be a representative man of the struggling cause. In 1783, he bore its standard across the Alleghanies to the waters of the Youghiogheny. From 1786, he served it with preëminent success for twelve years, as a Presiding Elder. Asbury nominated him for the Episcopate. 'From the first,' says one of the best antiquarian authorities of the Church,† 'he performed all the work of a Methodist preacher with fidelity and success, and for twenty-six years his name appears without a blot upon the official records of the Church among his brethren.' During the time, he filled every office, except that of Superintendent, and was designated for that place by Bishop Asbury, in a letter addressed to the Conference at Wilbraham, 1797. The preachers refused to comply with the request, simply upon the ground that it was not competent in a yearly Conference to elect Bishops. Poythress, in a word, was to Methodism generally, and to the South-west particularly, what Jesse Lee was to New England—

* 1776.

† Rev. T. Scott.

an apostle. His name stands in the Minutes of 1802 for the last time, among the Elders, but without an appointment, after which it disappears, and we hear no more of him, until we are roused from our anxious thoughts concerning his probable fate by the startling announcement of Bishop Asbury."* The announcement referred to is found in Asbury's Journal. While traveling through Kentucky in 1810, on Monday, the 15th day of October, he says: "This day has been an awful day to me. I visited Francis Poythress, if thou be he; but O! how fallen!"† He had become insane.

In his Sketches of Western Methodism, Mr. Finley says:‡ "In the year 1800, he was sent to a District in North Carolina, embracing fifteen circuits. His removal to a new field, among strangers, and the subjection, if possible, to greater hardships than he had endured in his former fields, without a companion save the companionship which he gained at different and distant points among his brethren, preyed heavily upon his system, shattering his nerves, and making fearful inroads upon a mind naturally of a too contemplative, if not somber cast; and seasons of gloom and darkness gathered around him. He should at once have desisted, and sought that rest and society for which he so much longed, among the friends and companions of his youth; but, alas! the necessity that rested in those days upon a Methodist preacher, stern as fate, kept him at his post, and he toiled on

---

*Stevens's History M. E. Church, Vol. II., pp. 23, 24.

†Asbury's Journal, Vol. III., p. 349. ‡P. 131.

till his shattered frame, like the broken strings of a harp, could only sigh to the winds that swept through it; and his mind, in deep sympathy with his frame, became alike shattered and deranged. The next year he came back to Kentucky, but the light of the temple was gone, and the eye which shot the fires of genius and intelligence, now wildly stared upon the face of old, loving, long-tried friends, as though they were strangers. Here he remained till death released him and sent his spirit home. Poor Poythress! Bravely didst thou toil and endure hardness on the well-fought field. A campaign of twenty-four years of incessant toil in the gloomy wilds of the West, away from friends and loved ones at home, proved too much for thy nature to bear. But thou art gone where the wicked cease to trouble, and the weary are at rest."

The Rev. Thomas Scott, a cotemporary, as well as the intimate personal friend of Mr. Poythress, says: "He was, if we rightly remember, about five feet eight or nine inches in height, and heavily built. His muscles were large, and when in the prime of life, we presume he was a man of more than ordinary muscular strength. He dressed plain and neat. When we first saw him, we suppose he had passed his sixtieth year. His muscles were quite flaccid, eyes sunken in his head, hair gray, turned back, hanging down on his shoulders, complexion dark, and countenance grave, inclining to melancholy."* He again says: "Early in the year 1797, he was con-

* Western Methodism, p. 137.

fined by affliction; but whether his mind was affected during his affliction we are entirely uninformed. The last time we saw him, was in the winter of 1800. The balance of his mind was lost, and his body lay a complete wreck. His labors in the Church militant were at an end, but the fruits of his labors still remain. We are not aware that any hereditary taint existed, which in its ultimate range dethroned his reason; but we can readily imagine that the seeds of that dreadful malady were sown in his system by the constant exposure and suffering during the war of the Revolution, and the twelve years he traveled and preached in the then almost wilderness of the West. Among the eight pioneers of Methodism in Kentucky and Tennessee in the year 1788, the name of Francis Poythress stands preeminent. By those intrepid heroes of the cross the foundation of Methodism was laid in those States, on which others have since built, and others are now building. Their names ought to be held in grateful remembrance by all who love our Lord Jesus Christ in sincerity and truth; but among all, we are inclined to the opinion, there is not one of them to whom the members of our Church, in those States, owe a greater debt of gratitude than to Francis Poythress."* In devoting so much space to Francis Poythress, we have done so, because he was more intimately identified with the rise and progress of Methodism in Kentucky than any other minister. For ten consecutive years he had charge of the

---

* Sketches of Western Methodism, p. 141.

Kentucky District, and, in the absence of Bishop Asbury, presided over the Annual Conferences. "Grave in his deportment, chaste in his conversation, constant in his private devotions, and faithful in the discharge of his ministerial duties," he exerted an influence for Methodism, and contributed to its success in Kentucky, to an extent that can be claimed for no other man. When we recount his excessive and constant labors through twenty-four years, having "never been known to disappoint a congregation, unless prevented by sickness or disease," with the weight of so many Churches resting upon him, we are not surprised that his physical strength should have given way; and to the Church it is a cause for gratitude to God, that his noble intellect did not become impaired in the morn or noon of his life. It was not until he had entered "its sere and yellow leaf" that he gave any indications of the overthrow of his reason. The last years of his life were spent with his sister, Mrs. Susanna Pryor, twelve miles south of Lexington, Kentucky, where, in 1818, he passed away.

Peter Massie was among the first-fruits of Methodism in Kentucky.* He entered the itinerant work this year, after having long resisted his convictions on this subject; but when he yielded, he gave himself wholly to the work. He was a young man of "good personal appearance," but of delicate constitution. Living in close communion with God, deeply imbued with the spirit of his mission, wholly

* Western Methodism, p. 67.

consecrated to the work of the ministry, and educated amid the dangers of the wilderness, he gave great promise of usefulness to the Church. His manners pleasant, his voice soft and plaintive, as often as he preached, he wept over the people, and in most touching strains invited them to the Saviour. He was styled "the weeping prophet." One who knew him well says: "I heard him preach the gospel frequently, and I do not think I ever heard him but when tears rolled down his manly cheeks, while he warned the people to flee from the wrath to come."*

Of Benjamin Snelling, who also entered the ministry this year, we know but little. After traveling one year on the Lexington Circuit, we find him the second year of his ministry on the Fairfax Circuit, Virginia. He only remained in Virginia one year, when he returned to Kentucky, and was appointed to Madison Circuit. His name the next year disappears from the Minutes, probably by location, though this is not specified.† He settled in Bath county, Kentucky, where he finally died.

A very large proportion of the first two years in Kentucky was spent by the missionaries in hunting up and organizing into societies those members of the Church from other States, who had preceded Messrs. Haw and Ogden to the District. In the accomplishment of this work the local preachers had been faithful auxiliaries; and now to push for-

---

* John Carr, Christian Advocate, Nashville, February 5, 1857.

† We have previously referred to the want of information that marks the early Minutes.

ward the Redeemer's kingdom, they united heart and hand with their pious leaders. Sacrifice, toil, and suffering were endured, and the local preachers shared it. They shunned no hardship, they avoided no danger, but anxious to save souls and to assist in planting Methodism in the land that was to be the home of their children, they labored by the side of Poythress and Haw, Lee, Williamson, Snelling, and Massie. Their labors were crowned with success. God poured out his Holy Spirit upon the people. The sacred flame spread far and wide. Hundreds were converted and added to the Church, and at the close of the Conference-year they report eight hundred and sixty-three members.

CHAPTER III.

FROM THE CONFERENCE OF 1789 TO THE CONFERENCE OF 1790.

Interesting letter from James Haw—Barnabas McHenry—Stephen Brooks—Cumberland Circuit—James Haw—James O'Kelly—Interesting account of James Haw, by Learner Blackman—James O'Cull: his style of preaching—Poor support of preachers—Kindness of the Baltimore Conference.

IN the commencement of the year 1789, James Haw addressed the following letter to Bishop Asbury:

"Good news from Zion: the work of God is going on rapidly in the new world; a glorious victory the Son of God has gained, and he is still going on conquering and to conquer. Shout, ye angels! Hell trembles and heaven rejoices daily over sinners that repent. At a quarterly meeting held in Bourbon county, Kentucky, July 19 and 20, 1788, the Lord poured out his Spirit in a wonderful manner, first on the Christians, and sanctified several of them powerfully and gloriously, and, as I charitably hope, wholly. The seekers also felt the power and presence of God, and cried for mercy as at the point of death. We prayed with and for them, till we had reason to believe that the Lord converted seventeen or eighteen precious souls. Hallelujah, praise ye the Lord!

"As I went from that, through the circuit, to another quarterly meeting, the Lord converted two or three more. The Saturday and Sunday following, the Lord poured out his Spirit again. The work of sanctification among the believers broke out again at the Lord's table, and the Spirit of the Lord went through the assembly like a mighty rushing wind. Some fell; many cried for mercy. Sighs and groans proceeded from their hearts; tears of sorrow for sin ran streaming down their eyes. Their prayers reached to heaven, and the Spirit of the Lord entered into them and filled fourteen or fifteen with peace and joy in believing. 'Salvation! O the joyful sound! how the echo flies!' A few days after, Brother Poythress came, and went with me to another quarterly meeting. We had another gracious season round the Lord's table, but no remarkable stir till after preaching; when, under several exhortations, some bursted out into tears, others trembled, and some fell. I sprang in among the people, and the Lord converted one more very powerfully, who praised the Lord with such acclamation of joy as I trust will never be forgotten. The Sunday following, I preached my farewell sermon, and met the class, and the Lord converted three more. Glory be to his holy name for ever!

"The first round I went on Cumberland, the Lord converted six precious souls, and I joined three gracious Baptists to our Church; and every round, I have reason to believe, some sinners are awakened, some seekers joined to society, and some penitents converted to God. At our Cumberland quarterly meeting, the Lord converted six souls the first day, and one the next. Glory, honor, praise, and power be unto God for ever! The work still goes on. I have joined two more serious Baptists since the quarterly meeting. The Lord has converted several more precious souls in various parts of the circuit, and some more have joined the society, so that we have one hundred and twelve disciples now in Cumberland—forty-seven of whom, I trust, have received the gift of the Holy Ghost since they believed; and I hope these are but the first of a universal harvest which God will give us in this country. Brother Massie is with me, going on weeping over sinners, and the Lord blesses his labors. A letter from Brother Williamson, dated November 10, 1788, informs me that the work is still going on rapidly in Kentucky; that at two quarterly meetings since I came away, the Lord poured out his Spirit, and converted ten penitents, and sanctified five believers, at the first, and twenty more were converted at the second; indeed, the wilderness and solitary places are glad, and the desert rejoices and blossoms as the rose, and, I trust, will soon become beautiful as *Tirza* and comely as *Jerusalem*.

"What shall I more say? Time would fail to tell you all the Lord's doings among us. It is marvelous in our eyes. To him be the glory, honor, praise, power, might, majesty, and dominion, both now and for ever! Amen, and amen."

This letter breathes the spirit of a minister of Jesus Christ, whose soul was wholly devoted to the great work of doing good; and it also suggests to us the firm hold that Methodism, at that early day, was taking on the hearts of the people. We may not be able to appreciate the sufferings and hardships endured by this extraordinary man and his faithful colleagues, in planting the gospel here, surrounded by savages, and their lives continually exposed; but we can admire the success that, under such embarrassments, attended their labors. Already had Methodism reached every section of the inhabited portion of the District of Kentucky, and was contributing its influence, not only in ameliorating the condition of the people, but in their social and moral elevation.

At the Conference held in 1789, Thomas Williamson—a man whose labors had been so greatly blessed in Kentucky—was removed to another field of ministerial labor.* We take leave of him for the present, but will meet him again, prosecuting his work with a holy zeal, and winning trophies to the Redeemer.

The names of Barnabas McHenry and Stephen Brooks appear this year in the appointments for Kentucky. Barnabas McHenry, the son of John McHenry, was born December 6, 1767, in the State of North Carolina.† When Barnabas was about

---

* General Minutes, Vol. I., p. 34.

† Dr. Abel Stevens says, in the third volume of his History of M. E. Church, page 293, that Barnabas McHenry "was born December 10, 1767, in Eastern Virginia." The time and place above given of his

eight years of age, his father removed to Washington county, Virginia. He made a profession of religion when only fifteen years old, and joined the Methodist Church, and in the twentieth year of his age, entered on his itinerant career. His first appointment was to the Yadkin Circuit, in North Carolina. He spent the subsequent year in Kentucky, probably in the Lexington Circuit, to which Peter Massie had been appointed, though his name appears in connection with the Cumberland.

In a letter to one of the pioneer preachers,* Mr. McHenry says: "Soon after I reached the Kentucky settlement—which was on the 11th of June, 1788—Brother Haw formed the design of placing me on Cumberland Circuit, to which he then intended to accompany me, and make a short stay; but, before he had executed his purpose, he was superseded by Brother Poythress. The consequence was, that Brothers Haw and Massie went to Cumberland, and I continued in Kentucky that year, according to the original intention of that appointment. Brother Haw, it would seem, communicated his arrangements previous to the printing of the Minutes, which occasioned my name to be inserted as appointed to the Cumberland Circuit." †

The next year, (1789,) he was appointed to Danville Circuit, with Peter Massie for his colleague.

---

birth, is on the authority of a letter to the author from his grandson, Hon. John H. McHenry, of Owensboro, Kentucky, who copied for us from the family record.

* Rev. Lewis Garrett.

† Recollections of the West, pp. 97, 98.

The personal appearance of Mr. McHenry was commanding, his manners attractive, his intellect of the highest order, and his voice strong and well-trained. Soundly converted in early life, he consecrated himself to the work of the ministry. Regarding Methodism as the best exponent of Christianity, he devoted his noble life to the vindication of its heavenly truths. With Kentucky Methodism he was destined to become intimately identified, and in the formation of its character to take a conspicuous part. By the probity of his life, his sterling integrity, his invincible purpose to make every thing subservient to his religious obligations, as well as by the power he displayed in the pulpit, he wielded an influence for the cause of truth that is now deeply engraven in the hearts of the Church, though he has passed away. His cotemporaries speak of him in terms of highest praise. Rev. Jacob Young, in his Autobiography, in speaking of meeting, on one occasion, with several Kentucky gentlemen of distinction, says: "The most distinguished man I met was Barnabas McHenry. I may truly say he was a man by himself." Rev. Lewis Garrett,* referring to his death, says: "In him the Church lost a tried and able minister, and the cause of Christianity an efficient and firm advocate;" and, in later years, Dr. Bascom,† who never bestowed undue praise on either the living or the dead, said: "His preaching was mainly expository and didactic.

---

* Biographical Sketches, p. 30.

† Quarterly Review, Vol. III., pp. 421, 422.

The whole style of his preaching denoted the confidence of history and experience. All seemed to be real and personal to him. The perfect simplicity, and yet clear, discriminating accuracy of his manner and language, made the impression that he was speaking only of what he knew to be true. He spoke of every thing as of a natural scene before him. There was an intensity of conception, a sustained sentiment of personal interest, which gave one a feeling of wonder and awe in listening to him. You could not doubt his right to guide and teach. One felt how safe and proper it was to follow such leading. His style was exceedingly rich, without being showy. There was no effervescence. It was not the garden and landscape in bloom, but in early bud, giving quiet but sure indication of fruit and foliage. His language was always accurate, well chosen, strong, and clear. All his sermons, as delivered, were in this respect fit for the press—not only remarkably free from error on the score of thought, but from defect and fault of style and language. His whole manner, too, was natural, dignified, and becoming. Good taste and sound judgment were his main mental characteristics. Of imagination proper he had but little, and still less of fancy. Reason, fitness, and beauty were the perceptions by which he was influenced. The intrinsic value of things alone attracted him. The outward show of things made little or no impression upon him, under any circumstances. The inner man—the hidden things of the heart—controlled him in all his judgments and preferences."

Such was Barnabas McHenry, who was destined to be so closely identified with the history of Methodism in Kentucky, and to be a standard-bearer in its ranks.

Of the parentage and early life of Stephen Brooks we know but little, nor have we any information as to the date of his conversion. He was admitted on trial in 1789, and appointed to the Lexington Circuit with James Haw and Wilson Lee. The next year we find him on the Danville Circuit, laboring with zeal and with energy. In 1791, his name disappears from the Minutes; * but, in 1792, it makes its appearance again, at which time he is appointed to Sevier Circuit, East Tennessee; and, in 1793, he locates and settles in East Tennessee—after which we can learn nothing in reference to him, until, in the year 1796, we find him a member of the Convention that framed the Constitution of the State of Tennessee.† As a gentleman, he is represented as courteous and affable; as a Christian, a perfect model; as a minister of Christ, of the first order of talents. In "labors abundant," with the most unyielding devotion to his mission, he endeavored to make "good proof of his ministry." Regardless of the sacrifices required of him, he exposed himself to the rains of summer, the frosts of autumn, and the snows of winter, that he might achieve success. The perils of the wilderness, and

---

* I presume, by mistake, as no reason is assigned; and the next year it appears again in the same way. The early Minutes are full of errors.

† Christian Advocate, March 19, 1857.

the frequent massacres committed by the savages, did not for a moment induce him to hesitate. By "the suavity of his manners, and the gentleness of his deportment, he became a universal favorite with the people." His preaching was characterized by a sound logic and a holy zeal. His exhortations were pungent, searching, "powerful." He succeeded, too, in "bringing souls to Christ." * "His labors," says one who knew him, "were owned and blessed of God, by the turning of many from darkness to light." † Of him a gentleman once said: "If he had to hear but one sermon before dying, he would choose Stephen Brooks to preach it."

We regret to record that this year closed the labors of James Haw in Kentucky. ‡ He had been a faithful minister. For four years he had traversed the wilderness of Kentucky, often without shelter and without home; but he had the satisfaction of knowing that his labors had been blessed, that Churches had been planted, circuits formed—and now he goes to another field, where he would be exposed to hardships and dangers similar to those through which he had already passed. But he had left behind him "written epistles, to be known and read of all men," while the mellow influence of his

---

* John Carr, Christian Advocate, March 19, 1857.

† John Carr, Christian Advocate, March 19, 1857.

‡ Stevens, in his History of the M. E. Church, Vol. II., p. 368, in a note, says: "Burke says his labors (James Haw's) closed 1789." Dr. Stevens, however, misunderstands Burke—who says: "The Conference of 1789 closed the labors of James Haw in Kentucky."—*Western Methodism*, p. 73.

holy life and untiring zeal was destined to be felt by many then unborn. On the Cumberland Circuit, to which he was appointed the next year, amid abundant labors and great success, his constitution became impaired, and his health gave way. The testimony is that "he literally wore himself out." He married a Miss Thomas in Kentucky, and settled in Sumner county, Tennessee, "where the people, because of their affection for him, gave him a tract of land embracing six hundred and forty acres, on which he located."

In the Minutes of 1791, the question is asked: "Who are under a location through weakness of body or family concerns?" In the answer, with eight others, stands the name of *James Haw*.

On the Cumberland Circuit, on which Mr. Haw closed his labors as an itinerant preacher, he was eminently successful. We have before us the unprinted manuscripts of the Rev. Learner Blackman. In reference to James Haw he says: "James Haw was stationed in Cumberland in 1790. He continued here several years. It seemed at one time, after the arrival of the Methodist preachers in Cumberland, that all the people would embrace religion." *

We deeply lament that one who had done so much for Methodism should have been seduced from its paths and its principles by any influence whatever.

In the year 1792, the Rev. James O'Kelly, a

* After Mr. Haw's location, he settled, as before stated, in Sumner county, in the bounds of Cumberland Circuit. The MSS. of Mr. Blackman were placed in our hands by Dr. Summers.

popular and talented minister, and at the time the Presiding Elder of one of the largest and most influential Districts in the State of Virginia, became dissatisfied with the economy and government of the Methodist Episcopal Church, and withdrew from its communion. For fifteen years, as an evangelist, he had labored successfully in North Carolina and Virginia. In every department in which he labored, he exhibited those qualities that so eminently fitted him for usefulness. During the eight years in which he presided over Districts, "he wielded a commanding influence over the preachers of the South." There was no minister in the Connection who enjoyed the confidence of Bishop Asbury to a greater extent—and no man abused that confidence more than he. In his journal, he speaks of him as "a warm-hearted, good man," and says: "James O'Kelly and myself enjoyed and comforted each other: this dear man rose at midnight, and prayed most devoutly for me and himself." *

In his dissatisfaction with the Church, he was particularly hostile to Bishop Asbury, and heaped upon him the most bitter invective. Not contented with the organization of the "Republican Methodist Church"—the name by which the new faction was distinguished—he endeavored to "raze to the foundations" the fair and sightly edifice to the erection of which he had contributed so many of the best years of his life. By the influence he exerted he induced a large number of ministers to

---

* Asbury's Journal, Vol. I., p. 383.

follow his example—the most of whom, however, afterward returned to the Church from which, for a brief period, they had been estranged.

Among those who were led away by the pernicious teachings of Mr. O'Kelly, was James Haw. A man who had stood so prominently in the foreground of Methodism in the West, and whose life had been devoted to its success, could take no step of any importance without exerting an influence for good or for evil. Enjoying the confidence of the people, many of whom had been brought to Christ through his instrumentality, it is no matter of surprise that the position taken by him should induce so many others, both among the laity as well as the ministry, to embrace the delusion. A writer,* on whom we may rely, says: "Mr. Haw embraced the views of O'Kelly, and, by his influence and address, brought over the traveling preachers, and every local preacher but one, to his views, in the county in which he had located;" and that "considerable dissatisfaction obtained in many of the societies." In the unpublished manuscript of the Rev. Learner Blackman, in our possession, he says: "From the time Methodism was first introduced in Cumberland till about the year 1795, Methodism had been increasing. Birchett, Wilson Lee, and Buxton, and others of the first preachers stationed in Cumberland, will not soon be forgotten. None were more useful than Mr. Haw, till he became disaffected toward the Methodist discipline and govern-

* Rev. Wm. Burke.

ment, which, in effect, cut off his influence as a preacher, and did much injury to the cause of Methodism." It frequently occurs that the first departure, on the part of a Methodist preacher, from the Church whose prosperity had been promoted by his labors, is only the precursor of disquietude and unrest. The history of the Church presents but few examples of ministers who had been prominent in labors and in usefulness, and who, from any cause, had sought the communion of other denominations, who did not lose their hold on public confidence, and whose usefulness was not for ever impaired. It was so with James Haw. He had been the zealous advocate of the doctrines and economy of the Methodist Episcopal Church. Every feature that belonged to it was dear to his heart—to achieve its success he had performed labors and braved dangers, undaunted; and now, in his strugglings to turn away from his "earliest love," he lost much of the religious warmth and spirit that had distinguished his former life.

Mr. Hinde,* the author of a series of excellent articles on "Early Western Methodism," in his animadversions on both James Haw and Benjamin Ogden, says "they both went to nothing." There is certainly nothing in their history that justifies so harsh a verdict. However much Mr. Haw may have lost of the influence he had exerted in former years, and to whatever extent he may have gone in the departure from his former spirit, it is a source

* Methodist Magazine, 1819, p. 186.

of gratification to us that he always maintained a reputation for piety. But, his influence gone in the Methodist Church, in the year 1801 he joined the Presbyterian Church, in which he lived an example of piety, and died, some years after, a minister in that Communion.

His children, however, and his descendants, to the present time, so far as they have become connected with any Church, have sought that of their father's early love; or, if unconverted, have been attached to its interest.

The following account of James Haw, from the hitherto unpublished manuscript of the Rev. Learner Blackman, will be read with interest:

"James Haw ultimately left the Methodist Episcopal Church, and called himself a Republican Methodist. Mr. Spear, who was stationed in Cumberland in 1794, states that he found Haw intent on representing Bishop Asbury in the most unfavorable point of light, though he made no open avowal to leave the Methodist Episcopal Church at that time, but used his influence to get the young preachers and members of the society disaffected with Bishop Asbury and the Discipline of the Methodist Episcopal Church. In 1795, Mr. Haw held a conference with the preachers he had influence with; at which Joseph Brown and Jonathan Stephens were licensed as Republican Methodist preachers. They had both been previously licensed to preach by the Methodist Episcopal Church. Haw's design now was no longer a secret. It was now notorious that he was influenced by the same principles and prejudices of James

O'Kelly, and that his prejudices had the same object. About the time of the great and increasing difficulty caused by Mr. Haw, William Burke, an itinerant preacher, arrived in Cumberland. He requested Mr. Haw to meet him at Mr. Edwards's, and adjust the differences, if possible. Mr. Haw met, according to appointment, at the request of Mr. Burke; but the attempts to adjust the differences with the parties were ineffectual. Haw declared himself no more a Methodist. Mr. Burke farther stated that most of the officials of Cumberland had become disaffected to our government, in consequence of Haw's influence, but that they were all reconciled, except Haw and Stephens. Joseph Dunn came back to the Methodist Episcopal Church, after about six weeks. Stephens backslid and became a wicked man. A very few joined Haw. He held one sacrament, and it is said that himself and wife were the only communicants. But very few, if any, were either awakened or converted under Haw's ministry, after he left the Methodists. But, in consequence of William Burke, who did himself much honor, an almost expiring cause was saved. William Burke must be regarded as the principal cause, under God, of diverting the dismal cloud that seemed to be hanging over the infant Church.

"In the time of the revival among the Presbyterians and Methodists, about the year 1800, Haw joined the Presbyterians. At that time, the Presbyterians were friendly with the Methodists; Methodists and Presbyterians preached and communed together. But when Haw joined the Presbyterians, as he had said many things disrespectful of Bishop Asbury and of the form of Discipline, after he withdrew from the Church, the existing union was likely to be broken. John Page and Thomas Wilkerson were stationed in Cumberland at that time. They very unreservedly stated their objections to Mr. Haw, and that, if he continued among them, he must make such acknowledgments as would satisfy the Methodists; and, if he did not, the union must be, in the nature of things, broken. The Presbyterians determined that Mr. Haw should make such public acknowledgment, that the existing union might not be interrupted.

"The charges were stated, which were the following:

"1. For falsely representing Bishop Asbury as having a libidinous thirst for power.

"2. For making attempts to disunite the Methodist Society in Cumberland.

"3. In attempting to destroy the Methodist Discipline—charges that Haw did not deny. But it was requested that he should make his acknowledgments publicly.

"Accordingly, on Sunday morning, at camp-meeting, before thousands, Mr. Haw made acknowledgments full and satisfactory. He acknowledged he had misrepresented Bishop Asbury and the Methodist Discipline.

"After this, Mr. Haw seemed to rise in the esteem of the people, and gain some influence as a preacher. He continued with the Presbyterians while he lived.

"We have reason to believe that his sun went down in peace—that he died in the faith."

We devote so much space to Mr. Haw, because the truth of history demands it. However much we may lament his departure from primitive Methodism, we rejoice in that grace by which he maintained a Christian character and found sweet consolation in the hour of death.

As yet, we had but two circuits in Kentucky. The Danville Circuit included one-third the entire State,* while the Lexington embraced the counties of Fayette, Jessamine, Woodford, Franklin, Scott, and Harrison.

Among the ministers whose labors contributed so much to the advancement of the cause of truth during this year, the name of James O'Cull ought not to be omitted. He was a native of Pennsylvania, and by birth and education a Roman Catholic. When quite a young man, he attended a Methodist meeting, and was awakened under the preaching of the gospel; and, immediately upon his conversion, began to persuade others to seek the salvation of their souls. In 1789, he came to Kentucky, a local preacher, and traveled two years under the Presiding Elder. In 1791, he joined the Conference, and was appointed to the Cumberland Circuit as colleague to Barnabas McHenry. Naturally of a feeble constitution, he was unable to endure the privations and perform the labors required of him

---

*Quarterly Review of Methodist Episcopal Church, South, Vol. III., p. 416.

on that circuit, and before the close of the year he was compelled to retire from the work, to enter it as an itinerant no more. In Kentucky, however, as well as on the Cumberland Circuit, he was successful as a minister. Through his instrumentality, many souls were awakened and converted to God—among whom was the husband of Mrs. Jane Stamper, referred to in a former chapter. As a preacher, Mr. O'Cull stood high. His sermons were not only distinguished for their zeal and fervor, but also for their strength and discrimination. To the doctrines and economy of the Methodist Church he was deeply attached, and to vindicate them, whenever assailed in his presence, was the joy of his heart.

Subsequent to his labors on the Cumberland Circuit, his health was so feeble that he could preach but seldom, and frequently in only a whisper, yet a peculiar unction always attended his ministrations. One who knew him well gives the following account of a sermon he heard him preach: *

"I once heard him preach a characteristic sermon on the parable of the Prodigal Son. He brought the whole subject simply but forcibly before the congregation. First he described the prodigal leaving home, thoughtless and gleeful—the very expression of wealth and fashion. He followed him to the resorts of pleasure and dissipation, where he was surrounded by flattering sycophants, who complimented his person, his talents, and, above all, his liberality. He sailed on a smooth sea while his

---

* Rev. Jonathan Stamper.

money lasted, but when it failed, his associates turned from him with disdain, and called him a fool. When he applied for aid to those who had flattered and ruined him, they kicked him out-of-doors as a spendthrift and vagabond, unworthy of relief or pity. Penniless and ragged, he sought a livelihood by feeding swine—a most disgraceful employment for a Jew, but it afforded him no relief: he would fain have satisfied his hunger with the husks which the swine did eat. Alas! luckless boy, what a sad reverse!

"At length, however, he came to himself, and thought of the happy home he had left, of the kindness of his father, and the plenty with which his house abounded. Ah, should he ever see that home again? His pride revolted at the thought of so humiliating a return, for pride will follow a man to the very swine-yard, and curse him even there. But necessity pinched and want distressed him, and he said, 'I will arise and go to my father, and say unto him, Father, I have sinned against Heaven and before thee, and am no more worthy to be called thy son; make me as one of thy hired servants.'

"The Saviour gives us no items of his travel home, but I reckon the poor fellow had a hard time of it. No doubt he begged his way, probably traveling upon his bare feet. How very different the circumstances of his return from those of his departure! He went away in rich attire, with abundance of gold, finely mounted and attended. But look at him now! He is in sight of his native home, covered with rags, barefoot, and bleeding!

He moves slowly, his head droops down, and an old hat, with a tow-string for a band, hangs about his ears. The father, sitting in his veranda, and looking down the long, shaded avenue, sees the sad, bent figure, slowly and painfully halting toward the house. He feels a strange yearning toward the wretched creature. 'Who is it?' he inquires. The servant does not know, but would judge it to be some beggar coming to tax his well-known liberality. But ere the answer was ended, his heart had told him that the stranger was his long-lost son! With eager haste he runs to meet him: the son confesses: the father, not waiting to hear, cries out for joy, 'My son that was dead is alive again!' falls upon his neck, kisses him, and bathes his thin cheeks with a father's warm tears.

"After applying the history to illustrate the loving-kindness of our Heavenly Father to his wandering creature, man, he called in the most simple manner upon the prodigals present to return to their insulted but forgiving Father, assuring them that they should meet a merciful reception. And though the whole discourse was of this simple narrative style, and delivered in a low and measured tone of voice, the congregation was so convulsed with emotion that there was scarcely a dry eye in it.

"He seldom preached without producing a similar result."

He lived for many years after the failure of his health, and passed away to the "rest that remaineth to the people of God."

Methodism, during this year, assumed a more

permanent form. The experience of Poythress and of Haw—the sound and logical preaching of McHenry—the persuasive eloquence of Wilson Lee, and of Brooks, with the holy zeal, the pathos, and the tears of Peter Massie, and the earnestness of James O'Cull, under the blessing of Heaven, invested Methodism with a commanding influence. At the close of the year, they report one thousand and ninety members, being an increase of two hundred and twenty-seven.

During this year, the support of the preachers was very defective. Small as the allowance was, the people were unable to meet it. Hence, at the Conference held in Baltimore on the 6th of September, we have the following record: "At the Baltimore Conference, there was a collection of £72 9s. 6d; and, as the brethren in the Kentucky and Ohio Districts happened to be in the greatest need, the Conference generously voted two-thirds of the said sum as a partial supply for the preachers in the Ohio District, and one-third for the brethren in Kentucky—the whole to be sent in books." *

It was truly fortunate that the support of the preachers at that day did not require large amounts. They were all, then in Kentucky, unmarried men, and their appointments were so remote from each other that they could have no settled home, but lived among the people.

* General Minutes, Vol. I., p. 39.

Engraved by John Sartain Phil^a Expressly for History of Methodism in Kentucky.

FIRST METHODIST CHURCH IN KENTUCKY.

NEAR LEXINGTON.

CHAPTER IV.

FROM THE FIRST CONFERENCE HELD IN KENTUCKY, IN 1790, TO THE CONFERENCE OF 1792.

Bishop Asbury's first visit to Kentucky—The first Annual Conference in the District held at Masterson's Station, near Lexington—Richard Whatcoat—Hope Hull—John Seawell—First Methodist Church in Kentucky—Peter Massie—John Clark—The Conference composed of six members—Limestone and Madison Circuits—Henry Birchett—David Haggard—Samuel Tucker—Joseph Lillard—Death of Samuel Tucker—Bethel Academy—Madison Circuit disappears from the Minutes—Salt River Circuit—Barnabas McHenry—Death of Peter Massie—Life and death of Simeon.

IN the spring of 1790, Bishop Asbury made his first visit to Kentucky, where, for the first time, an Annual Conference was held. He was accompanied by Richard Whatcoat—afterward elected Bishop—and also by Hope Hull and John Seawell, men well known in those days as ardent, zealous, and useful preachers. The Conference was held, commencing on the 15th of May, at Masterson's Station, about five miles north-west of Lexington, where the first Methodist Church* in Kentucky—a plain log structure—was erected. To reach the seat of the Conference, required a journey of several days through a dreary wilderness, replete with dangers and

* This house is still standing (1868). See engraving.

infested by savages. "A volunteer company was raised to guard the Bishop through this dreary waste." This company was composed of the Rev. Peter Massie and John Clark, with eight others.

On the seventh day of their journey, they reached Richmond, the county-seat of Madison county, and three days afterward, reached Lexington. In alluding to this journey, Bishop Asbury says:* "I was strangely outdone for want of sleep, having been greatly deprived of it in my journey through the wilderness—which is like being at sea in some respects, and in others worse. Our way is over mountains, steep hills, deep rivers, and muddy creeks—a thick growth of reeds for miles together, and no inhabitants but wild beasts and savage men. I slept about an hour the first night, and about two the last. We ate no regular meals; our bread grew short, and I was much spent." On his way, he "saw the graves of the slain—twenty-four in one camp"—who had, a few nights previous, been murdered by the Indians.

The Conference was composed of six members, namely, Francis Poythress, James Haw, Wilson Lee, Stephen Brooks, Barnabas McHenry, and Peter Massie.

Bishop Asbury, in his journal,† in speaking of the Conference, says: "Our Conference was held at Brother Masterson's—a very comfortable house and kind people. We went through our business in great love and harmony. I ordained Wilson Lee,

---

* Journal, Vol. II., p. 83.

† Vol. II., p. 84.

Thomas Williamson, and Barnabas McHenry, elders. We had preaching noon and night, and souls were converted, and the fallen restored. My soul has been blessed among these people, and I am exceedingly pleased with them. I would not, for the worth of all the place, have been prevented in this visit, having no doubt but that it will be for the good of the present and rising generations. It is true, such exertions of mind and body are trying; but I am supported under it: if souls are saved, it is enough. Brother Poythress is much alive to God. We fixed a plan for a school, and called it *Bethel*, and obtained a subscription of three hundred pounds in land and money toward its establishment."

The Conference lasted only two days; for, on Monday, the 17th, we find Bishop Asbury again in the saddle, and "preaching ten miles from Lexington." The session was attended by a large number of people. The preaching was with divine power. One who was present* says: "The house was crowded day and night, and often the floor was covered with the slain of the Lord, and the house and the woods resounded with the shouts of the converted."

The visit of Bishop Asbury to Kentucky was of the highest importance to the infant Church. Although his labors had been abundant, they had been bestowed on the older settlements of the country. That he might fully understand the condition and the wants of the Church here, it was requisite that

---

*Rev. Lewis Garrett.

he become personally familiar with the perils by which it was surrounded. No Bishop of our Church had ever preached in the District. Bishop Asbury was the first preacher of any denomination, holding that high and sacred office, who exercised its functions in Kentucky. It was necessary to organize a Conference in Kentucky; and it was proper, in an eminent degree, that its organization should take place under the auspices of such a man as Bishop Asbury. Privations had to be endured, sacrifices made, difficulties surmounted, and dangers encountered, by the missionaries—and who was so well prepared to whisper words of cheer as one who had trodden the path of trial, and planted the standard of the cross amid discouragements before which stout hearts had paled?

Bishop Asbury was no ordinary man. "He was the only son of an intelligent yeoman of the parish of Handsworth, Staffordshire." * From early childhood, he was seriously impressed upon the subject of religion. Converted to God when quite a youth, "at the age of seventeen he began to hold public meetings, and before he was eighteen began to preach;" † and started out as an itinerant before he was twenty-one years of age. At the age of twenty-six, he was appointed by Mr. Wesley to America; and, at the Christmas Conference of 1784, held in the "Lovely Lane Chapel," in the city of Baltimore, he was *unanimously* elected to the office of Bishop.

---

* Stevens's History of M. E. Church, Vol. I., p 111. † Ibid., p. 115.

Possessed of a high order of talent, with a mind well cultivated and richly stored with useful knowledge; with a will to execute; thoroughly imbued with the spirit of his mission; entirely consecrated to the service of God; devoting every energy to the prosecution of the work to which he had been called—to this man American Methodism and American Christianity is more largely indebted than to any minister of the gospel of the present or the past. He was a Bishop according to apostolic rule. While many of the prelates on the Continent were reposing on their beds of down, and priests of the Established Church, in silken robes, were reeling before the altars of God, like the unwearied sun, he was "moving from day to day in his journey around this vast continent, of five thousand miles, annually," and diffusing his benign influence from center to circumference.

To the infant Church in Kentucky, his visit, though brief, gave a fresh impulse. The revival of religion that commenced at the session of this Conference spread through many portions of the State, so that this year was far more prosperous than any that had preceded it.

The Conference was an humble one—only six* preachers; but small as it was in the beginning, these ministers were destined to go forth, "a flame

*Collins, in his History of Kentucky, says twelve; but Mr. Collins counts visiting preachers. The Minutes report only six, and the list of appointments adds four, and deducts three, namely, James Haw, Wilson Lee, and Peter Massie. These latter were appointed to the Cumberland Circuit.

of fire," as the heralds of the cross, shedding the mellow light of Christianity, and spreading the triumphs of the gospel, through every settlement of the State; winning many trophies to the Redeemer from the ranks of sin. It was their mission to lay the foundations of a system, deep and wide, whose teachings should bless the nations; to plant here, upon this virgin soil, the evergreen-tree of Christianity—which, though the storms of opposition should gather around it, and the lightnings of persecution play upon it, should continue to grow, until its boughs should spread over every hill-top and upon every vale—offering a shelter to the weary and way-worn pilgrim on his journey to the grave.

Hitherto there had been but two circuits in Kentucky: the Minutes this year report four, adding the Limestone and Madison;* and nine preachers, instead of six, are appointed to cultivate this field. The names of Henry Birchett, David Haggard, Samuel Tucker, and Joseph Lillard, appear on the roll for this department of the work, for the first time.

Henry Birchett had entered the itinerant ministry in 1788, and, before coming to Kentucky, had traveled on Camden and Bertie Circuits, in North Carolina. He was a Virginian by birth. Surrounded in childhood with the comforts of life, and reared amid ease and abundance, he cheerfully consecrated

*The Cumberland Circuit is in the Kentucky District; but as it was almost exclusively in Tennessee, we do not refer to it as a part of Kentucky Methodism.

himself to the work of the ministry. To leave the comforts of home and the society of friends, and become identified with the fortunes of the itinerant work was, at that day, no ordinary sacrifice. The wants of the Church in Kentucky required ministerial help, and Mr. Birchett cheerfully volunteered for this distant and dangerous field. In the circuits he traveled, he was eminently useful and remarkably popular. His talents were good. He was regarded "an excellent preacher;" while his zeal scarcely knew any bounds. Nor did he confine himself to the labors of the pulpit. He looked on the children as the future hope of the Church, and in their moral and religious instruction he took the deepest interest. "In every neighborhood where it was practicable, he formed the children into classes, sang and prayed with them, catechised them, and exhorted them."* For many years after he had "entered into rest," his memory was green and his name was fragrant among the young people.

David Haggard accompanied Mr. Birchett into Kentucky. He was admitted to the ministry in 1787, and had labored on Banks and Anson Circuits, North Carolina, and on Halifax, in Virginia. In connection with Henry Birchett, he was, this year, as well as the succeeding, appointed to Lexington Circuit. In 1792, he was sent to New River Circuit, Virginia; and, in 1793, to Salisbury, North Carolina; after which his name disappears from the Minutes. He, however, returned to the East, and

---

*Western Methodism, p. 69.

became connected with the O'Kelly schism; but finally joined the New Lights, and died in their communion.* During the two years of his labors in Kentucky, and indeed during all the time of his connection with the itinerancy, he was a faithful, acceptable, and useful preacher.

Joseph Lillard was a Kentuckian by birth. He was born not far from Harrodsburg,† and this year entered the traveling connection. His appointment was to the Limestone Circuit, with Samuel Tucker. He traveled his second year on the Salt River Circuit, as colleague to Wilson Lee; after which his name disappears from the Minutes. After his location, he settled near Harrodsburg, Kentucky, not far from the place of his birth, where, among his friends and neighbors, he lived to a good old age. In his local relation to the Church, although as a preacher he was unpretending, yet, by the sanctity of his life, and by his devotion to the Church, he was very useful. In his home the weary itinerant always found a cordial welcome and a place of rest, while by his liberality he contributed largely to the promotion of the Church. Neither the precise date nor the manner of his death is known.‡

---

*Collins's Kentucky, p. 126.

†Collins, in his History of Kentucky, p. 127, makes this statement. If correct, Lillard must have been very young when he entered the itinerancy.

‡In a letter to the author, the Rev. S. X. Hall, of the Kentucky Conference, says: "The best information I can get in reference to the Rev. Joseph Lillard is, that he was born in Kentucky, in what is now Mercer county. He was esteemed to be a good man, truly

Samuel Tucker, just admitted on trial, was also appointed this year to the Limestone* Circuit, but did not live to enter upon his work. On his way to Limestone, in descending the Ohio River, at or near the mouth of Brush Creek, the boat was attacked by Indians, and the most of the crew killed. We also learn that Mr. Tucker exhibited that most extraordinary coolness during the attack, by which the brave man is always distinguished. He continued to defend the boat with his rifle, until every man was killed except himself, and he mortally wounded. He reached Limestone alive, but soon died of his wounds. His remains now lie, with no stone to mark his grave, in the cemetery at Maysville.

In alluding to the death of Mr. Tucker, the Rev. William Burke, in his Autobiography,† says:

"There is one thing worthy of notice, and that is, that, notwithstanding the constant exposure the traveling preachers were subjected to, but two of them fell by the hands of the savages, and both of them by the name of Tucker. One was a young

---

pious, but somewhat eccentric. He is said to have been a very ordinary preacher. About nine miles from Harrodsburg there is a large brick church, with a somewhat prosperous membership, principally built by the Rev. Joseph Lillard, and bearing the name of Joseph's Chapel, named for its builder. He died some fifteen years ago, while on his way from Missouri to Kentucky. It is not known how, when, or where he died. His friends and relatives think he was murdered."

*The point where Maysville now stands was originally called Limestone.

†Western Methodism, p. 44.

man, descending the Ohio on a flat-boat, in company with several other boats—all were family boats, moving to Kentucky. They were attacked by the Indians, near the mouth of Brush Creek, now Adams county, Ohio. Several boats were taken possession of by the Indians, the inmates massacred, and the property taken by them. Every man in the boat with Tucker was killed, and Tucker wounded mortally. The Indians made attempts to board the boat, but, notwithstanding he was wounded, the women loaded the guns, and Tucker kept up a constant fire upon them, and brought off the boat safe; but before they landed at Limestone he expired, and his remains quietly repose somewhere in that place. Brother James O'Cull assisted in burying him, and is the only man now living who could designate the spot. I think the Kentucky Conference should erect a monument to his memory. The other was shot near a station south of Green River, not far from the present town of Greensburg."

The Rev. Jacob Young, himself a minister for more than half a century, gives the following interesting account in his Autobiography: *

"We had a great and good quarterly meeting at Tucker's Station, near Briceland's Cross-roads, between Steubenville and Pittsburgh. This was among the oldest stations west of the Alleghany Mountains. Father Tucker was living here at the time that Adam Poe had the famous battle with the Wyandot chief, 'Big-foot.' They were both brave

* Autobiography of the Rev. Jacob Young, pp. 414, 415.

men and true patriots. 'Big-foot' was fighting in the defense of his nation, and Poe in the defense of his country. This was certainly a dreadful conflict. Both gave full proof of their natural courage and dexterity. It had liked to have proved fatal to both. I apprehend the Wyandots were a noble race of men. It is a great pity the world cannot learn more of their nationality. I believe that the Poes descended from an excellent stock: we had full proof of this in the high-minded Daniel Poe, who died a martyr, in my opinion, in doing his part to evangelize Texas. A Christian soldier, he fell at his post; his manly form lies in a strange land, and his sweet-spirited missionary wife sleeps by his side. Their lovely children were left without father or mother, but were not forsaken and left to beg their bread.

"Father Tucker resided here during a long, dangerous, and bloody war with the Indians; raised a very large family, but one of whom distinguished himself—I think his name was William.* His father might have said of him, as old Priam said of Hector, that William was the wisest and best of all his sons. He became pious when he was very young, and before he was twenty years of age commenced preaching the gospel. Although born and reared on the frontiers, by close and constant application he acquired a pretty good English education. He bore a very active and successful part in trying to civilize and Christianize the people in the country

---

* The Minutes give the name as Samuel.

where he resided. His zeal increased with his years; and, while he was yet a young man, he volunteered as a missionary to go to Kentucky: he well knew the danger to which he would be exposed—for the Indian war was raging at the time in its most dreadful forms—but a desire to save souls elevated him above the fear of death. While he was going down the Ohio River, the boat in which he was descending was attacked by a large company of Indians, and as he was well acquainted with the mode of Indian warfare, he took the supervision of all the boats in the company, and had them all lashed together with ropes. Taking his stand in the middle boat, that the whole company might hear the word of command, he ordered the women and children to keep close to the bottom of the boats, lest the Indians might shoot them, and directed the men to arm themselves with axes and bars of iron, etc., so that, if the Indians attempted to come on board, they might mash their fingers and hands. In this way they crippled many of their warriors, and defended themselves for a long time. At length, the cunning Indians found out where the commander stood, and, in a canoe, got round to the end of the boat where the steering-oar works, and shot him through the hole. He saw that he had received his death-wound. He advised them all to get into one boat, leave their property, and try to save their lives. Having given them the best direction he could, he kneeled down, made his last prayer, and expired. They made their escape from the Indians, and landed at Limestone, where they buried their beloved minister. I have stood and looked at his grave with mingled feeling. I will here say that I received this minute information through an uncle of mine, who owned one of the boats, and was an eye-witness of the whole scene."

The Rev. Lewis Garrett, in his "Recollections of the West," p. 17, in referring to the death of Mr. Tucker, expresses the opinion that he labored the greater portion of the year on the Limestone Circuit, and near its close returned home "to the old settlements;" and, on his return to Kentucky, was killed by the Indians. He says: "Samuel Tucker, a young man, who was this year (1790) admitted on trial as a traveling preacher, was remarkably successful in preaching the gospel: he was, indeed, a herald of the cross; and in him was exemplified that prediction, 'His ministers shall be a flame of fire.' Under his labors there was a mighty turning to God, and these were days of grace, and times of refreshing from the presence of the Lord. But his race was short, and his work soon accomplished. Perhaps about the close of this year, he had occasion to go to the old settlements, to assist in removing some of his relatives or friends. In descending the Ohio River, the boat, laden with emigrants to Kentucky, was fired upon by the Indians. Mr. Tucker received a mortal wound; but report said that he fought with valor and much presence of mind, so that the boat was saved—but he died soon after, rejoicing in God."

The Rev. Dr. Stevenson, in his "Fragments from

the Sketch-book of an Itinerant," after alluding to the voyage of his father down the Ohio River to Kentucky, gives the following account of the murder of Mr. Tucker:

"Widely different, however, was the fate of the next lot of boats that attempted the same dangerous passage. A little below the mouth of the Scioto, they were attacked by the Indians, in great numbers, from both sides of the river, as well as from their numerous bark canoes in the stream itself. Two of the boats were soon overpowered by superior force, and an indiscriminate slaughter of men, women, and children ensued. The third and only remaining boat of the company was closely pursued for several hours. At times the issue of the conflict was considered doubtful. The most of their active and valorous men were either killed or wounded, and their remaining force was by no means sufficient to manage the oars and successfully resist a direct assault from their blood-thirsty pursuers. The women, however, at length, came forth to the rescue from their places of security and protection. Some took the oars, and others commenced reloading the guns, leaving the few fighting men, who had been mercifully preserved from the balls of the enemy, with nothing to do but to watch the movements of the insidious foe, fire to the best advantage, and as often as they pleased. It was a long and hard-fought battle. The Indians, at length, began to haul off: the fire from the boat had become too constant and well directed to meet their views, and soon the last warlike craft disappeared on the distant waters, and the poor bullet-riven boat was left to float on without farther molestation. Early the next day, they landed at the 'Point.' My father was among the first on board. The scene was inexpressibly horrible. The living, as well as the dead and dying, were literally covered with blood. Among the latter was a Mr. Tucker, a respectable local preacher* of the Methodist Church. He had received a mortal wound in his chest, soon after the commencement of the attack; but, nothing daunted by the near and certain approach of death, he continued to fight on—loading and firing his own long rifle, until his fading vision shut out the enemy from his sight. He breathed his last, in submission to the Divine will, soon after the boat reached the landing, and was buried by my father and others, amid the lofty forest trees that then overhung, in primitive grandeur and sublimity, the beautiful bottom where now the tide of business and commerce rolls on unmindful of the past. The place of his interment is known to none now living. The light of eternity will alone reveal the hallowed spot."†

It is proper to state that Dr. Stevens, in his History of the Methodist Episcopal Church, quoting from an article in the Methodist Magazine for 1819, written by the Rev. Mr. Hinde, fixes the date of the murder of Mr. Tucker in 1784. Dr. Stevens says: "As early as 1784, local preachers began to enter it

* He was a traveling preacher. His name stands on the General Minutes, Vol. I., p. 37.

† Nashville Christian Advocate, Oct. 9, 1856.

(Kentucky), both as settlers and as pioneers of their faith. In this year, one of them, by the name of Tucker, while descending the Ohio in a boat, with a number of his kindred—men, women, and children—was fired upon by the Indians: a battle ensued; the preacher was immediately wounded; but, falling upon his knees, prayed and fought till, by his self-possession and courage, the boat was rescued. He then immediately expired, shouting the praise of the Lord." Mr. Hinde, to whom we are indebted so largely for his interesting Sketches of Early Western Methodism, has doubtless fallen into an error as to the time of the massacre of Mr. Tucker. From the Minutes of the Conference, as well as from the testimony of the Rev. Lewis Garrett, we learn that he was admitted on trial into the traveling connection in 1790; and the Rev. William Burke refers to him as a traveling preacher.* Rev. Jacob Young says, "He volunteered as a missionary to go to Kentucky."† As no missionaries were sent to Kentucky previous to 1786, the date of Mr. Hinde, as quoted by Dr. Stevens, must be incorrect. We are also convinced that the Rev. Lewis Garrett is mistaken in the belief he expresses, that Mr. Tucker had spent the year, until "about its close," on his circuit in Kentucky. His useful labors, to which he makes such touching reference, must have been "in the country in which he resided," where, the Rev. Jacob Young informs us, "he bore a very active and successful part in trying to civilize and

* Sketches of Western Methodism, p. 44.

† Autobiography, p. 415.

Christianize the people," before "he volunteered as a missionary to go to Kentucky." From all, however, we can learn concerning him, he was reared amid the dangers of Indian warfare; "became pious when very young, and, before he was twenty years of age, commenced preaching the gospel." In the work of the ministry he was remarkable for his zeal, and cheerfully left home and friends that he might aid in the erection of the temple of Methodism in Kentucky. But God ordered otherwise. The spot where he was to commence his labors was to be the scene where his final triumph would be witnessed. It may be that the "shout of joy" which fell from his lips so soon after the boat on which he lay dying landed at Limestone, in the hearing of those to whom he had been appointed to "proclaim the unsearchable riches of Christ," made an impression more enduring than might have been made by his labors, if he had lived. The Minutes of the next year make no mention of his death.

This year, Thomas Williamson, who left Kentucky in 1789, returned, and was appointed to the Danville Circuit, where he remained for two years; and, having "literally worn himself out in traveling and preaching,"* asked for a location. During all the period of his connection with the itinerancy, he was a very successful preacher. He ended his days in great peace, near Lexington: the precise time of his death, however, is not known.

Allusion has already been made to the revival of

---

* Western Methodism, p. 68.

religion with which the first Conference in Kentucky was blessed. The summer and autumn of the previous year had passed away amid extraordinary manifestations of Divine power. Under the ministry of the word, hundreds were convinced of sin, and bowed before the cross, and the shouts of triumph had ascended to heaven from souls converted to God. The spring of 1790 exhibited no abatement of religious interest or prosperity. Wherever the gospel was preached, the presence of the Lord was manifested, and his power felt. Indian depredations and cruelties were of common occurrence. The noble Tucker had fallen by their hands, but nothing daunted, these preachers of the cross, true to their obligations and their trust, shunned no danger in the performance of duty. They inscribed "success" upon their banners, and they achieved it. They preached a present Saviour: they expected immediate results, and were only satisfied with the realization of their hopes and wishes.

At the close of the year, they report one thousand five hundred and fifty-three members, being an increase over the former year of four hundred and sixty-three—the largest of any year since the organization of the Church in Kentucky.

The Methodist Church in Kentucky, anxious to aid in the educational interests of the District, was the first of the Christian denominations to undertake any movement that looked to the establishment of an institution of learning. At the Conference held in April of this year, at Masterson's Station, Bishop Asbury says: "We fixed a plan for a school, and called it *Bethel*, and obtained a subscription of upward of three hundred pounds in land and money toward its establishment." It was "principally built through the influence and exertions of the Rev. Francis Poythress, the first Presiding Elder on the Lexington District."* It was located in Jessamine county, and stood on a high bluff on the Kentucky River. The Rev. William Burke, in his Autobiography, published in "Sketches of Western Methodism," pp. 42, 43, in referring to Bethel Academy, says:

"In the county of Jessamine, situated on the cliffs, was Bethel Academy, built entirely by subscriptions raised on the circuits. One hundred acres of land were given by Mr. Lewis as the site for the academy. The project originated with Mr. Asbury, Francis Poythress, Isaac Hite, of Jefferson; Col. Hyde, of Nelson; Willis Green, of Lincoln; Richard Masterson, of Fayette, and Mr. Lewis, of Jessamine. A spacious building was erected—I think, eighty by forty feet, three stories high. The design was to accommodate the students in the house with boarding, etc. The first and second stories were principally finished, and a spacious hall in the center. The building of this house rendered the pecuniary means of the preachers very uncertain, for they were continually employed in begging for Bethel. The people were very liberal, but they could not do more than they did. The country was new, and the unsettled state of the

---

*Rev. Jonathan Stamper, in Home Circle, Vol. I., p. 360.

people, in consequence of the Indian wars and depredations, kept the country in a continual state of agitation. The legislature, at an early period, made a donation of six thousand acres of land to Bethel Academy. The land was located in Christian county, south of Green River, and remained a long time unproductive; and while I continued a trustee, till 1804, it remained rather a bill of expense than otherwise. In 1803, I was appointed by the Western Conference to attend the legislature and obtain an act of incorporation. I performed that duty, and Bethel was incorporated, with all the powers and privileges of a literary institution. From that time, I was removed to such a distance that my connection with the academy ceased. The Rev. Valentine Cook was the first that organized the academical department; and at first the prospect was flattering. A number of students were in attendance; but difficulties occurred which it would be needless to mention, as all the parties concerned have gone to give an account at a higher tribunal; but such was the effect that the school soon declined, and Brother Cook abandoned the project."

However much we may lament the fate of the Bethel Academy, it affords us pleasure to look back to that early day, when Kentucky was only a District, not having been admitted as one of the States into the Union, and behold that noble little band of Methodists, with only six preachers and less than one thousand Church-members under their supervision, laying the foundations of educational enterprise, and projecting schemes for the literary advancement of the rising generation. They looked to the future. They plainly foresaw the coming prosperity and glory of the State; and if Methodism would occupy its proper place with sister Churches in the regards and esteem of a free and prosperous people—if their labors would be crowned with permanent success—the supporting layer on which they must build, must necessarily embrace in its provisions the literary culture, as well as the moral and religious instruction, of the youth of the country. Methodism has ever been friendly to education, as sanctified learning has ever been the handmaid of religion. Rejecting the theory that no man should preach the gospel of Christ, whose literary attainments are not of the highest classical character, Methodism, at the same time, has numbered among her ministers in Kentucky many who have stood preëminently high for their scholastic attainments; whilst, among her large and rapidly increasing membership, in the learned professions, and in the higher walks of life, she is ably represented in every community. At this early day, many of the most influential families in the State had entered her communion, amongst whom were the names of Hardin, Thomas, Hite, Lewis, Easland, Masterson, Kavanaugh, Tucker, Richardson, Letamore, Brown, Garrett, Churchill, Jeffries, Wickliffe, Hoard*—names, most of which are prominently known at the present time in Kentucky Methodism.

* Western Methodism, p. 66.

The failure of the Bethel Academy to meet the wants and wishes of the Church, did not, by any means, paralyze their efforts, or shake them in their purpose to succeed. It seemed only to fit them for new and untried exertion, at another point, where we shall meet them again arduously laboring to accomplish the same ends.

At the Conference in 1791, the Minutes report the same number of circuits as the former year. The name of the Madison Circuit, however, does not appear, it having been absorbed in the Danville; and the Salt River Circuit is added. There is also one preacher less this year.

The circuits, at that date, were not of the convenient size in which the minister who now enters the itinerant field finds them.

"The *Limestone Circuit* lay on the north side of Licking River. It included Mason and Fleming counties.* It was bounded on the east, south, and west, by the frontier settlements, and on the north by the Ohio River.

"*Lexington Circuit* contained the counties of Fayette, Jessamine, Woodford, Franklin, Scott, and Harrison—bounded on the east and north by the Hinkstone Circuit, and on the west by the frontiers. Frankfort, now the seat of government, was then a frontier station.

---

*Several of the counties mentioned were not formed at this date. Previous to 1792, only nine counties had been formed, namely, Fayette, Jefferson, Lincoln, Nelson, Bourbon, Madison, Mercer, Woodford, and Mason. Mr. Burke means the territory embraced in these counties when formed.

"*Salt River Circuit*, the most difficult in the bounds of the Conference, included Washington, Nelson, Jefferson, Shelby, and Green counties—bounded on the north by the Kentucky River; on the east by Danville Circuit; on the south by the frontier settlements on Green River, including where Greensburg and Elizabethtown are now situated.

"*Danville Circuit* included Mercer, Lincoln, Garrard, and Madison counties. The west part of the circuit included the head-waters of Salt River and Chaplin on the north, and bounded by the Kentucky River south and east, extended as far as the settlements."*

The Cumberland Circuit lay chiefly in Tennessee. It extended, however, into Kentucky, and embraced, besides Middle Tennessee, what is now known as Logan, Warren, and Simpson counties. To travel through so large a territory; to preach almost daily; to form societies, and to perform other duties that belong to the profession of the ministry, required an amount of labor to which but few men are equal, and which, in a short time, would impair the health of the most stalwart.

Joseph Tatman was admitted on trial into the Conference this year, and appointed to Danville Circuit, as colleague to Thomas Williamson. He only traveled one year. At the next Conference, his name disappears from the Minutes, after which all trace of him is lost.

In a previous chapter, we have shown that,

---

*Burke's Autobiography.

although the General Minutes announce the appointment of the Rev. Barnabas McHenry to the Cumberland Circuit, in 1788, he did not take charge of this work until 1791. This year he leaves Kentucky, to cultivate "Immanuel's lands" elsewhere.

During the three years of his absence from Kentucky, his labors were abundant. The first was spent on the Cumberland Circuit; the second as Presiding Elder over the Holston, Green, New River, and Russell Circuits, spreading over a vast extent of territory in Virginia and Tennessee; the third as the Presiding Elder over the Bedford, Bottetourt, Greenbrier, and Cow Pasture Circuits, in Western Virginia. In 1794, he returns to Kentucky, and is appointed to the Salt River Circuit—the most laborious in the Conference. During this year he was married to Miss Sarah Hardin, daughter of Col. John Hardin; and, at the close of the year, located, and, in that sphere, for many years rendered valuable service to the Church.

Before parting with Barnabas McHenry for the present, we will quote a letter written by him to the Rev. Lewis Garrett,* which will be read with interest, and convey to us a correct idea of the toils, the privations, and the dangers endured by those devoted men on whose labors we have entered:

"MOUNT PLEASANT, near Springfield, Ky., May 15, 1823.

"DEAR BROTHER:—After the reception of your favor of the 24th of March, rummaging some of my

---

* Recollections of the West, pp. 92–101.

old papers, I found a journal, (or fragment of a journal,) including a part of the first year of my itinerant labors in what is now West Tennessee, then called Cumberland Circuit.

"In company with Brother James O'Cull, I reached Philip Trammell's, on one of the forks of Red River, not very far from the place which has since been called 'Cheek's Tavern,' on Wednesday, May 25, 1791. The circuit was a four-weeks' circuit. Clarksville, near the mouth of Red River, was the lower extremity of the circuit, *and of the settlement.* We had one stage between that and Prince's Chapel, near the mouth of the Sulphur Fork; we had one or two preaching-places up the fork, besides one on Whip-poor-will, a large creek that falls into it on the north side; whence we proceeded on, or near, to the northern limits of the settlement, (which did not then include all the upper waters of Red River,) preaching at a few places where we had some societies, till, some distance above Trammell's, we turned across to Sumner Court-house, which was a *cabin* near Station Camp Creek. The upper end of the circuit was the eastern extremity of the settlement, Col. Isaac Bledsoe's, near Bledsoe's Lick. The population, for some miles down, consisted of a narrow string between the river and the ridge. Indeed, there was then no population on the south side of Cumberland River, Nashville and a very small part of the adjacent country excepted. There were but four regular preaching-places on that side of the river, although the preachers aimed so to regulate their stages that all the inhabitants of the country should have circuit-preaching convenient to them. I do not remember a single instance of their refusing to visit any neighborhood, nor even any *station*, on account of danger, though, in some instances, *guards* met them, where risk was thought to be uncommonly great.

"I find in my old journal the following, viz.: As I had no company on Monday, 18th of July, I yielded to persuasion, and deferred riding up to Col. Sanders's until the next day. And perhaps it was well I did; for, not far to the right of the way I must have gone, the Indians fired upon four persons that evening, and killed Mr. Jones. Again: Thursday, August 4th:—The guard did not meet me at Mr. Hogan's, according to promise; so I tarried here till Saturday, etc.

"I happened to be in the same part of the circuit, when a man much beloved—Maj. George Winchester—was killed in the neighborhood of the place where Gallatin now stands.

"In one case the hand of God has appeared *to me* so evident in my preservation, that I cannot think it improper to give you the circumstances in detail. I have told you that Clarksville was the extreme point of the settlement down the river. Mr. Denning's, where I put up, was the upper house in the place—a cabin, standing fifty or sixty yards (I conjecture) from any other, near the bank, having the door fronting the river. Being much engaged with a book that had just fallen into my hands, when others had retired to rest one night, I again sat down to read, with my face toward the door; the table upon which my candle was placed standing by the wall, between me and the door. Observing that the door was not closely shut, I rose, shut and bolted it, or rather barred it, and again sat down to my book till quite late. The next day, I preached in one of the cabins in the town, (as it was even then called,) intending to spend the following night at Mr. Denning's, for the purpose of reading; but a young gentleman having come about fifteen miles, in order to ride with me that afternoon, I changed my purpose, and went on with him. That very night the Indians attacked the house of Mr. Denning. Firing in at the door, which was standing a little open, (as it had stood the preceding night,) they shot a Mr. Boyd, who was sitting, or in some way resting, on the table, standing in the very place where it had stood when I sat reading at the end of it. It afterward appeared (the Indians relating it themselves to a white man with whom they were acquainted, and whom they met in the Spanish territory, where they were professedly at peace) that they had crossed the river the night before on purpose to murder the people in that house; but, growing fearful that there were too many men in it, they shrunk from the attempt, lay concealed all the next day, and at night rose and made the assault.

"Had I tarried there that night, as I had designed to do if Mr. Pennington had not come to meet me, I had in all likelihood been their mark, sitting with my breast toward them, on the opposite side of the candle, within a few feet of the muzzles of their guns. And how probable is it, that, if the door had not been noticed and closely shut the preceding night, the light of the candle would have invited their approach. It would have shown, at a late hour, both that all was still, and that there was a favorable opportunity of looking in. But *the hairs of my head were numbered.* The *Strength of Israel was my refuge.*

"Although blood continued to flow, from time to time, till I left the circuit, in April, 1792, the country was not by any means as it had before been—particularly in 1789, when Brother Thomas Williamson was on the circuit. He was my intimate and particular friend, and gave me by letter an affecting history of their perilous situation. He expressed his doubts whether he would ever see me 'any more in this world,' as God permitted the barbarous enemy to slay the righteous with the wicked. He mentioned two or three young men who had been powerfully converted, and soon afterward murdered. But I have to regret that I have not preserved any of his letters.

"In *that country*, and in *this*, the course pursued by the circuit-preachers was pretty much the same, and so likewise were their dangers and their difficulties. They had counted the cost, and no form in which Death or any of his precursors presented seemed to appall them. Each circuit in Kentucky embraced *dangerous frontiers*, in which, in some places, paths made by stock or wild beasts might lead the traveler astray. By one of these, in the summer of

1788, Brother Wilson Lee was conducted so far beyond the limits of the settlement that he had to spend a dreary night in the wilderness alone. One of the preachers appointed to Danville Circuit, in the spring of 1789, was quietly enjoying his nightly repose, about a mile from the place where I now write, when a company of Indians, not far from the little cabin in which he lay, were catching the horses which the family had ridden home from meeting late that evening. In the course of that year, William Wilson and Charles Burks, two class-leaders belonging to the circuit, were killed. In some places the preachers could not retire to the woods or fields for the purpose of reading, meditation, and prayer, without probable danger of being shot or tomahawked. This was the more sensibly felt, as the houses in such places afforded little or no convenience for retirement. Our 'advantages' consisted principally in *peace and love.* United in the holy fellowship of the gospel ministry, we were, in a great measure, *of one heart and of one soul.* The same spirit, in no small degree, happily pervaded our societies. We served a simple-hearted, teachable people, who received us as the messengers of God. The Churches, augmenting by an accession of members of this description, were '*our glory and joy;*' though, in weariness and painfulness, in watchings often, in hunger and thirst, in fasting often, in cold and nakedness, (tattered raiment,) we 'eat our' *coarse fare* 'with *gladness* and singleness of heart, praising God, and having favor with the people.'

"You will see, by an extract of a letter in the Arminian Magazine, Vol. II., p. 202, that Brother James Haw went from this country to Cumberland in August, 1788; and that he and Brother Massie were there in the following winter. They remained there till the next spring.

"Soon after I reached the Kentucky settlement—which was on the 11th of June, 1788—Brother Haw formed the design of placing me on Cumberland Circuit, to which he then intended to accompany me, and make a short stay; but, before he had executed his purpose, he was superseded by Brother Poythress. The consequence was, that Brothers Haw and Massie went to Cumberland, and I continued in Kentucky that year, according to the original intention of that appointment. Brother Haw, it would seem, communicated his arrangements previous to the printing of the Minutes, which occasioned my name to be inserted as appointed to Cumberland Circuit. Brother Combs never went there. He was taken sick, and desisted from traveling. Brother Haw did not travel much in 1790. For particulars respecting his latter years, I refer you to Brother John Page. Brother Ogden married in Kentucky, in the spring of 1788, and immediately started to the eastward. He returned in the latter end of 1790, and has been a citizen of this country ever since. At one period, influenced by considerations which I am not prepared to explain, he withdrew from the Church; and, after continuing several years not regularly connected with any religious community, rejoined it. The latest account, he was living near Eddyville, a local preacher. Probably Brother Holliday can give you some account of him. His son, John Wesley Ogden, occupies the pulpit, we are told, among the Cumberland Presbyterians.

"A few years ago—I think it was in 1818—Brother Poythress died, *insane*, in Jessamine county, Kentucky, about twelve miles from Lexington, at the house of his sister, Mrs. Susanna Pryor, with whom he had lived, *in a state of derangement*, for a considerable time. My acquaintance with him began in the forty-fourth year of his age, (as he told me in July, 1788.) I have long thought that his mental powers had even then begun to fail. Be that as it may, his mind was certainly sinking, though sinking very gradually, for several years before. In the fall of 1800, if I remember rightly, he retired from the work. His exemplary piety, his zealous and *useful labors*, and his faithful (I do not say *able*) attention to the duties of his station, secured to him a degree of confidence and affection which made most of his friends *blind to his condition*. When he left his District, he came to his sister's without much delay, and, excepting a little while that he spent in Lexington, about the latter part of the year 1801, continued there the remainder of his days.

"At an early stage of his total derangement, he conceived an opinion that *he never had been pious*. He said that he had been *sincere* in his religious profession, but had always been mistaken in thinking that he was a Christian. In combating this opinion, his friends sometimes drew from him the strongest arguments, as he conceived, which recollection could supply, to prove that he must have been radically wicked even in his last days. Some have thought that on these occasions he furnished divine proof of the uprightness of his character. His memory was unimpaired; and it was thought that the man must be circumspect indeed who knew nothing worse of himself. He had a strange notion that he was suffering under the operation of a malignant influence proceeding from *mankind en masse*, and even those who as individuals regarded him with *good-will* were somehow compelled to aid in inflicting the evil.

"My helper on Cumberland Circuit, Brother O'Cull, labored with great zeal till some time in the fall of 1791, when he broke himself down so entirely that he has never recovered to this day. True, he sometimes preaches—and preaches, I am told, in a very impressive strain—but he has to speak slowly and in a very soft tone of voice. Indeed, it is in this manner only that he can hold conversation. He resides in Fleming county, in the northern part of this State, and has reared a family. After he broke down, Brother Stephen Brooks, by the direction of the Presiding Elder, took his place on the Cumberland Circuit till next spring.

"In 1794, I succeeded Brother Lurton, in August, and returned in November, being superseded by Aquila Sugg. I recollect nothing worth relating that fell under my notice in Cumberland Circuit, that year. Moses Spear was the helper. He lives somewhere in your bounds, I believe. Perhaps you can get some useful information from him. My health suffered frequent interruptions in the past winter. An intermittent headache in the month of March reduced me very much. I am still exceedingly feeble, but try to preach at least every Sabbath. My family are in common health. I know but little about the state of religion in the bounds of this Conference. My expectations are not elated. I think a great change in the ministry must take place before we shall see days of general prosperity. Pray for the peace of Jerusalem. God hath not cast away his people. May he speedily revisit us, and cause *our reproach* to be rolled away!

"I am yours in Christ Jesus,

"BARNABAS MCHENRY."

We now part for several years with this distinguished preacher of the gospel. We shall, however, meet him again—a giant in the itinerant ranks—devoting the prime of his manhood and the evening of his life to the promotion of Methodism. We will follow him to the close of his earthly career, and catch the last notes of triumph that fall from his dying lips.

Although the returns of this year do not indicate the prosperity that attended the labors of the previous year, yet "there was considerable religious excitement," and many accessions to the Church. There was an increase of membership on all the circuits. The largest increase was on the Salt River Circuit—the most laborious in the Conference: it was one hundred and twenty-six. On the

Danville Circuit, the increase was ninety-three; on the Lexington, twenty-three, and on the Limestone, thirteen. The total increase was two hundred and fifty-five.

Up to this period, not a single death had occurred among the itinerants of Kentucky, if we except that of the Rev. Samuel Tucker, who fell before entering upon his work. The first of the noble band who had devoted their lives to the cultivation of "Immanuel's lands," in these Western wilds, was Peter Massie.

> "Is it not a noble thing to die
> As dies the Christian, with his armor on?
> What is the hero's clarion, though its blast
> Ring with the mastery of a world, to this?
> What are the searching victories of mind—
> The lore of vanished ages? What are all
> The trumpetings of proud humanity,
> To the short history of him who made
> His sepulcher beside the King of kings?"

The composure of the Christian in the hour of death has excited the admiration of mankind in every age, since the establishment of Christianity, and in every clime where its ensign has floated and its truths been proclaimed. His motto, "Holiness to the Lord," and his hope, the reward of the blessed—ever impressed with the conviction that "to die is gain"—he has always been able to look upon death, though with feelings of solemnity, yet as the precursor of his rest, and the avenue through which he may enter the abodes of the redeemed. The teachings of Christianity are, that this world is not man's home—it is only the vestibule of his being—the stepping-stone of his existence; and that, beyond "the valley and the shadow of death," there is a land where spring is perennial, and amid whose glories he may repose for ever and ever! With the Christian, Death, the "king of terrors," and the terror of kings, is divested of his power to alarm, and is regarded as a friendly messenger, to "break the golden bowl," and to "loose the silver cord" of life. How oft have we seen the Christian die, and, amid weeping friends, heard the last words of triumph as they fell from his expiring lips and floated out on the pure, ambient air of heaven! It was the triumph of the soldier, returning from the empurpled field with victory inscribed upon his banner. The contest had been severe, but the triumph is complete. It is more: it is the inexpressible joy of the child of God, who, with earth's sorrows past, is now standing beside the river on whose banks there grows no living thing, and upon whose leaden waters there floats not a wreck of all that was—looking back, with emotions of pleasure, upon a life that had been consecrated and devoted to God; and then, beyond the swelling stream, to the "land afar off," and, in the light of Revelation, contemplating the glories that await him. It is the rapture of the soldier of the cross, who, with life's battle fought and its warfare ended, leaning his head upon the breast of his Redeemer, bids adieu to earth—the theater of his conflicts—and enters upon eternal rest. If this be so with the Christian who may have filled only an humble sphere in life, may we not expect the faithful minister of Christ, whose life had been devoted to the weal of others, to approach the margin of the river undaunted and composed? It has been often and truly said, that "a man's life is the proper index to his death. Tell me how he lived, and I will tell you how he died." This, as a rule, is correct, with proper qualifications. Apply it to the subject before us, and how gratifying to linger and contemplate his character!

Peter Massie was the first itinerant minister of the Methodist Church, identified with its fortunes in Kentucky, to die—as he was the first man, converted in the State, who became an itinerant. He was among the first-fruits of the revival of 1786* in Kentucky. Soon after his conversion, he was impressed with the conviction that he ought to devote himself entirely to the work of the ministry. Feeling properly the great responsibility of the "high and holy calling," and his "insufficiency for these things," he endeavored to drown the voice of conscience, and to suppress his impressions on this subject. The result was the loss of his religious enjoyment—retaining, however, "the form of godliness," and his membership in the Church. While in this backslidden state, "in company with two others, he crossed the Ohio River into the Indian

---

*In Finley's Sketches of Western Methodism, p. 66, the Rev. William Burke, referring to the revivals under the labors of James Haw, says: "Out of this revival was raised up some useful and promising young men, who entered the traveling connection, and many of them made full proof of their ministry, and lived many years to ornament the Church of God. I will name a few of them: Peter Massie, who was termed the weeping prophet, was among the first-fruits."

country, and gathered some horses. On their return, the Indians overtook them on the bank of the Ohio, fired on them, and killed all the company, except Massie. Seeing no chance for flight, he sprang into a sink, and concealed himself among the weeds. He could see the savages butchering his comrades, whom they cut to pieces and scattered around him."* Surrounded by such imminent danger—his escape uncertain—he turned to the only sure refuge for such an hour. He fervently prayed for deliverance, and promised, if his life was spared, he would hesitate no longer in entering the ministry. He faithfully kept his promise. In 1788, he entered the connection, and traveled successively the Lexington, the Danville, the Cumberland, and the Limestone Circuits. The Limestone Circuit—the last to which he was appointed—was the smallest in its territorial limits of any on which he had labored; and yet it spread over a large tract of country. In the various charges he filled, he was eminently useful. As often as he preached, he wept over the people. He was styled "the weeping prophet." A writer† says: "He was a feeling, pathetic preacher. The sympathetic tear often trickled down his manly cheek while pointing his audience to the Lamb of God slain for sinners." His talents as a preacher were fair; his personal appearance attractive; his voice soft and plaintive—a good singer; fascinating in his address, and re-

---

* Recollections of the West, p. 19.

† Rev. Lewis Garrett.

markable for his zeal. He was about thirty years of age. It is to be regretted that one so useful, so devoted, and so universally beloved, should so early be called away. He died in the bounds of the Cumberland Circuit, on which he had traveled the previous year, and to which he had gone probably on a visit to his friends. On the evening of the 18th of December, 1791, he reached the house of Mr. Hodges, four miles west of Nashville. The family of Mr. Hodges was in the fort, for protection, and Mr. Hodges himself was in his cabin, alone, and quite ill. The only person at the cabin, besides, was a negro boy named Simeon, who had on that evening escaped from the Indians, and reached the house of Mr. Hodges. Simeon had become acquainted with the preacher on the Cumberland Circuit, and had been converted through his instrumentality. Mr. Massie was "an afflicted man." His constitution, always feeble, had become greatly impaired by his excessive labors, and, on reaching the house of his friend, he complained of indisposition. He suffered considerably during the night, but on the next morning was able to take his place at the table. While in conversation with Mr. Hodges, it was observed to him "that he would soon be well enough to travel, if he recovered so fast." To which he replied: "If I am not well enough to travel, I am happy enough to die."* These were his last words. In a few moments he fell from his seat, and suddenly expired. In any country the

*Rev. Learner Blackman's unpublished manuscript.

death of such a man would be deeply felt; but where the "harvest was so plenteous, and the laborers so few," the loss of so useful a minister would spread a shadow over the Church. But he has passed away—the first of a noble line of self-sacrificing and devoted ministers of Christ—"having washed his robes and made them white in the blood of the Lamb."

When nearly a half century had elapsed, the Tennessee Conference felt a considerable anxiety to find the place of his burial. No stone had been left to mark his grave; or, if so, it had fallen away. A committee was appointed to find the sacred spot; but, after an ineffectual search for years, the hope of success was abandoned. Seven years later, the Rev. Thomas L. Douglass was preaching near Nashville, and in the close of his sermon referred with much feeling to the hope he anticipated of meeting in heaven with Wesley, Asbury, McKendree, and others who had passed over the flood. In the congregation there sat an aged African, with tears coursing their way down his furrowed cheeks, and the frosts of nearly eighty winters resting upon his brow. He too was deeply moved, and, thinking of another whom he hoped to see again, exclaimed in a clear voice: "Yes, and Brother Massie!" and then, continuing his soliloquy, he added: "Yes, Simeon, with these hands, with no one to help, you dug his grave, and laid him away in the cold earth; but you will see him again, for he lives in heaven!" A member of the Tennessee Conference* sat just

*Rev. A. L. P. Green, D.D.

in front of old Simeon, and heard what he said. After the close of the services, he took him aside, and inquired of him as to what he knew of the death and burial of Peter Massie. His eyes sparkling with the fire of other years, he replied that he was at Mr. Hodges's at the time of the death of Mr. Massie; that Mr. Hodges himself was sick, and unable to assist in his burial, and that the painful pleasure of the interment devolved on him alone; that he had no plank of which to make a coffin; that he cut down an ash-tree and split it in slabs, and placed them in the grave which he had dug, and, after depositing the body, placed a slab over it, and then filled the grave with the earth. He was under the impression that he could find the precise spot where the remains of Massie lay; but he could not. When he buried him, the whole country was a wilderness; but at the time he made the search for his grave, civilization had changed its entire appearance.

> "His ashes lie,
> No marble tells us where. With his name
> No bard embalms nor sanctifies his song."

Angels keep their vigils over his grave, and in the first resurrection he shall have a part.

We now propose to close this chapter with a brief sketch of Simeon, by whom Peter Massie was buried. He was a native African, and stated to Bishop Paine that he belonged to the nobility of that country. When only a child, he was brought to the United States. He fortunately fell into the hands of Mr. Dickinson, an elegant gentleman of Tennessee; and, under the preaching of Peter Massie, in 1790, was awakened and converted to God. He soon became impressed with the conviction that he ought to preach the gospel; and, although uneducated, he entered at once upon the work of the ministry. For more than fifty years he lifted the ensign of the cross among the colored people of Tennessee, and was remarkable for his success in winning them to Christ. His preaching was "not with enticing words of man's wisdom, but in demonstration of the Spirit and with power," and exerted an influence that was felt far and near. With the people of his own color he enjoyed a popularity that belonged to no other man in the community in which he lived, and over them he exercised an authority for good. The purity of his life so won upon the affections and confidence of his master, that, in early manhood, he emancipated him, and gave him a small farm near Nashville, which was voluntarily returned by him in his last will and testament. The deep concern that he felt for the African race was not confined to those around him, but his sympathy extended to his countrymen in their native land.

In 1823, he called on Bishop McKendree, and presented to him, in forcible language, the wants and the condition of his people in Africa, and urged the appointment of a missionary to that benighted land. The Bishop became deeply interested in the scheme, and decided to comply with his wishes. The Rev. Robert Paine (now Bishop Paine) was then a young preacher, and stationed at Franklin and Lebanon. Mr. Paine offered himself for the work, making only one condition—that Simeon should accompany him. To this Simeon readily consented; but the entire arrangement was defeated by the remonstrance of the Church at those places against the removal of their preacher.*

In his personal appearance he was superior to all his race around him. Although a full-blooded African, his face would have commanded attention anywhere. With a high and well-formed forehead; with penetrating, searching eyes; with a countenance full of the expression of benevolence, and with a mind far above ordinary—he would have commanded respect in any community. Added to these, a life unblemished by vice, developing every day the practical duties of Christianity, it is no wonder that he enjoyed the confidence, as well as commanded the respect, of those among whom he lived. Not only did he minister to the spiritual wants of his own people, but often was he sent for to kneel and offer prayers to God at the bedside of the sick and the dying among the white people.†

In 1847, he passed away. After a long and useful life, he was called from "labor to reward." While dying, a member of the Church was kneeling beside him, who said to him: "Father Simeon, what hope have you beyond the grave?" With his eyes swim-

---

*I have these facts from Bishop Paine.

†Samuel P. Ament informed me that he had often found him praying with white families in sickness.

ming in death, he raised his right hand, and replied: "Up, up, up!" He spoke no more. Thus died this venerable servant of Jesus Christ—respected in life, and lamented in death, by all who knew him.

CHAPTER V.

FROM THE CONFERENCE OF 1792 TO THE CONFERENCE OF 1793.

Kentucky admitted into the Union—Isaac Shelby the first Governor—The imperiled condition of the State—Preparations for its defense—The counties of Lincoln, Fayette, Jefferson, Nelson, Bourbon, Madison, Mercer, Woodford, Mason, Green, Hardin, Scott, Logan, Shelby, and Washington—The Conference of 1792—Bishop Asbury present—Religious condition of the State—Col. John Hardin—He is sent on a mission of peace to the Indians—Is massacred—Col. Hardin a Methodist—Isaac Hammer—John Sewell—Richard Bird—Benjamin Northcutt—John Ray—Anecdotes of John Ray—John Page—Dr. McFerrin's testimony—Letters of John Page—Bishops Asbury, Whatcoat, and Coke—Wilson Lee leaves Kentucky.

Kentucky was admitted as a sovereign State into the Union in 1792. On the 4th of June, under the first Constitution, Isaac Shelby, the first Governor, took the oath of office. Mr. Shelby was of Welsh descent, but was born in the State of Maryland, near Hagerstown, where his ancestors had settled, on their first arrival in America from Wales. In early manhood, he removed to Western Virginia. At twenty-four years of age, he distinguished himself by the conspicuous part that he bore in the memorable and bloody battle fought with the Indians on the 10th of October, 1774, at the mouth of the Kanawha, under the command of the famous chief, Cornstalk.*

Mingling with the stirring events of the Revolution, and having borne an active part in our struggle for independence, he won for himself a reputation for martial prowess that gave him a place in the confidence and affections of his countrymen more enduring than granite. In 1783, he came to Kentucky, where "he established himself on the first settlement and preëmption granted in Kentucky," on lands that he had "marked out and improved for himself," during his first trip to the District, in 1775. Desirous to live in retirement, in the peaceful pursuit of agriculture, and to enjoy the quietude of home, he addressed himself with energy to the improvement of his lands. The unsettled condition of the District—the frequency of Indian depredations—the unprotected condition of the frontier—the dangers to which the settlers were continually exposed—all called for efforts too active to allow such a man the enjoyment of rest. He was a member of the Conventions held in Danville in 1787 and 1788, for the purpose of obtaining a separation from the State of Virginia; and also a member of the Convention of April, 1792, which formed the first Constitution of Kentucky. In the succeeding month he was duly elected Governor of the State. Entering upon the discharge of his official duties under the most trying circumstances, he turned his attention at once to the defense of the State against

* The father of Bishop Morris was in the same battle.—*Morris's Miscellany*, p. 87.

Indian incursions, and entered upon defensive operations for the protection of the entire frontier. The safety of the people—their growth and prosperity—as well as their religious advancement, and the promotion of Christianity, were intimately associated with the devising of such measures as would be a guarantee for protection. War has never been friendly to the advancement of religious truth, and no wars have probably ever been more demoralizing than those between the early Kentuckians and the Indians. Commenced and waged with shocking cruelties by the savage, retaliations equally severe were not unfrequent. The administration of Gov. Shelby—the signal advantage to the State with which he discharged his duties as the Chief Executive—belong not to our history, but to that of the State.

The county of Kentucky, which had been formed in 1776, by the Legislature of Virginia, out of Fincastle county, was divided, in 1780, into three counties—Lincoln, Fayette, and Jefferson. The former was named in honor of Gen. Benjamin Lincoln, an officer of distinction in the Revolutionary war; Fayette county was so called for Gen. Lafayette, the generous young Frenchman who offered his services to Washington in defense of American liberty; and Jefferson county was named in honor of Thomas Jefferson. Besides these, six other counties had been formed previous to 1792: in 1781, Nelson, named in honor of Gov. Nelson, of Virginia; in 1785, Bourbon and Madison counties were formed—the former named for the Bourbon family, in

France, and the latter for James Madison: Mercer county was formed in 1786, and was named in honor of Gen. Hugh Mercer; in 1788, Woodford, and in 1789, Mason counties, were formed—the former named after Gen. William Woodford, and the latter in honor of George Mason, an eminent statesman of Virginia.

In 1792, six additional counties were formed, namely, Green, Hardin, Scott, Logan, Shelby, and Washington.*

The Conference of 1792 was appointed to be held on Monday, the 1st of May; but from Bishop Asbury's Journal, the time appears to have been anticipated. The Bishop says:

"KENTUCKY—*Tuesday, April* 3. We reached Richland Creek, and were preserved from harm. About two o'clock it began to rain, and continued most of the day. After crossing the Laurel River, which we were compelled to swim, we came to Rockcastle Station, where we found such a set of sinners as made it next to hell itself. Our corn here cost us a dollar per bushel.

"*Wednesday, April* 4. This morning we again swam the river, and also the West Fork thereof. My little horse was ready to fail in the course of the day. I was steeped in the water up to the waist. About seven o'clock, with hard pushing, we reached the Crab Orchard. How much I have suffered in this journey is only known to God and myself. What added much to its disagreeableness,

*Collins's Kentucky.

is the extreme filthiness of the houses. I was seized with a severe flux, which followed me eight days: for some of the time I kept up, but at last found myself under the necessity of taking to my bed.

"*Tuesday*, *April* 10. I endured as severe pain as, perhaps, I ever felt. I made use of small portions of rhubarb, and also obtained some good claret, of which I drank a bottle in three days, and was almost well, so that on Sunday following I preached a sermon an hour long. In the course of my affliction I have felt myself very low. I have had serious views of eternity, and was free from the fear of death. I stopped and lodged, during my illness, with Mr. Willis Green, who showed me all possible attention and kindness.

"I wrote and sent to Mr. Rice, a Presbyterian minister, a commendation of his speech, delivered in a convention in Kentucky, on the natural rights of mankind. I gave him an exhortation to call on the Methodists on his way to Philadelphia, and, if convenient, to preach in our houses.

"*Tuesday*, *April* 11. I wrote an address on behalf of Bethel school. The weather was wet, and stopped us until Friday.

"*Friday*, *April* 20. Rode to Clarke's Station; and on Saturday preached on David's charge to Solomon.

"*Sunday*, *April* 22. I preached a long and, perhaps, a terrible sermon, some may think, on 'Knowing, therefore, the terror of the Lord, we persuade men.'

"*Monday, April* 23. I rode to Bethel. I found it necessary to change the plan of the house, to make it more comfortable to the scholars in cold weather. I am too much in company, and hear so much about Indians, convention, treaty, killing, and scalping, that my attention is drawn more to these things than I could wish. I found it good to get alone in the woods and converse with God.

"*Wednesday, April* 25. Was a rainy, damp day. However, we rode to meet the Conference, where I was closely employed with the traveling and local preachers—with the leaders and stewards. I met the married men and women apart, and we had great consolation in the Lord. Vast crowds of people attended public worship. The spirit of matrimony is very prevalent here. In one circuit both preachers are settled. The land is good, the country new, and indeed all possible facilities to the comfortable maintenance of a family are offered to an industrious, prudent pair.

"*Monday, April* 30. Came to L.'s. An alarm was spreading of a depredation committed by the Indians, on the east and west frontiers of the settlement. In the former, report says one man was killed. In the latter, many men, with women and children. Every thing is in motion. There having been so many about me at Conference, my rest was much broken. I hoped now to repair it, and get refreshed before I set out to return through the wilderness; but the continual arrival of people until midnight, the barking of dogs, and other annoyances prevented. Next night we reached the

Crab Orchard, where thirty or forty people were compelled to crowd into one mean house. We could get no more rest here than we did in the wilderness. We came the old way by Scaggs Creek and Rockcastle, supposing it to be safer, as it was a road less frequented, and therefore less liable to be waylaid by the savages. My body, by this time, is well tried. I had a violent fever and pain in the head, such as I had not lately felt. I stretched myself on the cold ground, and borrowing clothes to keep me warm, by the mercy of God I slept four or five hours. Next morning we set off early, and passed beyond Richland Creek. Here we were in danger, if anywhere. I could have slept, but was afraid. Seeing the drowsiness of the company, I walked the encampment, and watched the sentries the whole night. Early next morning we made our way to Robinson's Station. We had the best company I ever met with—thirty-six good travelers, and a few warriors; but we had a pack-horse, some old men, and two tired horses—these were not the best part."

The preachers appointed to the work were mostly new men. The zealous and indefatigable Lee and Birchett, with Francis Poythress as the Presiding Elder of the District—men who had contributed so largely to the success that had crowned the labors of Methodism, thus far, in Kentucky—were still continued in this department. The names of John Ray, John Page, Benjamin Northcutt, John Sewell, Richard Bird, and Isaac Hammer, appear this year, for the first time, in the list of the Kentucky Appointments. Allusion has already been made to the difficulties with which the pioneer preachers had to contend in propagating the truths of Christianity amongst the first settlers of Kentucky. As yet, there was no abatement in their trials. Very few settlements had been made outside the forts, and there was no diminution of the vigilance or cruelty of the Indians. The nation had just emerged from a long and bloody war, in their struggle for independence. The early settlers in Kentucky had, in the States from whence they came, been active participators in the exciting scenes of the Revolution. We have already said that war is demoralizing; and protracted, as was the Revolutionary war, through several years, there was left upon the minds of the people an irreligious taint, if not the impress of infidelity. Religion had been, to a great extent, neglected. Besides, the perils to which they were exposed, together with the frequent massacres which occurred, kept the mind in such a state of continual excitement as to repel religious truth.

It was in December of this year that Col. John Hardin was killed by the Indians. Among the brave and patriotic of the State he had but few peers. Descended from one of the best families of Virginia, he had served with marked distinction in the Continental army. Enjoying in the highest degree the esteem and the confidence of Gen. Daniel Morgan, to whose command he was attached, he was frequently selected for enterprises of peril, the success of which depended upon prudence and daring. As early as 1780, he came to Kentucky, but returned to Virginia. In 1786, he, with his wife and family, came again to Kentucky, and settled in Nelson (afterward Washington) county. In the wars against the Indians he had taken an active part. "After his settlement in Kentucky, there was not a single expedition into the Indian country in which he was not engaged, except that of Gen. St. Clair, from which he was prevented by an accidental wound, received while using a carpenter's adze."* In the spring of this year, he was sent by Gen. Wilkerson with overtures of peace to the Indians. The impression rested upon his mind that he would never return; but, true to the instincts of a brave and noble nature, he accepted the dangerous trust, willing, if need be, to sacrifice his life to his country's good. He reached an Indian camp, on his way to the Miami villages, attended by an interpreter—about a day's journey from where Fort Defiance was afterward built. He remained during the night with the Indians, who, in the morning, massacred him.

The loss of Col. Hardin to the State of Kentucky was deeply felt. No man had contributed more than he to the protection and safety of the settlers. The cause of Christianity, too, lost one of its brightest ornaments. As early as 1787, he embraced religion, and joined the Methodist Church, and, by his zeal, his influence, and his piety, had contributed much to its growth and prosperity.

---

*Collins's Kentucky, p. 339.

But in his home the stroke was felt with the greatest severity. For several months hope was entertained of his safety—that he was only a prisoner, and might still return.

On the 13th of the following April, Bishop Asbury, on his way to the Conference in Kentucky, visited Col. Hardin's family, and makes the following record in his journal: "From the quarterly meeting we came to Col. Hardin's. He has been gone some time to treat with the Indians: if he is dead, here is a widow and six children left. I cannot yet give him up for lost."

With deepest solicitude—with feelings of mingled fear and hope—his devoted wife waited for his return. The frosts of autumn came, and the snows of winter followed, and then the sad intelligence of his massacre. How desolate then his home! His impressions were prophetic: he never returned!

The cultivation of this field of ministerial labor required not only intellectual endowments of a high character, but also a devotion that no difficulties or trials could impair, and a resolution that no influence could shake. For more than two generations, the names of Ray, and Northcutt, and Page, occupy a place in the columns of the passing history of the Church.

The itinerant career of both Isaac Hammer and John Sewell was short. There is no account of the admission of Isaac Hammer into the Conference. His name appears in the Minutes of this year (1792) for the first time, as colleague to Henry Birchett on the Salt River Circuit; after which he unaccountably disappears from the roll. The failure of his health, in all probability, rendered him unequal to the task of an itinerant preacher, and compelled him to retire from a work that he had not the strength to perform.

John Sewell was admitted into the Conference in 1791, and traveled the Holston Circuit, in Virginia, one year, before entering on his labors in the wilderness of Kentucky. His appointment for this year was to the Lexington Circuit, with Benjamin Northcutt and John Page as his colleagues. His labors, however, in the Conference were brief. In 1793, he traveled the Danville Circuit, and located at the close of the year.

Richard Bird entered the traveling connection this year, and was appointed to the Danville Circuit. Wilson Lee, whose memory is so fragrant to the Church, was the preacher in charge. The subsequent year, Mr. Bird traveled on the Hinkstone Circuit; in 1794, the Limestone; after which he is transferred to Virginia, and travels successively on the New River, the Bottetourt, and the Greenbrier Circuits; and then his name disappears from the list of appointments.

It is but seldom that three such names appear so closely together, in answer to the question in the General Minutes, "Who are admitted on trial?" as those of Northcutt, Ray, and Page. Each, a giant in his sphere, was well qualified to assist in laying the foundations of the temple of Methodism amid the perils of the West.

Benjamin Northcutt was born in North Carolina,

January 16, 1770, and came to Kentucky in 1786. In the twentieth year of his age he was converted to God, and united with the Methodist Episcopal Church. The year after his conversion he was licensed to preach, and was employed the same year as helper on the Lexington and Danville Circuit. The following year he joined the Conference, and was appointed to the Lexington Circuit, and the next year to the Limestone. He remained, however, but a short time in the itinerant work.

No man, in a local sphere, labored more assiduously than he, or did more toward the development and growth of the infant Church; and but few in the itinerant ranks have contributed more largely toward the prosperity and elevation of Methodism in Kentucky. The principal societies in Fleming, and many in Mason, Nicholas, and Bath counties, were formed by him; and in the extraordinary revivals of religion which pervaded the State about the close of the last and the commencement of the present century, he was remarkably prominent as an efficient instrument in producing that glorious work of God. Reared amid the privations of frontier life, and conversant with the great revival of 1790, he was well prepared for the toil and the enjoyment connected with those remarkable demonstrations of Divine power—the subject of so much speculation—with which our State was favored at a later period. Side by side, at Cane Ridge, at Indian Creek, at Sugar Ridge, and in other portions of the State, with Ray and others, he labored day and night for the salvation of the people; and in later life, so far from being weary of the noble work, he not only preached on Sabbaths, but often devoted whole weeks together in attending meetings, both near and remote from his home. On camp-meeting occasions, he was a powerful preacher. In every department of the ministerial work he was perfectly at home. Whether in the altar, pointing the penitent to Christ, or standing before the vast multitude, pleading with sinners that they might be saved, he never faltered. In preaching, his voice, at first low, yet soft and musical, would gather compass and strength as he proceeded in the discussion of his subject, until he could be distinctly heard by the largest assembly. He resided in Fleming county, and in the community in which he lived his influence was more commanding than any other minister. It was not only his extraordinary intellect, but, added to this, the firmness of his Christian character, and the purity of his life, that endeared him to the people. One* who knew him well, said of him: "Few men have been permitted to live an age in one community, and go down to the grave with the universal testimony that their lives were of unimpeachable purity. Yet this was the lot of Benjamin Northcutt."

He died at his residence, in Fleming county, February 13, 1854, of cancer. His sufferings were great, but he bore them with Christian patience.

When spoken to in reference to his future prospects, he always expressed himself with great confi-

---

* Rev. Jonathan Stamper, in Home Circle, Vol. III., p. 30.

dence. To his pastor he said that his unwavering confidence in his Redeemer was astonishing, even to himself—that death was no terror to him; and thus he passed to the rest that awaited him.

The name of John Ray appears on the Minutes of this year, for the first time, though the testimony of his family is that he entered the Conference one year earlier.* He was born January 21, 1768. We have no information as to the denominational influences, if any, under which he was brought up. Without the advantage of early education, and reared on the frontier, he was familiar with the hardships incident to such a life. Indifferent to the subject of religion, he spent his boyhood and youth in the sports of that period, in which he greatly excelled.

"When the Methodists visited his neighborhood, he was one of the first converts, and, forsaking his gay and trifling companions, turned his feet to the house of God."† Soundly converted, and impressed with the conviction that he ought to preach the gospel, he soon offered himself to the Conference, and was cordially received by his brethren. His first and second years were spent on the Limestone Circuit, in Kentucky. In 1793, he was appointed to Green Circuit, in East Tennessee; and the three following years he labored in Virginia; and, from the year 1797 to 1800, inclusive, he traveled extensively in North Carolina, until, worn down by incessant toil and constant exposure and hard-

* In a letter from his daughter, Mrs. Lavinia Moss, to the author.

† Rev. Jonathan Stamper, in Home Circle, Vol. II., p. 284.

ship, he was no longer able to perform the duties incumbent on an itinerant minister. He then sought rest in a local sphere. In the great work to which he had been called, "his labors were abundant, and through his instrumentality many were awakened and converted to God." Whether on the banks of the Ohio, in the mountains of East Tennessee, traveling over the rich lands of Virginia, or threading the waters of the Roanoke, in North Carolina, his zeal knew no bounds, save his wasting strength.

In 1801, he located, and returned to Kentucky, and settled in Montgomery county, three miles east of Mt. Sterling, where his family resided, until 1831; when, in consequence of his antislavery sentiments, he removed to Indiana.

In his local relation to the Church, he was not idle. He preached with untiring energy in the great revivals with which Kentucky was blessed at that period. He had regular appointments, and never failed to meet them when able to do so. He was preëminently successful in the altar; and wherever he labored, he was instrumental in the salvation of souls.

Mr. Ray remained local until 1819, when he was reädmitted into the Kentucky Conference, and appointed for two years to the Lexington Circuit; after which he successively traveled the Limestone, Madison, Danville, and Hinkstone Circuits. The following two years he sustained a superannuated relation to the Conference, after which he was appointed to the Hinkstone Circuit; and then his name appears no more on the effective roll.

From 1828 until 1836, he was on the list of superannuated preachers, when his name disappears, without any record on the Minutes.

The following year, in the sixty-ninth year of his age, he calmly passed away, at his residence in Putnam county, seven miles north of Greencastle, Indiana, where he had lived since 1831, "esteemed and beloved by all who knew him." *

During his connection with the ministry—which lasted through nearly half a century—he maintained an irreproachable character, and in his Conference relations was reverenced by the young, esteemed by the aged, and respected by all.

Judge Scott, late of Chillicothe, Ohio—himself a pioneer preacher in Kentucky—thus describes him, as he appeared about the year 1795: "The Rev. John Ray was a rather tall, well-proportioned man, with a very pleasant countenance; and, on account of his meek, courteous manners, and chaste, instructive conversation, was held in high estimation by all who knew him. He was a very faithful and useful minister of the gospel, but did not rank as high as some few of our ministers of that day."†

Many amusing incidents are related of him, among which we give the following, from the "Autumn Leaves:"‡

---

* His death was caused by a lingering and painful affection of the bronchia.—*Home Circle*, Vol. II., p. 284.

† We are indebted to Rev. W. T. Harvey, pastor of the Methodist Episcopal Church, Chillicothe, Ohio, for a copy of the manuscript left by Judge Scott, in reference to early Methodism in Kentucky. We shall quote from it frequently.

‡ Rev. Jonathan Stamper, in Home Circle.

"On one occasion, an old gentleman of some wealth and influence had been guilty of very unfair conduct in the settlement of certain matters; for which, Ray, who was immediately concerned, unhesitatingly remarked that the old man was a great rascal. The person so complimented, hearing of it, said that Ray should take that back, or he would thrash him. A short time afterward, Ray was passing along the road where the old gentleman was out with his hands at work. He immediately called out:

"'Mr. Ray, I want to see you a moment.'

"'Very well,' said Ray, 'what is your will?'

"'I understand that you said I was a rascal.'

"'Yes, I did say it, and I said precisely what I thought.'

"'Well, sir, I said I would thrash you the first time I saw you.'

"'And did you think that that would make you an honest man, or alter my opinion of you? It would do neither the one nor the other, so that my whipping would go for nothing. I think you would be acting very foolishly. Now, if you want to find out which of us is the stouter man, we can settle that in a more decent way than by having a fight. Let us try it by lifting at that log. If you can raise it higher than I can, I will acknowledge that you are the stouter; but if I lift it higher than you—which I am pretty well persuaded will be the case—then you must acknowledge yourself beaten.'

"'Well, Mr. Ray, don't you acknowledge that

you slandered me in saying I was a rascal? and won't you take it back like a Christian?'

"'No; I shall always look upon you as a scoundrel until you repent, and give evidence of the sincerity of your repentance by making restitution.'

"The old man flew into a rage again, and repeated vehemently that he would flog him.

"'I think,' said Ray, 'you are a little rash. If you were to attempt such a thing, you could not do it.'

"'What! you a minister of the gospel, and threatening to fight!'

"'You had better not provoke me. I don't know what I might do; only this, I certainly am not going to let you beat me.'

"'Ah! well, Mr. Ray, let us make it up, and have no more quarreling.'

"'Agreed,' said Ray. 'I will take back what I have said when you repent and make restitution; but, until then, I shall hold you as a dishonest man.'

"The old man did not get angry again, and Ray rode away, leaving him in a better humor, but still feeling that he was regarded by him as a dishonest man.

"Brother Ray was a stranger to fear. I once saw him tried in circumstances where most men would have quailed. He, with several others, had prosecuted a man for kidnapping a family of free negroes. This person had carried off two lads and sold them in West Tennessee. In order to save himself from the State-prison, he was compelled to send and purchase the negroes at an enormous advance, and surrender them to the court. He was greatly exasperated, and determined to seek revenge on his prosecutors. Not long afterward, Ray and myself, with two other persons, were returning from the city of Lexington, where we had attended a Conference. We had not traveled far before we found ourselves pursued by a party of five men, armed to the teeth, with knives and pistols. They followed us until we reached a certain place, when they rode up, swearing that they would be revenged by shedding Ray's heart's blood. He received them as coolly as if they had been harmless travelers. 'If you think,' he said, 'to frighten me by this maneuver, you are mistaken. I know well that you are a set of cowards, or you would not come up armed against an unarmed man. It is dastardly. You are young men; I am an old man: why all this parade?'

"I and the other brethren present told them that if they touched Ray, it would be at their peril, and urged them to desist for the sake of their own reputation, if for no other reason. We finally succeeded in dissuading them from their purpose, but through it all, the intended object of their vengeance remained perfectly unmoved."

A member of the Kentucky Conference,* who knew him well, writes thus:

"The Rev. John Ray, about forty years ago, was a minister of very marked character, of the Kentucky Conference of the Methodist Episcopal Church.

---

*Rev. Dr. Ralston, in a letter to the author.

He was a man of large stature—tall, well-proportioned, rather portly, erect, noble, and commanding in appearance. His features were regular, of a strong, masculine cast. Benignant humor, independent boldness, uncompromising firmness, and biting sarcasm, were strongly written upon his countenance. His step was firm and elastic. He was of graceful and commanding mien. His complexion, though dark, was not swarthy. His hair—though doubtless originally a deep-brown—when I first saw him, was a magnificent iron-gray, standing nearly erect upon his forehead, and hanging down, from ear to ear, in bushy curls upon his shoulders.

"A man of such personal appearance, we may reasonably suppose, would be a marked and decided character in whatever sphere he might move. And such he was. I have been informed that, in early life, his advantages were few, his education limited, and his training rough and little refined. He was a ringleader in all the frolicsome amusements and rough sports of the neighborhood. He could outrun, outjump, outfiddle, outdance, and outbox the most celebrated of his associates.

"But when converted, he was equally bold and decided. He soon became a minister; and though, to use his own language, he often 'drew the bow at a venture,' he seldom failed to 'send the arrow to the heart' of some of 'the King's enemies.' He was certainly no book-worm. He read comparatively but little, except the Bible and the standard works of the Church; yet he was a man of great quickness of perception, and keen, practical sense. He thought much and closely. His ideas were clear; his reasoning strong and logical; his method simple and natural; his voice strong, melodious, and manly; his emphasis was correct and impressive, and his manner dignified and earnest. Though ignorant of etymology and syntax, his language was generally in accordance with grammar.

"With him, shrewdness of mother-wit supplied, to a great extent, what culture had denied. In the pulpit, as well as in the social circle, he abounded in pithy, epigrammatic remark. His illustrations, though always taken from the common affairs of life, and sometimes coarse, were pointed and forcible—always understood and seldom forgotten.

"Many amusing incidents, illustrative of his ready wit and repartee, have been told, and are yet in the memory of his friends. He became noted in Kentucky, in his day, for his strong opposition to slavery; and was quite rough, and sometimes offensive, in the manner in which he obtruded that subject, especially upon people of the world. He would seldom lodge at the house of a slave-holder, if he could well avoid it. Often, at his appointments, when invited home with a stranger, his prompt interrogatory would be: 'Have you any negroes?' In the Annual Conference, whenever a preacher was proposed for admission, every eye would be turned to Father Ray, expecting him to arise, as was his custom, and say: 'Mr. President, has he any negroes?'

"Once, in his presence, a young preacher was

rather boasting that he was very popular on his circuit with a certain denomination. 'It is a bad sign, young man,' said Father Ray. 'That only shows that you are both *impudent* and *ignorant;* for those are the passports to popularity in that quarter.'

"In his own neighborhood resided a Baptist minister named John S., familiarly called 'Raccoon S.,' who also was a man of much wit. These ministers had many a friendly sparring together. One day they met in the road, in the presence of some friends—Ray returning from a camp-meeting, and S. from an Association.

"'How do you do, Brother Ray?' said S. 'You seem to be returning from camp-meeting; and I suppose you had the devil with you, as usual.'

"'No, sir,' replied Ray; 'he had not time to leave the Association.'

"Ray generally rode a very superior horse. Once, as he was riding through the town of M., a group of young lawyers and doctors, seeing him approach, plotted that they would 'stump' him, in some way, when he came up. On his arrival, their chosen spokesman commenced:

"'Well, Father Ray, how is it that you are so much better than your Master? He had to ride on an ass, but you are mounted on a very fine horse. You must be proud. Why do n't you ride as did your Master?'

"'For the simple reason,' said Ray, 'that there are no asses now to be obtained—they turn them all into lawyers and doctors.'

"They said no more.

"These amusing incidents, though of little consequence in themselves, serve to illustrate the character of the man. We add but one more:

"He was celebrated for his capacity to command order, and tame the ruffians who sometimes infested camp-meetings. On one occasion, he had asked some young men to leave the seats appropriated to the ladies. They did not obey; whereupon he left the stand, and was approaching toward them, when he overheard one of them say to his companion: 'If he comes to me, I'll knock him down.' Ray very coolly replied: 'You are too light, young man;' and, taking him by the hand, led him quietly to his appropriate seat. He misbehaved no more.

"Though years have elapsed since the subject of this sketch passed from earth away, numbers are now living who trace their religious impressions to his labors.

"He remained in Kentucky some years after he had superannuated, but, previous to his death, he had removed to Indiana.

"Hundreds are yet living—not only in Kentucky, but in Indiana, Illinois, and Missouri—who once knew him well, and can call up, with the freshness of yesterday, the swelling melody that rolled from his clear, musical voice, as he would lift it up in his favorite hymn:

"'Our souls by love together knit,
Cemented, mixed in one!'

"But this laborious servant of God now rests from his labors in his Master's kingdom. He and his son Edwin, of precious memory in the Indiana

Conference, are now doubtless singing together the 'song of Moses and the Lamb.'"

John Page was born in Fauquier county, Virginia, November 22, 1766. In 1791, he was married to Miss Celia Douglas; and, in 1792, he entered the itinerant field.

Of his early life and training we have no record, nor are we informed in reference to the date of his conversion, nor of the instrumentality through which he was brought to Christ. He was twenty-six years old when his name first appears on the roll of the Conference.

Judge Scott, from whom we have already quoted, says: "The Rev. John Page was a large, splendid-looking man, of an open, manly countenance. He possessed a sound, discriminating judgment, and was regarded as an able, useful minister of the gospel, wherever he traveled."

From 1792 to 1859, his name is found on the roll of the Conference, with the exception of the period embraced in the years between 1804 and 1825—during which time he sustained the relation to the Church of a local preacher.

The first four years of his itinerant ministry were spent in Kentucky, on the Lexington, Danville, Salt River, and Limestone Circuits. In 1796, he was appointed to Green Circuit, in East Tennessee; but in 1797, he was returned to Kentucky, and appointed to the Hinkstone Circuit; and, the following year, to the Salt River and Shelby.

In 1799, he had the distinguished honor of succeeding William Burke on the Cumberland Circuit, lying partly in Tennessee and partly in Southern Kentucky.

The General Minutes of 1800 place him on the Holston, Russell, and New River Circuits,* embracing a large extent of territory in East Tennessee and Western Virginia; but, we learn from a letter written by himself, as well as one written by Bishop Asbury—both of which are published in the South-western Christian Advocate, of March 22, 1844—that his removal from the Cumberland Circuit met with the dissatisfaction of the people whom he had served with much usefulness and success. He had hardly entered upon his new field of labor until Episcopal prerogative called him away.†

He says: "I was in New River Circuit when the letters of Bishops Asbury and Whatcoat were handed me, urging me to hasten to Cumberland with all speed. I had just finished my sermon. I took my dinner and started, and reached my destined place as soon as I could. The work—as it had been—was still going on."

---

*In the South-western Christian Advocate, of March 22, 1844, Mr. Page calls this appointment New River, Holston, and Clinch.

†Rev. Learner Blackman, in his manuscript, says: "In the year 1800, Bishops Asbury and Whatcoat, accompanied by Elder McKendree, in their visit to the Western country, passed through the settlements of Cumberland. The work of the Lord was going on in the most pleasing manner; but they saw that the Methodist cause was most likely to suffer in consequence of the neglect of Methodist Discipline. They immediately transferred John Page from New River Circuit, in Virginia. He had previously been stationed in Cumberland, and was one of the principal instruments, under God, of the great revival, so much talked of over the United States."

The work to which he alludes was that extraordinary display of Divine power, which began in 1799, in the Cumberland Circuit, and spread with unparalleled success throughout the settled portions of Northern or Middle Tennessee and Southern Kentucky. If this remarkable revival of religion did not owe its origin to the instrumentality of John Page, it certainly was promoted and extended through his pious labors and exertions. In the section of Kentucky and Tennessee in which he labored, among the many distinguished ministers of his day, he was always the central figure—the most commanding person. In the altar, in the pulpit, in the social circle—mingling now with the more wealthy and refined, and then in the humble cabins of the poor—he vindicated himself as a useful and faithful minister of Jesus Christ, until his name in all this region became a household word—the synonym of all that is good. No wonder Bishop Asbury said, in his letter to him: "Had I attended at the last Holston Conference, you should have returned immediately to Cumberland. I should have had the petition that was sent for your return. Had I known what had taken place, I should have dismissed you when I passed by you. I hope you will now hasten to that charge as soon as possible. The eternal God be your refuge and strength!"

Uncommon as it was to continue a preacher any considerable time in the same field of ministerial labor, yet we find that this remarkable man is continued on the Cumberland Circuit during the years 1801 and 1802, and in 1803 we find him in charge of the Cumberland District as Presiding Elder. This District—including only four separate charges, namely, Nashville, (formerly Cumberland,) Red River, Barren, and Natchez—was confided to the supervision of John Page; while he had for his assistants in the work such men as Thomas Wilkerson, Jesse Walker, James Gwinn, Jacob Young, and Tobias Gibson.

In the discharge of the functions of his office, his long rides, his constant exposure, together with his incessant labors, broke down a constitution that hitherto had refused to yield to the exertions of so many years; and at the close of the first year on the District, he asked for and obtained a location. After this period his name appears no more in connection with the Church in Kentucky.

In 1825, he was reädmitted into the Tennessee Conference, and remained a worthy member of that body until his death, which occurred on the 17th day of June, 1859—only eight years of which time he was able to preach regularly, sustaining the most of the time a superannuated relation to the Conference. In the ninety-third year of his age, and the sixty-eighth of his ministry, the "weary wheels of life stood still."

We make the following brief extract from the General Minutes:

"Just before his death, he declared that he was ready and willing to die, and would soon be done with old earth and all its troubles and afflictions—then fell into a sweet sleep, to wake up in the land of eternal life."

In contemplating the character of such a man, how gratifying to the Church that his life was so protracted! He had seen the Church in its infancy, when it seemed to be only "a reed shaken by the wind;" he marked it as it gradually developed and gathered strength; and he beheld it as his sun was setting—gigantic in its proportions, dispensing its blessings all over the land. When he entered the itinerancy in Kentucky and Tennessee, there were but *two* Districts, embracing *nine* Circuits, and only *nineteen* traveling preachers, and only *twenty-six hundred and seventy-four* white, and *two hundred and one* colored members. At the time of his death there were, in the same territory, five Annual Conferences, embracing *forty-four* Districts, and *four hundred and eighty-six* Stations, Circuits, and Missions, *six hundred and eighty-nine* traveling, and *sixteen hundred and seventy-six* local preachers, and a membership of *one hundred and fifty-five thousand five hundred and eighty-four* white, and *thirty thousand seven hundred and ninety-six* colored!

If, in the morning of his life and the strength of his manhood, it was to him a source of pleasure to devote his energies to the Church, how great must have been the satisfaction he derived, as, in its evening, he contemplated the success and the triumph Christianity had achieved!

The following letters—published in the Southwestern Christian Advocate, of March 22, 1844, and entitled "Early Methodism in the South-west," with which we close this sketch—will be read with interest, and show the estimation in which Mr. Page was held by the chief pastors of the Church. They are thus introduced by the editor of that paper, the Rev. John B. McFerrin:

"There are yet among us a few of the fathers, who were the associates of Bishop Asbury, and who were among the pioneers of Methodism in the South-west. We venerate these men, and shall ever cherish them tenderly. When we remember that long before we were born, and when this vast country was a wilderness, with only here and there a thinly populated settlement, exposed to the barbarity of savage tribes, these men, constrained by the love of Christ, risked all to preach to the poor the gospel of the grace of God, we should be justly chargeable with ingratitude, were we not to highly esteem them for their work's sake.

"We number in this class the Rev. John Page, who still holds a place in the Tennessee Annual Conference, and usually visits our body at our annual meetings, and who is always hailed with pleasure by the younger members. 'Father Page,' as he is familiarly called, is one of those sweet-spirited servants of God, whom the wear and tear of years has not wrecked. He still loves God and loves the Church, and is a beautiful sample of a simple, plain, old-fashioned Methodist preacher.

"In his palmy days he could perform as much labor and endure as much suffering as any of his colleagues, and was in the midst of the glorious revival which swept over this country about half a century ago. He has favored us with two letters which have never been published—one from Bishop Asbury, the other from Dr. Coke. These are accompanied with a short note from Father Page, which we take the liberty to lay before our readers. Father Page's letter, though dated December 3, 1843, was retained by him until a few days past. This was owing to our absence during the winter."

"Dear Brother McFerrin:—I send you, with these lines, the Bishops' letters, to read and examine. Do with them what you may think best, only take care of them. Publish all or any part, as you may think proper. It may be necessary for me to state why I was sent to Cumberland in 1799. Brother William Burke preceded, and had a controversy with James Haw, an O'Kellyite, who expected to get the whole circuit to join him; but he failed in his attempt, and did not so much as influence his wife to join him. When Burke left, he promised to send me, (as the members of the circuit told me when I came.) When I did come, I found no opposition, and that year all was quiet, and God blessed us with a good revival; and the last part of the year I was invited into two of their meeting-houses, they having no pastor at Shiloh. I left in March for Holston Conference, and from thence to Baltimore. The Bishop then appointed me to New River, Holston, and Clinch. I was in New River Circuit when the letter of Bishops Asbury and Whatcoat was handed to me, urging me to hasten to Cumberland with all speed. I had just finished my sermon. I took dinner and started, and reached my destined place as soon as I could. The work—as it had been—was still going on. Arminius* has greatly misrepresented the work in Cumberland. He states that the revival first began at Gasper, or Muddy River, among Presbyterians. This is not so. It might have begun there among the Presbyterians, but not among us: we had a good work in Nashville Circuit the year before. John and William Carr are men acquainted with the whole revival scenes of that day. Alexander Rasco, one of our local preachers, got religion in 1799. I have troubled you with my scribbling. Bear with and believe me to be your friend and brother in Christ Jesus, JOHN PAGE.

"Smith county, Tennessee, December 3, 1843."

"The date of Bishop Asbury's letter is torn off; but we gather from it and Father Page's note, that it was written at Van Pelt's, ——, 1799.—*Ed. Adv.*"

LETTER OF BISHOP ASBURY.

"MY DEAR PAGE:—I have only time to write a few lines. * * * * Had I attended at the last Holston Conference, you should have returned immediately to Cumberland. I should have had the petition that was sent for your return. Had I known what had taken place, I would have dismissed you when I passed by you. I hope you will now hasten to that charge as soon as possible: the eternal God be your refuge and strength. To save

*Arminius is a writer who gave, some years since, sketches of early Methodism in the West.—*Ed. Adv.*

time, I hope Brother Watson will take your place, and Brother Hunter, Brother Watson's. Green must be left. If I can send help from South Carolina, I will. When you come to Cumberland, you will see if Brother Young or Grenade will be best spared to come to Green. We borrowed two jackets of yours, we will leave at Van Pelt's. I purpose riding half the year, upon horseback, upon the frontiers of the work. We shall always attend the Western Conferences, while able.

"I am, with great affection, thine,

"FRANCIS ASBURY."

POSTSCRIPT BY BISHOP WHATCOAT.

"MY DEAR:—Hitherto the Lord hath helped us. Glory to his great name! We cannot do too much for so gracious a benefactor. I hope you think no labor too great nor cross too heavy to bear for him that bought you with blood. The Lord hath given the alarm—the set time to visit Zion has now come. What thy hand findeth to do, do it with thy might. May Israel's God be thy strength and thy salvation!

"With due respect, thy brother in Christ,

"R. WHATCOAT."

LETTER OF DR. COKE.

"MY VERY DEAR BROTHER:—The great revival on the Continent rejoices me exceedingly—yea, more, I can truly say, than a revival in any other country in the world. I have read to thousands, and shall read, God willing, to tens of thousands, the accounts I have already received of the progress of the work in Maryland, Delaware, and Tennessee. I am glad to find that my old venerable colleagues are able, by traveling separately, to preside at all the Annual Conferences. I frequently travel with them in spirit, and never forget them and my other American brethren any night whatever, while I am bowing my knees before the throne. I am yours to command; and consider my solemn offer of myself to you at the General Conference before last, to be as binding on me now as when first made; and nothing shall keep me from a final residence with you, when I, God willing, meet you at your next General Conference, but such an interference of Divine Providence as does not at present exist, and such as shall convince the General Conference that I ought to tear myself from you. Nothing less, I do assure you, shall prevail with me to leave you.

"The work of God still goes on in a very blessed manner in Ireland. I lately returned from taking a tour of that country. There is nothing at present very remarkable in the work in Britain; but I am in hopes that I shall stir up my British brethren to jealousy, by first reading to them, and then printing, the delightful and animating accounts I have received from several of my American brethren. I am glad that Brother Cooper has published the Irish account. I intend soon to draw up and print another account of the farther progress of the work in Ireland.

"I bless the Lord, I am happy, constantly happy

in God; and I feel myself more than ever drawn toward my American brethren by the cords of love. Let me hear from you by some merchant-ship, directing to me at the New Chapel, City Road, London—whence all letters are safely sent to me, if I be not there.

"I am glad to find, by Brother Asbury, that you universally press upon your believing hearers the necessity of sanctification and entire devotedness to God; and that you guard them from seeking this, as it were, by the deeds of the law; and that you urge them to believe now on a present Saviour for a present salvation. Point out also in every sermon the absolute necessity of the knowledge of salvation by the remission of sins—the witness of the Spirit—the bright evidence of our interest in the Saviour's blood. Lukewarm endeavors are not sufficient now to pull down the fortresses of infidelity. They must be attacked by all the power of God; and, as humble instruments, we must get at the hearts of our hearers. Blessed be the Lord, the wretched formalists are disappearing like the dew of the morning; and we can fight infidelity without a screen betwixt. Let us, then, dear brethren, aim at being cities set upon a hill—at being the lights of the world—at being the salt of the earth; and, poor earthen vessels as we are—weak things, and things that are not—victory itself shall be enlisted on our side, because Almighty God will be on our side. O what a ravishing view the Lord sometimes favors me with of your immense continent, filled with inhabitants, and filled with sons of

God! The word of promise is on our side, ratified by the blood of the Lamb. It therefore must be so, for God hath spoken it.

"Pray for your faithful friend and brother,

"T. COKE.

"Liverpool, March 3, 1802.

"Do write to me once, before I see you, if you possibly can. I enjoy excellent health—the blessing of God; and I do assure you, my brother, I have no other intention but to pass the remainder of my poor life with you, from the next General Conference, God willing. T. C."

This year closed the labors of Wilson Lee in Kentucky. He had entered the District in 1787, and for six years he had been untiring in his energy in preaching the gospel of the Redeemer. But now, with wasted health and constitution broken, unable longer to remain and labor for the cause he loved so well, he naturally turns his thoughts to the older settlements, cherishing the hope of a return of health. Many hearts were touched at his departure. He had wept and prayed, and labored and suffered, with the infant Church, and had seen the fruit of his toil. Of him one of his cotemporaries* thus speaks:

"Wilson Lee was one of the most successful preachers among those early adventurers. He was a man of fine talents, meek and humble, of a sweet disposition, and not only a Christian and Christian

---

*Rev. William Burke, in Western Methodism, pp. 68, 69.

minister, but much of a gentleman. During his stay in Kentucky—from 1787 to 1792—he traveled over all the settlements of Kentucky and Cumberland, much admired and beloved by saint and sinner. In the spring of 1792, in company with Bishop Asbury, he crossed the wilderness from Kentucky to Virginia, where I met him at Conference on Holston; and from thence to the eastward, and attended the first General Conference at Baltimore, November 1, 1792; and remained in the bounds of the New York, Philadelphia, and Baltimore Conferences, till he departed this life, in 1804, at Walter Worthington's, Anne Arundel county, Maryland. The last time I had the pleasure of seeing him was in Georgetown, District of Columbia, on my way to the General Conference of May 1, 1804. He was then in a very feeble condition. His affliction was hemorrhage of the lungs, of which he died. During the time he traveled in Kentucky he passed through many sufferings and privations, in weariness and want, in hunger and nakedness, traveling from fort to fort, sometimes with a guard and sometimes alone—often exposing his life."

The causes, to which a reference has already been made, as having a tendency to retard the growth of the infant Church, were in no degree lessened: in addition to which, the minds of the people were occupied to a great extent by the questions that would necessarily grow out of the organization of the Government of the State.

Notwithstanding much had been done since the

first arrival of Messrs. Haw and Ogden, in 1786, yet we have to lament a smaller increase this year than any that had preceded it. Only ninety members more are reported than the previous year.

CHAPTER VI.

FROM THE CONFERENCE OF 1793 TO THE CONFERENCE OF 1794.

Conference held this year in Kentucky at Masterson's Station — Dangers encountered by Bishop Asbury to reach Kentucky — His immense labors—Jacob Lurton—James Ward—William Burke—John Ball—Gabriel Woodfield—Death of Henry Birchett.

THE Conference for the West, for the year 1793, was held in Kentucky, at Masterson's Station—the same place at which it convened three years previous. The session commenced on Tuesday, the 30th of April, and embraced the first and second days of May.*

To reach the seat of the Conference, Bishop Asbury again encountered the dangers of the wilderness. His route from Tennessee to Kentucky led him by "Doe River, at the fork, and through 'the Gap,' presenting a most gloomy scene, not unlike the Shades of Death in the Alleghany Mountains." On his way he held "a Conference at Nelson's, near Jonesboro," where they had "sweet peace." Anticipating trouble from the Indians, he expresses trust in God, and feels sure that, "if God

*The Rev. William Burke says: "On the 15th of April, 1793, the Conference met at Masterson's Station." (Western Methodism, p. 36.) We, however, prefer to follow Asbury's Journal, Vol. II., p. 194.

suffer Satan to drive the Indians" on his company, "he will teach their hands to war, and their fingers to fight and conquer."

The session of the Conference was a delightful one. The deliberations were marked with candor—"openly speaking their minds to each other"—and it closed "under the melting, praying, praising power of God."

There was but little business transacted of which we have any record. The only entry made is, that "trustees were appointed for the school, and sundry regulations made relative thereto." They also "read the Form of Discipline through, section by section, in Conference."

The day after Conference he preached from Habakkuk iii. 2, and some of the "people were moved in an extraordinary manner;" and the next day he arrives "at Bethel, and holds a meeting with the newly elected trustees."

Bishop Asbury deeply laments the decay of moral power, and makes a touching allusion to "the want of religion in most houses."

During his brief stay in Kentucky—entering the State on the 10th of April, and leaving it on the 10th of May—he attended two quarterly meetings; one of which was held at Humphries's Chapel, and the other at Clark's Station. Almost every day he preached to listening hundreds, urging the Church to awake from its lethargy, and sinners to turn to God. He traverses nearly the entire of Central and South-eastern Kentucky—exposing himself to danger, preaching the gospel, and administering the sacraments—until, utterly exhausted by his immense labors, he says: "I cannot stand quarterly meetings every day: none need desire to be an American Bishop on our plan, for the ease, honor, or interest that attends the office." But amid all this exertion and labor, worn out with traveling and preaching, he exclaims: "Yet, blessed be God, I live continually in his presence, and Christ is all in all to my soul!"

During his stay in Kentucky, he had the pleasure of visiting the Rev. Francis Clark, the pioneer preacher of the Methodist Church, who, in a local relation, had formed the first class, previous to the arrival of Messrs. Haw and Ogden in the District.

Jacob Lurton, James Ward, William Burke, John Ball, and Gabriel Woodfield this year receive appointments in Kentucky. Messrs. Lurton, Ward, Burke, and Ball were present at the Conference.

There were five circuits in the State, and the Appointments were:

Francis Poythress, Presiding Elder. Salt River—Jacob Lurton, James Ward; Danville—William Burke, John Page, John Sewell; Lexington—John Ball, Gabriel Woodfield; Hinkstone–Richard Bird; Limestone—Benjamin Northcutt.

Jacob Lurton had entered the connection in 1786, and traveled that year on the West Jersey Circuit. In 1787, he labored on the Berkeley Circuit, in the State of Virginia; the following year he was appointed to the Redstone Circuit, in Pennsylvania. In 1789, he returns to Virginia, and travels the

Clarksburg Circuit; the subsequent year the Kanawha. He spends the years 1791 and 1792 in Maryland, on the Baltimore and Harford Circuits; and in 1793, he was transferred to Kentucky, and appointed to the Salt River Circuit—the most difficult to travel and the most laborious of any in the State.

In the various appointments on which Mr. Lurton had labored and suffered, he had been the instrument of good. Whether in West Jersey, Virginia, Pennsylvania, Maryland, or in the wilderness of the West, he was zealous in the promotion of the kingdom of the Redeemer. His last year in the itinerant ministry was 1794. His circuit was the Cumberland, but the latter six months of the year were spent on the Salt River Circuit. On both of these circuits he was useful and beloved.

In the Cumberland Circuit, under his labors, there was an interesting revival of religion, which extended into Kentucky. He carried the tidings of salvation into Logan county—at that time remarkable for its vice—and was the first to proclaim the story of the cross to the people there. In the humble cabin of Mr. Cartwright—the father of the Rev. Peter Cartwright—in that county, he "preached with great power," while the "congregation were melted to tears."

Soon, however, his health failed him, and in the retirement of a local sphere he spent the remainder of his days.

He married a Miss Tooley, on Beargrass Creek, in Jefferson county, and for many years resided on Floyd's Fork of Salt River—where, still faithful to the dispensation of the gospel committed to him, he continued to preach, as his health would permit.

He is said to have been "an original genius," as well as "a useful preacher." He at length removed to the State of Illinois, and settled near Alton, where he died in great peace.

James Ward, who this year was the colleague of Mr. Lurton, was admitted on trial in 1792, in the Baltimore Conference, and appointed to the Holston Circuit—at that time on the Western frontier.

With the exception of 1793, when his appointment was to the Salt River Circuit, in Kentucky, he spent the first fifteen years of his itinerant life in connection with the Baltimore Conference—preaching chiefly, during this period, in the rugged settlements of Western Virginia.

The four years previous to his transfer to Kentucky—which occurred in 1807—he presided over the Greenbrier District, where his labors were greatly blessed. During the entire period of his early ministry, he was one of the most useful, as well as one of the most laborious, of the pioneer preachers. Persons who knew him in the evening of his life, could scarcely form any adequate idea of his pulpit abilities when in the flower of manhood. He was born and brought up in Somerset county, Maryland. In early childhood he was left an orphan. His mother inclined to the Church of England, and endeavored to train him in obedience to the stiff forms of that Communion. He, however, was brought in contact with the Methodist preachers, and through their instrumentality, in the seventeenth year of his age, was awakened, converted, and brought into the Methodist Episcopal Church. His mother was strenuously opposed to the step he had taken, but the opposition was soon overcome by his zeal for religion and the sanctity of his life.

Impressed with the conviction that he ought to devote himself to the work of the ministry, difficulties of an embarrassing character seemed to hedge up his way. The care of the family had been left to him as a sacred legacy by his father, previous to his death; his mother strenuously opposed his entering the itinerancy; and the interest and the cares of home demanded his attention. Amid these obstacles he earnestly sought the path of duty. "The love of Christ constrained him." The victory was gained; and, not disregarding his filial obligations, but making ample provision for his mother and the remainder of the family, he entered upon the "hazardous enterprise of Methodist itinerancy."*

In 1789, he was licensed to preach; shortly after which "he was called out by the Rev. Richard Whatcoat, then Presiding Elder, to fill a vacancy on Dover Circuit, Delaware."† It was not, however, until 1792, that his name appears on the Conference roll.

From the very hour of his entrance into the Conference until his death—covering a period of

*Letter from his son, the Rev. Joseph G. Ward, of the Little Rock Conference.

†General Minutes M. E. Church, Vol. VI., p. 13.

sixty-three years—his devotion to the Church was characterized by untiring zeal; while, in the various charges he filled, the most extraordinary revivals of religion were, under God, the result of his labors.

During the early years of his ministry, while connected with the Baltimore Conference, "he labored chiefly in the valley and mountain sections of Virginia. Many pleasing reminiscences of his great success in winning souls to Christ still remain among the inhabitants of those regions. The men and women who were young two generations ago speak with raptures of his untiring zeal, his almost exhaustless energy, his overwhelming ministrations. They ranked him among the ablest and most successful men of his times." *

In 1807, he was regularly transferred to the Western Conference, and stationed on the Lexington Circuit, while his family resided on a farm in Jefferson county, which he had purchased.

At the General Conference of 1808, the Rev. William McKendree, the Presiding Elder on the Cumberland District, was elected to the Episcopal office. On the District Mr. Ward was his successor. At this time the Cumberland District comprised twelve separate pastoral charges, embracing within its territorial limits the whole of Southern Kentucky, a portion of Middle Tennessee, the territories of Illinois and Missouri, and the inhabited settlements of Indiana. To accomplish his work,

---

*General Minutes M. E. Church, Vol, VI., p. 13.

"he had, in some places, to carry his provisions with him, and lie out in the woods or prairies at night." * He remained on this District but one year, during which he astonished the people by his zeal; while great displays of Divine power were, everywhere within its bounds, seen and felt under his ministrations.

In the years 1809 and 1810, we find him on the Kentucky District, the successor of the illustrious William Burke. This District—embracing the country around Maysville and Flemingsburg—extended into the central portion of the State, including the settlements along the Licking River; the blue-grass lands of Fayette and Mercer counties—embracing Frankfort, Shelbyville, and Louisville, and throwing its lengthening lines across Green River, and to the banks of the Cumberland—was the field to be occupied by James Ward.

During the two years of his supervision of the Kentucky District, the same success that had everywhere previously crowned his labors was still to be seen. The following year he was appointed to the Shelby Circuit; and then for two years he presided over the Salt River District; when, with impaired health, and a growing family to support and to educate, he asked for and obtained a location; in which relation he continued until 1828.

In this sphere, however, he had no ease. His zeal for the cause of Christ found no abatement whatever. "Working diligently with his hands,

---

* Letter from the Rev. J. G. Ward.

he embraced every opportunity of preaching. He spent no idle Sabbaths when it was possible for him to get to church. He kept up regular appointments, and was always willing to assist the traveling preachers at camp-meetings and two-days' meetings, and spent much of his time from home." * Wherever he attended meetings, he bore an active part in the exercises—whether in the pulpit, making his appeals to sinners, or in the altar, impressing upon the penitent the "exceeding great and precious promises" of the word of God.

In 1828, he was reädmitted into the Kentucky Conference; but, after traveling three years, he became superannuated, which relation he sustained until 1833; and from that period until 1840, he traveled circuits, yet was unable to do more than meet his regular appointments, from which he was seldom absent.

In 1840, his name disappears from the effective list, to be placed on it no more. From that time until his death he sustained a superannuated relation.

In the controversy which arose between the two divisions of the Methodist Church, in the General Conference of 1844, he took his position with the Northern branch; and in 1848, he asked admittance into the Baltimore Conference, and "the Conference, without controversy, by a unanimous vote, directed that his name should be recorded upon the list of superannuated members."

---

* Letter from the Rev. J. G. Ward.

"On the 13th of April, 1855, in the eighty-fourth year of his age, and the sixty-third of his itinerant ministry, he departed this life, near Floydsburg, Kentucky. His death seems to have been less the result of any particular disease than the gradual wearing away of life's weary wheels. The heavenly inheritance was bright before him to the last moment. His sun went down without a cloud. His spirit, without a struggle, returned to his God." *

As a preacher, Mr. Ward was not what the world would call eloquent. There was nothing rhetorical in his gestures, nor did he appeal to the sympathetic passions of the people. His preaching was scriptural; and this, with the fact that he was a man of prayer, always trusting in God, was the basis of his great success.

He was a member of the General Conferences of 1804 and 1808. He was also elected to the General Conference of 1812, but through modesty declined.†

This year introduces the name of William Burke into the history of Methodism in Kentucky. Among the early Methodist preachers of the West, William Burke stood preëminently high. With the fortunes of the struggling cause he became identified the previous year, when he joined the Conference, and was appointed to Green Circuit, in East Tennessee. In 1793, in charge of the Danville Circuit, with Page and Sewell for his colleagues, he entered the ranks in Kentucky, and from that period until 1812 he spent the most of his time in this extensive

*General Minutes M. E. Church, Vol. VI., pp. 13, 14.

†Judge Scott.

field. Occasionally the demands of the Church elsewhere require his services, and he is found proclaiming a Redeemer's love on Guilford Circuit, North Carolina, and on Holston, in the State of Virginia. Two years of this time he traveled the Cumberland Circuit, lying chiefly in Middle Tennessee. In 1804 and 1805, his field of labor is the Ohio District, embracing the extensive territory along the waters of the Muskingum, the Little Kanawha, Hockhocking, Scioto, Miami, and Guyandotte Rivers. The remainder of the time, embracing thirteen years, he devoted his energy and strength to Kentucky. Prompted by motives of the sublimest character—the love of Christ and the salvation of the people—he enters upon his work with the certainty of success.

The declension in piety, to which allusion has already been made, had reached the Danville Circuit. Mr. Burke says:

"We received our appointments at the close of the Conference, and separated in love and harmony. I was this year appointed to Danville Circuit, in charge, and John Page as helper. We entered upon our work with a determination to use our best endeavors to promote the Redeemer's kingdom. The circuit was in but a poor condition. Discipline had been very much neglected, and numbers had their names on the class-papers who had not met their class for months. We applied ourselves to the discharge of our duty, and enforced the Discipline, and, during the course of the summer, disposed of upward of one hundred. We had some few additions, but, under God, laid the foundation for a glorious revival the next and following years. The bounds and extent of this circuit were large, including the counties of Mercer, Lincoln, Garrard, and Madison. The west part of the circuit included the head-waters of Salt River, and Chaplin on the north; bounded by Kentucky River south and east, and extended as far as the settlements—taking four weeks to perform the round. There were three log meeting-houses in the circuit: one in Madison county, called Proctor's Chapel; one in the forks of Dix River, Garrett's Meeting-house; and one on Shoenea Run, called Shoney Run. Not far from Harrod's Station, in Mercer county, during the course of this year, a new meeting-house was erected in Garrard county, considered the best meeting-house in the country, and they named it Burke's Chapel. I remained on Danville Circuit till the first of April, 1794, and on the 15th our Conference commenced at Lewis's Chapel, in Jessamine county, in the bounds of Lexington." *

Such is his own account of his labors for this year. In 1794, his appointment is to the Hinkstone Circuit, then including Clark, Bourbon, and Montgomery counties; † and in 1795, he has charge of the Cumberland, embracing Middle Tennessee and Southern Kentucky. We have already noticed the influence he exerted in the Cumberland Circuit, in arresting the tide of opposition to the Methodist

* Western Methodism, p. 37.

† He remained on Hinkstone only until the first quarterly meeting, when he was removed to the Salt River Circuit.

Episcopal Church, when almost the entire community had been enticed from its teachings by the leading advocate of the views of Mr. O'Kelly. The declaration of the Rev. Learner Blackman, that "an almost expiring cause was saved"—in his reference to the controversy between William Burke and James Haw—is a worthy tribute to the talents and devotion to the Church of the former. From this period the Methodist Church, embraced in what was then the Cumberland Circuit, took a more elevated position; and from that date to the present time, its influence within the same territory has been more commanding than that of any other denomination of Christians.

The following account of the debate with Mr. Haw is from William Burke himself:

"On inquiry, I found that James Haw, who was one of the first preachers that came to Kentucky, had located and settled in Cumberland, and embraced the views of O'Kelly, and by his influence and address had brought over the traveling and every local preacher but one in the country to his views, and considerable dissatisfaction had obtained in many of the societies. Under these circumstances I was greatly perplexed to know what course to take—a stranger to everybody in the country, a young preacher, and Haw an old and experienced preacher, well known, a popular man, and looked up to as one of the fathers of the Church, and one who had suffered much in planting Methodism in Kentucky and Cumberland. After much reflection and prayer to God for direction, I finally settled upon the following plan, namely, to take the Discipline and examine it thoroughly, selecting all that was objected to by O'Kelly, and those who adhered to him, and then undertake an explanation and defense of the same. I accordingly met Brother Speer at Nashville, and after preaching, requested the society to remain, and commenced my work. When I concluded my defense, I took the vote of the society, and they unanimously sustained the positions I had taken. Brother Speer also asked the privilege of making a few remarks. He stated to the society that he would consider the Church as a house that he lived in; and notwithstanding the door was not exactly in the place he should like it, or the chimney in the end that best pleased him, yet he could not throw away or pull down his house on that account; and therefore he concluded that he would not throw away the Church, although some things, he thought, could be improved in the Discipline. In consequence of this victory on my first attempt, I took courage, and proceeded with my work in every society; and, to my utter astonishment, I succeeded in every place, and saved every society but one small class on Red River, where a local preacher lived by the name of Jonathan Stevenson, who had traveled the circuit two years before, and located in that neighborhood. Haw and Stevenson appointed a meeting on Red River, and invited the Methodists all over the circuit to attend the meeting, for the purpose of organizing the new Church. The result was, that only ten or twelve members offered themselves, and the most of them had formerly belonged to the Baptist Church. Having failed in every attempt to break up the societies, the next step was to call me to a public debate. I accepted his challenge, and the day was appointed to meet at Station Gap, one of the most popular neighborhoods, and convenient to a number of large societies. Notwithstanding I accepted the challenge, I trembled for the cause. I was young in the ministry, and inexperienced in that kind of debate. He was an old minister, of long experience, and of high standing in the community. I summoned up all my courage, and, like young David with his sling, I went forth to meet the Goliath. The day arrived, and a great concourse of people attended. The preliminaries were settled, and I had the opening of the debate. The Lord stood by me. I had uncommon liberty, and before I had concluded, many voices were heard in the congregation, saying, 'Give us the old way!' Mr. Haw arose to make his reply very much agitated, and exhibited a very bad temper, being very much confused. He made some statement that called from me a denial, and the people rose up to sustain me, which was no sooner done than he was so confused that he picked up his saddle-bags and walked off, and made no reply. This left me in possession of the whole field, and from that hour he lost his influence among the Methodists, and his usefulness as a preacher. In this situation he remained until 1801; and when the great revival began in Tennessee among the Presbyterians and Methodists, he connected himself with the former, and ended his days among them as a preacher."* In 1796, he was appointed to Guilford, North Carolina; the following year, to Holston, in Virginia. In 1798, he returned to the Cumberland; and from that period until 1812, his labors were confined to Kentucky, with the exception of the years 1804 and 1805, which he spent on the Ohio District. In the great revival in the interior of Kentucky, in 1801, known as the Cane Ridge revival, he was the leading spirit. During the period of his ministry in Kentucky, revivals of religion followed his labors everywhere; and in those sections of the State favored with his ministrations, either as the Presiding Elder of a District, or in the relation of a pastor, Methodism assumed a more permanent and enduring form than it had done before. He was not only an earnest preacher of the gospel, but an able defender of the truth. In the religious controversies that disturbed the quietude of the Church throughout the State, Mr. Burke bore an active part. Calvinism, deformed as it always appears, was truly hideous under his mighty touch. In his controversy with the advocates of exclusive immersion, he always put them to silence and to shame. Challenged, on one occasion, to a debate with a Baptist minister, on the subjects and mode of baptism, near Mount Sterling, Kentucky, after "occupying about four hours on the subjects and mode of baptism, he turned to the Baptist preachers, who sat behind him in the stand, and

---

*Western Methodism, pp. 46, 47, 48.

told them if they had any thing to say, he would be glad to hear it. They consulted together, and then replied that they had nothing to say."* If the peculiarities and economy of Methodism were assailed, he was, on all occasions, equal to their defense. "He had become so notorious for his skill and success in controversy, as to be feared by all belligerent parties."† To preach the gospel to the people of Kentucky, no man was better prepared than he. The privations of frontier life could not discourage him. Bold and fearless, he was twice the leader of the company by whom Bishop Asbury was guarded into Kentucky. "He was" also "the first Secretary of an Annual Conference in America;"‡ and was a member of the General Conferences of 1804 and 1808. We will here, however, take leave of Mr. Burke for the present; but we shall frequently meet with him in the prosecution of our work.

John Ball, who also came to Kentucky this year, had entered the lists as an evangelist in 1790, although his name is not among the Appointments for that year—an error in the Minutes. In 1791, he traveled the Russell Circuit, in Virginia; and in 1792, the Cumberland, in Tennessee. In Kentucky, we find him, in 1793, on the Lexington Circuit, where he only remains for one year, when he is reäppointed to the Cumberland in 1794; at the close of which year he located. Of his success on the Lexington Circuit we have no information.

---

*Rev. Jonathan Stamper, in Home Circle, Vol. II., p. 282.

†Ibid.

‡Western Methodism, p. 20.

He is represented by one who knew him,* as a "son of thunder. He smote with his hands and stamped with his feet. He warned the people faithfully to flee from the wrath to come."

"He was about medium height, rather slender, but compactly built. He was firm, independent, and opinionated. He was regarded as a pious, useful minister, of the medium grade, and was well received wherever he traveled. He was a bold, intrepid man, who never turned his back on an enemy; and, if my information be correct, he and the Rev. William Burke were two of the guards, who, in 1793, met Bishop Asbury some distance east of the Cumberland Mountains, and conducted him to the Kentucky Conference and back again."†

The name of Gabriel Woodfield appears only for the present year on the roll of the Conference. Among the names of those "admitted on trial," that of Woodfield is omitted, and we only find him mentioned as one of the preachers on the Lexington Circuit. As a local preacher, he came to Kentucky from Pennsylvania at an early day. He was "of the first order of local preachers,"‡ and in that capacity "labored with success." Anxious to extend the sphere of his usefulness, he offered himself to the Conference; but, from some cause, only spent one year in the itinerant work. We afterward find him, in 1802, as a local preacher, faithfully dispensing the word of life—in his pulpit

---

*John Carr, in Christian Advocate, February 5, 1857.

†Judge Scott.

‡Western Methodism, p. 63.

labors "rising above all his clouds," and "preaching excellent sermons."* He removed from Fayette county, where he had settled on his arrival in Kentucky, to Henry county. Previous to his death, "he removed to Indiana, in the neighborhood of Madison." There he resided to a good old age; when, like a ripe sheaf ready for the garner, in the full enjoyment of the Christian's hope, he sweetly fell asleep, surrounded by his friends and connections.

Previous to this date but few churches had been erected in Kentucky, and they were humble ones. Besides the log structure at Masterson's Station—which was put up in 1787 or '88—a similar house had been built in 1790, in the Salt River Circuit, at Poplar Flats, and bore the name of Ferguson's Chapel—to which allusion has already been made—after the worthy local preacher who labored so faithfully in the cause of God in that section. About the same time a log meeting-house was erected in Jessamine county, near Bethel Academy, and called Lewis's Chapel; Proctor's Chapel, in Madison county; Garrett's Meeting-house, in the forks of Dix River, and a house on Shoenea Run, had also been built. During this year Burke's Chapel was built, in Garrard county; Humphries's Chapel had also been built—at which place Bishop Asbury had attended a quarterly meeting on the 13th of April of this year.

We are called upon this year to record the death

---

*Jacob Young's "Autobiography," p. 69.

of Henry Birchett, the third itinerant minister, who had been connected with the work in Kentucky, to pass away—including the Rev. Samuel Tucker, who was murdered by the Indians.*

Among the pioneer preachers who came to Kentucky, no one was more devoted to the work of the ministry, or prosecuted his calling with greater ardor, than the subject before us. He was born in Brunswick county, Virginia, (the time of his birth is not known.) After laboring for two years in the State of North Carolina, he freely offered himself as a missionary to the West. In the year 1790, he was appointed to the Lexington Circuit, where, with untiring zeal, he labored assiduously and usefully for two years. In 1792, he was removed to the Salt River Circuit, where, it is said, "he was eminently useful."†

No circuit in Kentucky was more trying to the constitution than this—spreading over a vast extent of territory, sparsely settled, accommodations poor, rides long, and preaching almost every day; "requiring more labor and suffering than any other in the country." His slender constitution necessarily gave way. At the close of the year it was the judgment of his friends that he ought to desist from preaching until he recovered. He was present at the Conference at Masterson's Station, "in a poor state of health," and was suffering from "weakness in his breast and spitting of blood." Owing to the scarcity of preachers, great difficulty

---

* See page 75.

† Western Methodism, p. 69.

existed in providing for the Cumberland Circuit, and it was decided to leave it without a preacher for the present. Under these circumstances Henry Birchett, wan and pale, asked the privilege of supplying it. He turned to Bishop Asbury and said: "Here am I; send me!" His brethren remonstrated against his going. Two hundred miles lay between the seat of the Conference and this distant field; the life of the traveler was every hour imperiled by the Indians; the small-pox was prevailing through all the country; and his health was already wrecked by labor and exposure. Every influence that could be, was brought to bear upon him to dissuade him from his purpose; but in vain. To all their arguments and remonstrances he replied: "If I perish, who can doubt of my eternal rest, or fail to say, 'Let me die the death of the righteous, and let my last end be like his'?" He entered upon his work soon after the adjournment of the Conference, and with commendable zeal pushed forward the victories of the cross, though in feeble health, until the summer and autumn had passed away, when he was compelled to cease his labors. James Hoggatt, a gentleman of wealth and of liberality, residing two miles west of Nashville, invited the weary and way-worn itinerant to the hospitalities of his home. There he remained, visited by friends who loved him—the recipient of every kind attention—until, in the month of February, 1794, he breathed his last, in hope of eternal life.

"James Haw asked him, in the time of his last illness, if he had any temptations. He replied he had, for he had too much anxiety to die; 'but, glory to God!' he said, 'I am resigned to the will of my Master.' Another person standing by discovered the blood settling under his nails, and told him the Master had come. He replied, 'I am glad of it,' and began crying, 'Glory, glory to God!' until his hands fell upon his breast, and he expired in peace." *

At his own request, he was wrapped in white flannel and committed to the silent grave.

No man had been connected with the ministry for so short a time, to whom the Church and his fellow-laborers in the work were more ardently attached. He was, perhaps, the best pastor in the West. He regarded the children as the future hope of the Church, and improved every opportunity that offered in their catechetical instruction, so that by the children he was remembered with affection long after he had entered into rest.

The printed Minutes say: "He was one among the worthies who freely left safety, ease, and prosperity, to seek after and suffer faithfully for souls."

Notwithstanding the zealous efforts that had been made to promote the cause of religion, the net increase for this year was only *eleven* members. There had, however, been a sifting throughout the Churches, and the most of them were in a more healthy condition than they were the previous year.

---

*Rev. Learner Blackman.

CHAPTER VII.

FROM THE CONFERENCE OF 1794 TO THE CONFERENCE OF 1796.

Gen. Anthony Wayne—Gen. St. Clair—His expedition against the Indians unsuccessful—The campaign of 1794—The battle near the rapids of the Miami—Gen. Wayne's victory complete—The Indian war brought to a successful termination—Treaty of peace concluded—The Conference of 1794—John Metcalf—Thomas Scott—Peter Guthrie—Tobias Gibson—Moses Speer—Conference of 1795—William Duzan—John Buxton—Aquila Sugg—Francis Acuff: his death—Thomas Wilkerson—Decrease in membership.

In the year 1792, Gen. Anthony Wayne, an officer of distinction in the United States service, was appointed by President Washington as successor to Gen. St. Clair, in the command of the army engaged against the Indians on the Western frontier. The depredations of the Indians upon Kentucky were not only incessant, but most disastrous to the safety of the people, as well as to the prospects of the Commonwealth. The efforts that had hitherto been made to secure the State against these incursions, had proved ineffectual. The expedition of Gen. St. Clair, a short time previous, had been not only unsuccessful, but calamitous. In the summer and autumn of 1793, Gen. Wayne began to make preparations for another campaign. The season, however, was too far advanced for active operations, and the invasion of the country of the hostile tribes was postponed until the following year. Before marching into the enemy's country that gallant officer made one more attempt to obtain peace, which, however, failed.

"On the morning of the 20th of August, 1794, he marched into the heart of the hostile country, and attacked the Indians in a formidable position which they occupied, near the rapids of the Miami." The victory was complete. The Indians were thoroughly defeated, and the war was brought to a successful termination; and in 1795, he concluded a definite treaty of peace, which was observed until the war of 1812.*

The Conference of 1794 met at Lewis's Chapel, in the Lexington Circuit. We find upon the Minutes of this year the names of three preachers who had not previously appeared in Kentucky: John Metcalf, Thomas Scott, and Peter Guthrie.

John Metcalf was admitted into the itinerancy in 1790. He had traveled four years before he came to Kentucky, three of which were spent in Virginia, and one in North Carolina. In 1794, he was transferred from the Virginia Conference to the work in Kentucky, and was stationed on the Lexington Circuit. We have no means at present of ascertaining whether or not he was successful on this circuit. The printed Minutes show a considerable decrease on the Lexington Circuit, yet this may be the result of change in the territorial limits

---

*Collins's Kentucky.

of the several pastoral charges in the State. After this his name disappears from the Minutes. We learn from Mr. Burke that he subsequently became Principal of Bethel Academy—the immediate successor of Valentine Cook.

Thomas Scott, who this year was transferred from the Baltimore Conference to Kentucky, deserves more than a passing notice. He was born in Alleghany county, Maryland, October 31, 1772. In the fourteenth year of his age he was soundly converted, and joined the Methodist Episcopal Church. Before he was seventeen years old he was received on trial into the Conference, and appointed to Gloucester Circuit; the subsequent year he was the junior preacher on Berkeley Circuit; and in 1791, we find him in charge of Stafford Circuit—all lying in the State of Virginia. In 1792, he traveled the Frederick Circuit, in Maryland; and the following year he was sent to the Ohio Circuit, a field of labor of great extent, stretching along the frontier settlements of the Ohio River in western Pennsylvania and Virginia. In the spring of 1794, he descended the Ohio River, to join the band of itinerants in Kentucky, and was present at the Conference which convened on the 15th day of April.

He embarked on a flat-boat at Wheeling, laden with provisions for Gen. Wayne's army, and landed where Maysville now stands. He was appointed to the Danville Circuit, on which, William Burke informs us, there was an extensive revival of religion. At the Conference of 1795, he located; but, in 1796, at the request of the Rev. Francis Poythress, the Presiding Elder, he took charge of the Lexington Circuit, in the place of Aquila Sugg, whose health had failed, until the ensuing Annual Conference. This circuit spread over the present territory of Fayette, Jessamine, Woodford, Franklin, Scott, and Harrison counties, and included portions of Bourbon and Clarke. The appointments were filled every four weeks, and the circuit had within its bounds the following preaching-places: Lexington, Reynolds's, Widow Prior's, Lewis's Chapel, Burns's, Versailles, Frankfort, Snelling's, Griffith's, Widow Waller's, Col. Thomas Morris's—below Cynthiana, Coleman's Chapel, Tucker's, Smith's, Matthews's, Col. Robert Wilmot's, White's, Ewbank's, and Bryant's. A class had been previously formed at each one of these points, and Mr. Scott represents the most of them as in a healthy condition. The one in Lexington, however, he speaks of as being small, though in it were "several excellent members, who were ornaments of society." * At the close of this year his labors as an itinerant minister ceased.

A short time afterward he was married, and turned his attention to secular pursuits. For a brief period he was a clerk in a dry-goods store in Washington, Mason county. He then turned his attention to the study of law, and while prosecuting his legal studies, in order to support his family, he worked at the tailoring business—some idea of which he had gathered, in early life, from his

---

* Judge Scott's manuscript.

father, who was a tailor. Anxious to render him every assistance, his wife devoted her leisure time in reading to her husband Blackstone's Commentaries and other law-books, while he plied his needle upon his board.

In the fall of 1798, he removed to Lexington, Kentucky, where, under the Hon. James Brown, he prosecuted his preparations for the bar. In 1800, he obtained license to practice law, and settled in Flemingsburg. In 1801, he emigrated to Ohio, and settled in Chillicothe, where he resided until his death.

In the State of Ohio he held various civil offices, and always discharged their functions to the satisfaction of those who had confided them to his trust. In 1809, he was elected by the Legislature of Ohio one of the Judges of the Supreme Court, and the next year was reëlected, and commissioned Chief Judge of that court. In 1815, "finding the salary insufficient for his support, he resigned his seat on the bench, and resumed the practice of law." He afterward held several offices, and filled positions of high responsibility.*

"On the 13th day of February, 1856, in the bosom of his family, and surrounded by friends, his spirit peacefully departed, without a struggle or groan, to the God that gave it."†

By his brethren of the bar he was held in high esteem. On the second day after his death the

---

* Finley's Sketches of Western Methodism.

† Extract from proceedings of the Ross County (Chillicothe) Bar.

members of the bar of Ross county met in Chillicothe, and adopted resolutions expressive of their high veneration for his memory. The Scioto Lodge of Masons also passed similar resolutions, in which they state that "he met death with calmness and manly resignation;" that, "after a long life of usefulness, honorable bearing, and beneficent liberality, he confronted death with an unquailing eye, and passed away from earth, to realize that future which God has promised to the pure in heart." But it was his Christian character that shone with brightest luster. As a pioneer preacher in Kentucky, he spent two years in the itinerant service of the Church, faithfully prosecuting the great work of the ministry; and then retiring to the local ranks, he still devoted every energy within his power to the welfare and prosperity of the Church he loved so well. To locate—hazardous as is always the step—did not release his conscience of the obligation to preach the gospel, nor did it weaken his desire for the salvation of the people. As long as he remained in Kentucky, he faithfully prosecuted his ministerial calling; and when he settled in Ohio, he at once became a representative man in the infant cause. Through a long and eventful life he held fast his profession, maintained his ministerial standing, and everywhere avowed himself a follower of the "meek and lowly Jesus." No wonder, then, that he met death with composure, and felt ready for the summons.

It is always a cause of regret to the Church, when a laborious and useful minister of the gospel retires from the itinerant field, and especially if in the flower of his manhood. There was, perhaps, no one among the early pioneers, who promised greater usefulness to the Church than Mr. Scott; and while it is a pleasing reflection that he never stained the judicial ermine by any act of wrong, nor soiled his Christian character as he mingled with the turmoil and strife of political life, yet our pleasure would be heightened if we could record that his noble life had been exclusively devoted to the work of the ministry.

Of Peter Guthrie we know but little. He entered the Conference this year, and was appointed to the Salt River Circuit, and the following year to the Cumberland; and then we lose sight of him altogether.

The name of Tobias Gibson is also in the list of the Appointments in Kentucky; but we likewise find him, for the same year, appointed to the Union Circuit, in North Carolina. The Minutes read: "Union—Tobias Gibson, *one quarter*." We do not find sufficient evidence to justify the belief that he spent any portion of this year in Kentucky. None of his cotemporaries, so far as we are advised, make any allusion to him in this department of the work; and in the brief account of his life and labors published in the General Minutes,* no reference whatever is made to his appointment to Kentucky. The probabilities are that he remained during the whole year in the South; yet it will not be improper to

---

* Vol. I., p. 125.

refer to him in this connection. He was a native of South Carolina, and was born November 10, 1771, in Liberty county, on the Great Pedee. He lived only thirteen years after he entered the traveling connection; three of which were spent in South Carolina, four in North Carolina, one on Holston; and the last five years in Mississippi, as missionary to Natchez—where he died on the 5th day of April, 1804.

Among the early Methodist preachers there was no one more self-sacrificing or more zealous in the prosecution of his labors than Mr. Gibson. His biographer says: "What motive induced him to travel, and labor, and suffer so much and so long? He had a small patrimony of his own, that, improved, might have yielded him support. The promise of sixty-four dollars per annum,* or two-thirds, or one-half of that sum—just as the quarterly collections might be made in the circuits—could not be an object with him. His person and manners were soft, affectionate, and agreeable. His life was a life of devotion to God. He was greatly given to reading, meditation, and prayer. He very early began to feel such exertions, exposures, and changes, as the first Methodist missionaries had to go through in spreading the gospel in South Carolina and Georgia—preaching day and night. His feeble body began to fail, and he appeared to be superannuated a few years before he went to the Natchez country. It is reported that, when he

---

*The salary, at that time, of a traveling preacher.

found his difficulties, after traveling six hundred miles to Cumberland, he took a canoe, and put his saddle and equipage on board, and paddled himself out of Cumberland into the Ohio River, and took his passage six or eight hundred miles in the meanders of the Great River.* What he met with on his passage is not known—whether he went in his own vessel, or was taken up by some other boat—but he arrived safe at port. Afterward it was reported to the Conference that he said he was taken up by a boat. Four times he passed through the wilderness—a journey of six hundred miles—amidst Indian nations and guides, in his land passages from the Cumberland settlement to Natchez. He continued upon his station until he had relief from the Western Conference, where he came and solicited help in his own person, and in the habit of a very sick man."†

The labors of Mr. Gibson as missionary to Natchez could not have been other than profitable to the cause of Christianity. Although the Minutes do not show large accessions to the Church during the four years he traversed the country around Natchez and preached to the people, yet he was laying the foundations of Christianity there, and preparing the ground that has since brought an abundant harvest. At the close of the Conference-year in which he died, there are reported on the General Minutes *one hundred* white and *two* colored members.

His last sermon was preached on the 1st day of

* The Mississippi.

† General Minutes, Vol. I., pp. 125, 126.

January, 1804. It was blessed to many of his hearers. Not only through his life, but in his last illness, "he was a pattern of patience, humility, and devotion," and hailed with joy the hour of death. He met the last enemy, not like the warrior on the blood-stained field, amid the excitement and enthusiasm of the battle, but with the resignation of the Christian, in the calmness of a trusting faith, reposing his hope of eternal life on the "exceeding great and precious promises" of the word of God; and in the contemplation of his priceless inheritance, he passed away.

The following letter to the author, from the Rev. Dr. C. K. Marshall, dated Vicksburg, February 10, 1868, in reference to Mr. Gibson, will be read with interest:

"While in feeble health, he remained with his relatives, and rode out and visited his friends and brethren, and went out occasionally to the nearest appointments of his brethren in the ministry. But as his health gradually failed, he declined giving out appointments to preach himself, though he could occasionally exhort after the delivery of the discourses of the regular pastors.

"One day, when he was out in the plantation of his kinsman, endeavoring to give a little assistance in the supervision of the place, he was caught in a very trying and perilous situation. A cane-brake had been set on fire, to clear the land for the purpose of planting. The fire had been set at several different points; and, while attending to other matters, and before any one was aware of the state of things, the negroes discovered that the fire had so encircled them that escape seemed impossible. A path leading over a bridge which was built across a bayou was the only way out, and the fire had reached that. They hurried at once into the bed of the bayou, now almost entirely dry, and lay down. The heat was, however, so intense as to nearly suffocate them, and nearly killed Mr. Gibson on the spot. After the fire had passed over them, the persons present helped to get Mr. Gibson back to the residence; but he had received a shock to his weak lungs and general system, which pushed him with accelerated movement toward the grave. But for this sad occurrence, his useful life might have been extended to many years.

"His remains were buried about five miles south of Vicksburg. In 1856, or about that time, his relatives and numerous friends united together and erected a handsome monument over his remains. The writer delivered an appropriate address on the occasion, and solemn religious services were conducted by assisting ministers. The grave where his remains repose is not far from, and in sight of, the public road, and is one of the loveliest and loneliest spots anywhere in the country."

Another honored name, though not in the General Minutes for Kentucky, properly belongs to this part of our history—that of Moses Speer.* He was born in Maryland, in 1766, and removed with

*He was the father of the Rev. Dr. Speer, of the Louisville Conference, and of the Rev. James G. H. Speer, a member of the Holston Conference, who died many years ago.

his father to Kentucky when quite a youth, and settled at the mouth of Beargrass, where Louisville now stands. Early in life he embraced religion, and united with the Methodist Episcopal Church; and soon afterward he entered the ministry. Under the direction of the Presiding Elder, he labored for some time on the Hinkstone Circuit, in Kentucky, evincing by his zeal and devotion his Divine call to the ministry. In 1794, he joined the Conference, and, with Jacob Lurton, was appointed to the Cumberland Circuit, where his labors were signally blessed. During this year he was married to Miss Amelia Ewing, of Nashville; and, in consequence of the difficulties in the way of the support of married preachers, at the close of the year he located. He settled near the city of Nashville, and for more than forty years he was in that vicinity, a faithful and useful local preacher. In 1839, his name appears in the Minutes of the Mississippi Conference, and his appointment to Montgomery, in the San Augustin District, Texas.* Mr. Speer had not the privilege of aiding, for any length of time, in the cultivation of this new and interesting field. His work was well-nigh done. Before another Conference met, he was called from labor to reward. In the seventy-fourth year of his age, full of faith and of hope, he closed his eventful and useful life.

Mr. Speer was the first minister of the Methodist Church who bore the standard of the cross beyond

*The missionary work in Texas was at that time connected with the Mississippi Conference.

the Ohio, into what is now the State of Indiana.* In his early ministry, he was the intimate friend of Haw, Ogden, McHenry, and Burke. He was among the first who were licensed to preach west of the mountains. He was also one of the brave band that was sent to meet Bishop Asbury near the Cumberland Gap, and guard him through the wilderness into the settled portions of Kentucky. He contributed by his labors much toward the planting of Methodism in Logan county, Kentucky; and he labored with the McGees in the great revivals at the close of the past and the beginning of the present century.

We have this year an increase of only *thirty-five* members.

The "Conference for 1795 was held at Masterson's Chapel, on the 1st day of May. Bishop Asbury

* Col. N. A. Speer, his son, writes, that in 1827, he found many of the old settlers in Jefferson, Bullitt, Nelson, Shelby, and other counties, who remembered the preaching and labors of Moses Speer; and who had known him from the time of his landing at the Falls, in 1780, until he was sent to the Cumberland, in 1794. He farther states that, in 1838, he formed the acquaintance of an aged gentleman at Evansville, named Robertson. Mr. Robertson informed him that Moses Speer was the first Protestant minister who preached west of the Ohio. Mr. Robertson stated that he and others had gone west of the Ohio River on a hunting tour, and, finding the game very abundant, they concluded to build a block-house and remain, and send for their families; which they did. They established themselves on a stream, afterward called Silver Creek. Soon after they had established themselves, one of their number visited the Falls, and requested Moses Speer to visit the settlers at Silver Creek Station, and preach to them. He consented, visited the station, and preached to them.

was not present. The Rev. Francis Poythress presided over the deliberations of the body. The Revs. John Buxton, Aquila Sugg, Francis Acuff, and Thomas Wilkerson had been transferred to Kentucky by Bishop Asbury, and reported themselves to the Conference, and were courteously received."* The name of William Duzan also appears for the first time. The "proceedings of the Conference were concluded harmoniously. The preachers were warmly united in the bonds of peace, and each started to his circuit with renewed zeal and fixedness of purpose, to discharge with greater fidelity the trust and confidence reposed in them by the great Head of the Church."†

William Duzan, who was admitted on trial at this Conference, was a resident of Washington county when he entered the ministry, and was, in all probability, one of the subjects of the revival of 1790, with which that county was visited. His first appointment was to the Salt River Circuit, with John Buxton and Barnabas McHenry. "He was a young man of unblemished reputation, pious, humble, deeply devoted to God, and greatly esteemed by all his acquaintances on account of his excellent qualities. He was small in stature, and of humble pretensions in the ministry."‡

He spent only one year in Kentucky, and at the subsequent Conference was appointed to Cumberland; and in 1797, to the Holston Circuit; at the close of which he located.

---

*Judge Scott. †Ibid. ‡Ibid.

John Buxton was admitted on trial in 1791, and appointed to Bertie Circuit, in North Carolina. The three following years he traveled in Virginia. In 1795, he was transferred to the West, and appointed to Salt River Circuit. He remained in Kentucky only one year, when he was removed to the Cumberland. The following year he traveled on Green Circuit, in East Tennessee. In 1798, he returned to Kentucky, where he spent two years—the first on the Lexington, and the second on the Limestone Circuit. In the year 1800, he returned to the Virginia Conference, and, after traveling successively the Sussex, Mecklenburg, and Greenville, the Portsmouth and Brunswick Circuits, he was sent to the Richmond District as Presiding Elder. The remainder of his itinerant life was spent on Districts. In 1805, we find him on the Norfolk District. At the close of this year he leaves Virginia, and is appointed to the Salisbury District, North Carolina. The subsequent year he has charge of the Newbern District, North Carolina, where he remains for two years, when he is reäppointed to Norfolk District, in Virginia. The three following years he has charge of Raleigh District; and in 1813, of the Tar River District—both in North Carolina; at the close of which he located.*

From the sketch we have given, it will be perceived that the life of Mr. Buxton was by no means

---

*All the appointments he filled from 1809 were in the Virginia Conference, which extended into North Carolina.

an idle one. In that early day the territorial limits of the circuits were generally more extensive than the Districts of a Presiding Elder at the present period, while the Districts of that time more than covered the boundary lines of our present Conferences.

In appearance, Mr. Buxton was tall and slender. His piety was fervent, and he was zealous and effective in his ministerial labors. His preaching was plain, sound, and both theoretical and practical. In his intercourse with others, he not only lacked those social qualities that so greatly endear a minister to his people, but was regarded as rather morose. During his connection with the Church in Kentucky, his ministry was greatly blessed. In the year in which he traveled on the Lexington Circuit there was a gracious revival of religion, and many persons were converted and added to the Church. The high estimation in which he was held by his brethren in the ministry is evinced by the very responsible positions confided to his trust. He was a member of the General Conferences of 1804, 1808, and 1812.

We have already referred to Aquila Sugg, as transferred to Kentucky. In 1788, he was admitted on trial, and appointed to Gloucester, in Virginia. The two following years he traveled on the Great Pedee and Edisto Circuits, in South Carolina. In 1791, he was appointed to the Canterbury Circuit; in 1792, to Salisbury; in 1793, to New Hope; in 1794, to Trent—all in North Carolina. In 1795, he came to Kentucky, and was appointed the first year to Lexington, and the following year to the Logan Circuit; and located at the Conference of 1797.

A writer in the Christian Advocate* says: "He was an excellent man, and his labors were blessed."

Judge Scott, in describing him, informs us that "he was about the medium size; of a feeble constitution; plain and neat in his dress; courteous in his manners, and instructive in his conversation with others." We also learn from the same authority, that "he was an easy, natural, and graceful preacher, and seldom failed to command the undivided attention of his hearers."

On neither of the circuits to which he was appointed in Kentucky, was he able to render efficient service. At the close of the first three months of his ministerial labor on the Lexington Circuit, his health entirely failed him, and he returned to the home of his parents. His place was filled by Mr. Scott, to whom we have already referred. Unwilling to be idle, he attempted to rally; and, believing his health equal to the duties of an itinerant, he was appointed to the Logan Circuit, which had just been formed under that name. Almost until the close of the year, he faithfully prosecuted his work, until the encroachments of disease too plainly indicated that his itinerant career must close. Broken down in health, he retires from the active duties of a work dearer to his heart than life itself.†

---

*John Carr, in Christian Advocate, February 12, 1857.
†Judge Scott.

Francis Acuff had only labored in Kentucky for a short time previous to his death. He was born in Culpepper county, Virginia, but brought up in Sullivan county, Tennessee. In 1793, he entered the itinerant field, and was appointed to the Greenbrier Circuit, in Virginia. The following year, his appointment was to the Holston; and in 1795, he became identified with the work in Kentucky, and was appointed to the Danville Circuit. In the enjoyment of excellent health, and blessed with a fine constitution, he entered upon his work with energy and zeal. Possessing a mind above mediocrity, and deeply devoted to the service of the Church, he soon won the esteem and the affections of his brethren. He, however, was not permitted to "occupy" his place in the Danville Circuit only for a short time. Before the summer passed away, he entered upon the peaceful calm of heaven. "He died in August, 1795, in the twenty-fifth year of his age. Thus dropped the morning flower—though flourishing in the morning, in the evening cut down and withered. He was soon called away from his labors in the vineyard to the rest that remaineth to the people of God."*

Bishop Asbury, in speaking of his death, says: "We came to Acuff's Chapel. I found the family sorrowful and weeping on account of the death of Francis Acuff."†

"As an instance of the strong attachment which

*General Minutes M. E. Church, Vol. I., p. 67.

†Asbury's Journal, Vol. II., p. 297.

was felt by those who were best acquainted with this man of God, I will give the following anecdote, on the authority of the author of 'Short Sketches of Revivals of Religion in the Western Country': 'An Englishman by the name of William Jones, on his arrival in Virginia, was sold for his passage. He served his time, four years, with fidelity, conducted himself with propriety, and was finally brought to the knowledge of the truth by means of Methodist preaching. As he had been greatly blessed under the preaching of Mr. Acuff, when he heard of his death, Billy, as he was called, determined to visit his grave. Though he had to travel a long distance through the wilderness, in which he had heard that the Indians often killed people by the way, yet his great desire to visit the grave of his friend and pastor impelled him forward, believing that the Lord in whom he trusted was able to protect him from savage cruelty, and provide for his wants. When I came to the rivers, said he, I would wade them; or, if there were ferries, they would take me across; and when I was hungry, the travelers would give me a morsel of bread. When I came to Mr. Green's, in Madison county, I inquired for our dear Mr. Acuff's grave. The people looked astonished, but directed me to it. I went to it; felt my soul happy; shouted over it, and praised the Lord.' Such a mark of strong affection in a single follower of Jesus Christ speaks volumes in favor of the man over whose grave those grateful recollections were so piously indulged." *

* Bangs's History M. E. Church, Vol. II., pp. 40, 41.

Another name that stands out with remarkable prominence is introduced this year into the annals of Methodism in Kentucky—that of Thomas Wilkerson. Mr. Wilkerson was born in Amelia county, Virginia, April 27, 1772. He had not the advantages of early religious training, as his parents were both unconverted. When about thirteen years of age, under the preaching of Methodist ministers, he was awakened to a sense of his condition as a sinner; but, by improper associations, his good impressions were effaced. Though only a child, he endeavored to drink in the poison of infidelity, but in its teachings found no relief. When about eighteen years of age, the neighborhood in which he was residing was blessed with a gracious revival of religion. Amongst the subjects of conversion were several of his associates. A determination on his part to dissuade them from a religious life, opened afresh the springs of conviction in his own heart, and decided him in a renewed purpose to seek religion. On the following Sabbath he joined the Church; and on the subsequent Saturday evening, about dusk, in the lone woods, and in a state of almost despair, he says: "As I was making my way through the bushes, I thought I saw a flash of lightning. Almost instantly it was repeated. I recollect nothing more till I found myself on my feet, with my hands raised, while loud shouts seemed to burst from the bottom of my heart." *

---

* Thomas Wilkerson, in a letter in South-western Christian Advocate, of June 26, 1841.

He soon filled the offices of class-leader and exhorter, in which positions his "efforts were crowned with success." Feeling a "necessity" laid upon him to preach the gospel, and, at the same time, his want of qualification and "insufficiency" for the work of the ministry, he shrank from the responsible office, until worldly misfortunes and the want of success in secular pursuits, together with the persuasions of friends and the reproaches of conscience, fully aroused him. Under the pastoral care of John Metcalf, then traveling the circuit in Virginia in which he resided, he was kept in the exercise of "gifts and graces," and finally persuaded to attend the session of the Virginia Conference held in Manchester, November 25, 1792. From this Conference "he was sent out to bear the fatigues and dangers of a pioneer itinerant life." His first appointment was to the Franklin Circuit, and the second to the Greenville—both in the State of Virginia. On the latter circuit he traveled only six months, when the demands of the Church elsewhere called for his services, and he was removed to Bertie Circuit, in North Carolina, where he spent the remainder of the year. In all these fields of labor, though in feeble health, he was greatly encouraged by the success that crowned his ministry—there being everywhere "living epistles known and read of all men." At the following Conference, held at Mayberry's Chapel, Virginia, a call was made for volunteers for Kentucky; and, with Buxton and others, Mr. Wilkerson offered himself for this arduous work, on which he was to enter in the following spring. During the winter he traveled with Mr. McKendree on the Bedford Circuit, in Virginia. His first appointment in Kentucky was to the Hinkstone Circuit. The country through which he had to pass, to reach his new field of labor, was sparsely settled, and the journey hazardous. He says: "We had to pack our provisions for man and horse for nearly two hundred miles; lie on the ground at night, having a guard stationed around us."* Feeble in health when he left Virginia, he steadily improved, so that he was able to undergo the hardships that awaited him. All along his journey he "preached to the people, in their forts and block-houses," the unsearchable riches of Christ. On his way, he says: "I met no D.D.'s to discuss doctrines, or make out reports about moral wastes. We had nothing from without to contend with, but the Indians and wild beasts."† His second appointment in Kentucky was on the Lexington Circuit. He was sent the next year to the Cumberland. After having traveled these several circuits, "with various success," he was sent, in 1798, to the Holston Circuit, with Tobias Gibson, whose health soon failed, when the duties of that laborious charge devolved on him alone. In the spring of 1799, he rejoined the Virginia Conference, and was sent to the Yadkin Circuit, in North Carolina, which, at that time, embraced that range of high mountains running through Buncombe county. Here he could "see but little fruit of his

---

*Nashville Christian Advocate, July 31, 1841. †Ibid.

labor." The following year, he traveled on the Baltimore Circuit, where he participated in "the most pleasing revival he ever witnessed." It commenced under the preaching of Wilson Lee, and in it were converted some persons who afterward "became distinguished in the Church." Again, at the Conference held in Kentucky, in the fall of 1800,* we find him on the Lexington and Hinkstone Circuit, in Kentucky, as colleague to William Burke. A gracious revival of religion crowned their labors. It was during this year, and on this circuit, that the whole power of Baptist enginery was arrested by Mr. Burke, "who met them so promptly, and so fully rebutted their arguments," that their attacks fell harmless to the ground.

In the Conference of 1801, he attempted to return to Baltimore, but was met by Bishop Asbury at the Holston Conference, and was solicited to return to Cumberland, where he remained for two years—the circuit, the latter year, taking, for the first time, the name of "Nashville."

His return to Kentucky in 1800, and his appointments for the several following years, threw him in the midst of the great revival which was then per-

*The General Minutes make his return to Kentucky, and his appointment to Hinkstone and Lexington, in 1801; but this error results from the change made, in 1800, in the time of holding the Western Conference, from the spring to the fall; so that two Conferences were held in the West in 1800—the first in April, at Dunworth, on Holston; and the second at Bethel Academy, in Kentucky, in October. The Conference, however, held in October, 1800, is published in the General Minutes as the Conference of 1801. This error runs through the Minutes for several years.

meating Middle Tennessee and the State of Kentucky, and in which he bore a prominent part. The labors he performed, the privations he met, and the exposures he underwent, were too much for his constitution, previously impaired. From a protracted illness, during which his life was despaired of, he recovered slowly, and met the Conference at the session of 1803. Still feeble in health, when Bishop Asbury met him, he said: "You look very slim;" and kindly offered him any appointment he might choose. Acting upon the proper principle, that the preacher who chooses his own field of ministerial labor, chooses, at the same time, any difficulties that may ensue, he promptly declined the proffered kindness. The Church in Lexington, Kentucky, had petitioned the Bishop to separate them from the circuit; and Mr. Wilkerson was appointed to the *station*—the first formed in Kentucky.*

During this year, at Lexington, his constitution again gave way, and he was able to preach but little. He says: "It was a year of affliction to my body and mind." He said he could see but little fruit as the result of his toil. In the midst of severe illness, when all hope of his recovery was abandoned, and his physician gave him the opinion that he could only survive a few days, he writes: "The language of my heart was, 'Though He slay me, I will trust in Him.' Death has no sting to

*The General Minutes read: "Lexington Town—Thomas Wilkerson."

me. Thank the Lord for the buoyancy of a gospel hope!"

At the next Conference he was permitted to rest. His untiring spirit, however, could enjoy this privilege but a short time. His health having slightly improved, he reported himself to the Rev. William McKendree, the Presiding Elder of the Kentucky District, as being able for efficient service, and was appointed to the Lexington Circuit until the next Conference.

In 1805 and 1806, he had charge of the Holston District, then covering a vast extent of country in East Tennessee, Western Virginia, and North Carolina. In traveling over this field—not only attending his quarterly meetings, but traveling through every circuit, and preaching constantly—we behold in him a true evangelist, "as he passes up and down, through gorges and defiles, over mountains and rivers, through a dreary wilderness—with scanty fare and threadbare clothes—with ruined health—that he might seek and gently lead into the fold of Christ the erring sons of men."

But now, again prostrated in health, he feels forced to retire from active participation in a work to which he had devoted the morning of his life and the prime of his manhood. He asked and obtained a location.

In 1828, his name reäppears in the Minutes, as the Presiding Elder on the French Broad District, Holston Conference. A single year is sufficient to impress his mind with the conviction that his itinerant labors must cease. From that period until his eventful life was closed, he sustained to the Conference either a supernumerary or superannuated relation.

As we review the life of such a man, we pause to express an admiration, not only for his character, but for the moral achievements of Christianity effected through his instrumentality, as well as for the heroism he so often displayed in the accomplishment of his work. Did dangers daunt him? Surely not.

"On one occasion, a hundred miles of unbroken forest lay between him and his work. He was detained, and his company had left him. Friendly settlers on the border of this mighty sea of woods described its perils, and attempted to dissuade him from his purpose to pass through it all alone. Tales of murder, of the savage's tomahawk and scalping-knife, which had been dripping with blood but a short time before in the depths of the very forest through which he had to pass, were rehearsed again and again to deter him. Duty called him to go, and he heeded not the dissuasions of his friends. Into the lonesome, solemn forest he plunged. He rode on and on, musing upon the loneliness of man isolated from humanity, and the still greater loneliness of him who is isolated from his God. Night came; he lay down and slept, and awoke to find 'his kind Preserver near.' As he pursued his lonely way, a chilling consciousness of his solitary, helpless condition, seized him. He apprehended danger near. Old tales of blood and savage torture recurred to his mind. He started at every rustle of a leaf. He looked behind, around, on either side. A moving object coming toward him startled him. He saw it was a human being; he felt it to be a savage. Turning as quietly as possible to one side, half concealed among the bushes, he awaited the event with throbbing heart. The footfalls sounded nearer and nearer; a swarthy, fierce-looking man stepped full in view, and, startled himself, grasped convulsively his rifle; but soon relaxed his grasp, and joyously greeted the affrighted preacher. Wilkerson found the stranger to be a way-worn, famished soldier, from Wayne's army, on his return home. He shared with him his loaf of home-made sugar, the remnant of his scanty provisions. After checking their hunger, and passing a few minutes in conversation, they knelt down and commended themselves to God, and reluctantly parted, each to pursue his journey alone.

"On another day, as Wilkerson was still urging his way to the field of his ministerial labors, he entered a dark ravine, whose depths the sun could scarcely penetrate, so completely was it walled in by hills, and covered with overarching oaks. As he plodded anxiously on, peering forward in hopes of catching a glimpse of light in front, where a more open prospect would present itself, his eyes fell on something white that lay a few rods beyond his path. A nearer approach disclosed a human skull, and the not uncertain marks it bore made him sure that the weapon of the savage had broken the golden bowl. A little farther on, arched ribs and another grinning death's-head repeated the terror-breathing story, and bade him tread softly, lest he should wake the fate that slept within this dell of death.

"But amid these scenes the Comforter came and ministered unto him. He was sustained; finding food for his own soul in the bread of life he broke to others.

"Although almost entirely uneducated, Wilkerson's fine native intellect, his sterling common sense, gave him a prominence among his brethren that many more highly favored as to educational privileges fail to reach. Prominence, however, he did not seek; it came, if at all, the free gift of those who knew and appreciated him. Indeed, his manner and his dress were the very reverse of those ambition assumes. He was remarkably affable and polite; but his politeness was not the hypocritical teachings of a book of etiquette. It seemed to be the gift of nature, and was often the subject of remark among those who knew him. It was difficult to account for the courtly smoothness and urbanity of the man, who had been born in humble life and trained in the wilderness.

"In dress he was scrupulously plain, always wearing a gray-mixed homespun suit, cut according to the primitive Methodistic style. He could never be induced to assume the *clerical black.* His reasons were cogent. He was met one day on the streets of Nashville by a prim young preacher, sleek in his raven-broadcloth, who accosted him with:

"'Well, Brother Wilkerson, why do you not wear black? It gives dignity to the appearance of a minister, solemnity to his air, and is so apt to insure him respect, that I think every minister should wear it.'

"Wilkerson replied: 'I have three reasons, my brother, why I do not wear black.

"'First: we are told that our message is *glad tidings, good news;* and such being the case, it seems to me that for the heralds of such a message to go clad in mourning is wholly inappropriate. In the second place: I once read a book entitled Dialogues of Devils, and I remember that Satan and Moloch, perhaps, were represented as being in conversation about ministers. Moloch was lamenting their power and influence, wielded, as it was, so powerfully, in opposition to the hosts of Pandemonium. Satan assured him he need not take much trouble to himself about that; for, said he, I have already induced them to put on my sooty livery, and I shall soon have them about my work. In the third place: I was taken up by God from the humbler rank in life; and if the dispensation of the gospel committed to me is to be delivered to any particular class, it is to the poor. It is with this class that I hope by my labors to be useful; and I wish by all proper means to commend myself to them. Hence I dress so as to make myself easy of approach by such, and wish by this means to make them feel that I am their equal, their brother, their friend, and not their lord or overseer—elevated so far above them as to have no sympathy with them.'

"Wilkerson was an earnest student of human nature; and so acute was his sense of the good and true, cultivated as it had been by the study of the character and attributes of his Maker, that the smallest deviations from rectitude were readily detected by him, and the internal springs of human action readily deduced.

"The peculiar plainness of his dress, he used to remark, gave him opportunity frequently for detecting the petty foibles that dwell in the heart of man.

"He was a delegate to the General Conference of 1828, which held its sittings at Pittsburgh, Pennsylvania. When he came forward to have his quarters assigned him, the committee looked at him, then looked at each other, seemed rather nonplussed, and turned aside to deliberate; all of which resulted in sending Wilkerson away off across the river, perhaps to the village of Alleghany. He made no remonstrance, but quietly submitted. In a few days, through a friend, an invitation was procured for him to go and dine at a wealthy man's table. He went; and after the usual courses of the dinner had been dispatched, wine was brought out. All the other guests were served first, when the host turned to him:

"'Will you have port, sir?'

"'No, I thank you, sir.'

"'Will you have sherry?'

"'No, sir.'

"'Perhaps, then, you will take a glass of small beer?'

"'If you please, sir.'

"'Ah, yes!' rudely responded the host, 'that is

about as high as we can elevate a backwoods Methodist preacher.'

"Wilkerson felt, but, with characteristic meekness, did not resent the ill treatment.

"The Committee on Public Worship waited upon him, and informed him that he was appointed to preach at a certain time and place. He told them, no; that he was out of the corporation, beyond their jurisdiction, and they must get some one else to do their preaching. They waited upon him a second time, and received the same reply. A third time they came, and mentioned his appointment, and fortified their authority by telling him that Bishop George said he *must* preach. He told them that if the Bishop said so he had no more to say, for he belonged to the Bishop and respected his authority. The appointment assigned was in one of the most prominent churches of the city, and it was a Sabbath-evening occasion. A great many of the preachers were present, and a great many citizens. The Holy Spirit aided him in a remarkable degree. He lashed the follies and vices that he daily saw exhibited, both among the preachers and the laity; and, after having fully secured the attention of the congregation, he burst forth into one of those appeals of melting tenderness which his heart was so capable of uttering, and to which the Spirit gave unusual power, and the whole audience was melted into tears. Mourners were invited to the altar of prayer. Numbers came. A time of refreshing from the presence of the Lord appeared, and sinners were happily converted. Wilkerson's star reached the ascendant; and now came what he disliked more than all the ill treatment his homespun had brought upon him.

"The man who had insulted him at his table met him on the street, and, extending his hand, exclaimed, in a very cordial manner: 'Why, how do you do, Brother Wilkerson? I have just found you out. You must come and make my house your home,' etc., etc. The preachers, very charitably, determined to make up a purse and buy him a suit of clothes. Several of them were speaking of it in the presence of good old Bishop George, who knew Wilkerson at home. A mischievous twinkle played in the corner of the old Bishop's eye as he remarked to them: 'Why, brethren, if you were blacked, he could buy half of you.'

"But above all the other characteristics of this estimable old man, his piety shone resplendent. It was a piety that begat meekness, gentleness, temperance, patience, long-suffering, brotherly kindness, charity; a piety that lived and breathed in all his words and acts; a piety that made him a most estimable citizen, a kind neighbor, a feeling and tender master, a devoted husband; a piety conspicuous in the pulpit, palpable in the social circle, resplendent around the fireside; a piety that maintained his spirits in cheerfulness and hope through the vicissitudes and reverses of a long life of eighty-three years; that enabled him to bear with meek resignation the loss of dear friends, and to say, despite the tears that bedimmed his eyes, 'The Lord gave, and the Lord hath taken away: blessed be the name of the Lord!' a piety that supported him through ten years of disease in the decline of life; that upheld him through more than six months of prostration, often suffering the most excruciating pain; finally, a piety that sustained him in the hour of death, and bore him triumphantly to the rest that remains to the people of God." * On his bed of death, a few weeks before he passed away, he said: "This old worn-out frame I shall willingly consign to the grave. The grave cannot hurt it. Storms may rage, the revolutions of earth may go on, the lightnings of heaven may flash, and her thunders resound, war with iron heel may tread my grave above; but my body shall be at rest. God has use for it, and he will take care of it till the judgment. My soul is his. He gave it; to him, blessed be his name! it will return." He was fearful of grieving the Spirit by being too anxious to depart. He said: "The grave is a quiet resting-place; death is a pleasant sleep;" for he was weary of life's long labors. The last connected words he uttered were: "If I had my time to go over, I would preach differently to what I have. I would preach more about eternity. I would strive to keep eternity always before the minds of my people. What is time but a vapor? Eternity is all." †

We close this sketch by the introduction of a letter from the Rev. W. G. E. Cunnyngham, of the Holston Conference:

* Rev. George E. Naff, in Home Circle, Vol. II., pp. 335, 336, 337.
† General Minutes M. E. Church, South, Vol. I., p. 674.

"He died at his residence, three miles east of Abingdon, Virginia, February 3, 1856, in the eighty-fourth year of his age. His death was peaceful and beautiful, as his life had been pure and useful. His sun went down calmly, in as bright a sky as ever faded into night. He had for years been standing on the margin of the river, waiting his time to pass over. He used to say, when talking on the subject of death: 'Its bitterness has long been past with me. The grave is but a subterraneous passage to a better world. I shall suffer only a momentary obscuration, and then rise with my Lord, to die no more.' He died in the midst of his family, surrounded by sympathizing and devoted friends. He was buried in rear of the Methodist Church in Abingdon, where he sleeps quietly, in company with four fellow-laborers of the Holston Conference.

"Father Wilkerson was a man of well-balanced character, distinguished for a sound understanding, lively fancy, tender sympathies, and profound piety. As a preacher, he was classed among the best of his day. To a thorough acquaintance with the Scriptures and Methodist theology, he added a deep knowledge of human nature, especially in its more profound and subjective experiences. Gentle and persuasive in manner, clear and logical in statement, his sermons were pleasing and instructive, and often overwhelmingly convincing. When inspired by his theme, he rose into the higher regions of pulpit eloquence. At such times he was one of the finest specimens of a gospel preacher ever heard in this country. He lived and died without the suspicion of a taint upon his spotless character."

We regret to report, at the close of this year, a decrease of *one hundred and ninety-four* members. This decrease was general throughout the State, embracing every circuit, except the Hinkstone, in which we had a small increase.

CHAPTER VIII.

FROM THE CONFERENCE OF 1796 TO THE CONFERENCE OF 1797.

The Conference of 1796 held at Masterson's Chapel—Jeremiah Lawson—Aquila Jones—Benjamin Lakin—John Watson—Henry Smith—John Baird—Increase in membership—Shelby Circuit.

THE Conference of 1796 was held at Masterson's Chapel, on the 20th of April. The Rev. Francis Poythress again presided, Bishop Asbury not being present. The session was harmonious throughout.*

Jeremiah Lawson joined the Conference this year. He remained in the Conference only three years, during which he traveled successively the Shelby, Danville, and Lexington Circuits; and then located. We, however, find him supplying the place of William Algood—who failed to come to Kentucky—during the spring and summer of 1800, on the Limestone Circuit, under the appointment of the Presiding Elder, William Burke. He lived to a good old age, honored and beloved by all who knew him, and then died at the residence of his son, the late Dr. L. M. Lawson, of Cincinnati, who stood for many years at the head of the medical profession in that city.

The names also of Aquila Jones, Benjamin La-

---

*Judge Scott.

kin, John Watson, and Henry Smith appear in the list of the Appointments.

Aquila Jones was admitted on trial in 1795, and appointed to the Holston Circuit. In 1796, he became connected with the ministry in Kentucky, and was appointed to the Hinkstone Circuit; the following year, to the Limestone; at the close of which he located.

The names of Lakin, Watson, and Smith, yet so fresh in the memory of many living, were familiar to the Church as useful ministers of Christ, through many successive years.

Benjamin Lakin, bearing the full name of his father, was born in Montgomery county, Maryland, August 23, 1767. The family from which he descended were originally from England. Left an orphan at nine years of age, by the death of his father, his moral and religious training was confided to the care of his only surviving parent. Soon after the death of her husband, Mrs. Lakin removed with her family to Pennsylvania, and settled near the Redstone Fort, in a region of country greatly infested by the Indians. About the year 1793, she emigrated with her family to Kentucky, and settled on Bracken Creek, within or near the limits of Mason county.

Under the preaching of the Rev. Richard Whatcoat, in 1791, and before the removal of the family to the West, during a season of religious interest, Mr. Lakin was awakened and converted to God.*

*Sprague's Annals of American Methodist Pulpit, p. 268.

Feeling divinely called to the work of the ministry, he became an itinerant preacher on the Hinkstone Circuit in 1794, under the direction of Francis Poythress, the Presiding Elder. In 1795, he joined the Conference, and was appointed to the Green Circuit, in East Tennessee. In 1796, he returned to Kentucky, and traveled on the Danville, and in 1797, on the Lexington Circuit.

During this year he married, and, finding it impossible to support his family in the itinerancy, he located at the close of the year. "Such was the prejudice that existed in the Church, at that day, against married preachers, that it was almost out of the question for any man to continue in the work if he had a wife."*

He continued in a local sphere for only a few years, when, in 1801, he was reädmitted into the Conference, and appointed to the Limestone Circuit. The two following years the field of his ministerial labor was on the Scioto and Miami Circuit, including all of Southern Ohio. In 1803, he was returned to Kentucky, where he remained for three years, and traveled successively the Salt River, Danville, and Shelby Circuits. In 1806 and 1807, he was again appointed to the Miami Circuit, and then traveled successively on the Deer Creek, Hockhocking, Cincinnati, White Oak, and Union Circuits—all lying beyond the Ohio River. In 1814, he again returned to Kentucky, where he preached and labored as long as he was able to be effective.

---

*Finley's Sketches of Western Methodism, p. 180.

His last appointment was to the Hinkstone Circuit, where he continued for two years.*

At the Conference of 1818, he was placed on the list of supernumerary preachers; but the following year, on the superannuated roll, which relation he sustained until his death.

For a few years after the failure of his health, he remained in Kentucky; but, at a later period, he removed to Ohio, and settled in Clermont county, near Felicity. Although unable to perform the work of an efficient preacher in the position he occupied, he never spent an idle Sabbath when it could be prevented. Having regular appointments at accessible points, when no longer able to perform the arduous labors that had characterized him in the strength of his manhood, even down to the grave, he determined to "make full proof of his ministry," by contributing his wasting life to the proclamation of the truths of the gospel. In the morning of his life, "he was one of those ministers who stood side by side, and guided the Church through that most remarkable revival of religion that swept like a tornado over the western world. In the greatest excitement, the clear and penetrating voice of Lakin might be heard amid the din and roar of the Lord's battle, directing the wounded to the Lamb of God who taketh away the sins of the world. Day and night he was upon the watch-tower; and in the class and praying circles,

---

* Mr. Lakin received into the Church, among others, the Rev. John P. Durbin, D.D., and Bishop Kavanaugh.

his place was never empty—leading the blind by the right way, carrying the lambs in his bosom, urging on the laggard professor, and warning sinners, in tones of thunder, to 'flee from the wrath to come.'"* From the time he joined the itinerant ranks until his name disappears from the effective roll, "he was abundant in labors, and never hesitated to tax a robust constitution to the extent of its ability."† In those religious controversies in Kentucky, which, in early times, not only disturbed the peace, but threatened for a while the very existence of the Church, he stood amongst the foremost in vindication of the truth, repelling with gigantic power the attacks of all opponents. Always fluent in speech, and often truly eloquent—not only a bold, but an able defender of the Church; sacrificing the pleasures of home to bear the tidings of a Saviour's love—Benjamin Lakin held as warm a place in the affections of the Methodists of Kentucky, of the past generation, as did any one of the noble men who were his associates in labor.

On the 28th of January, 1849, he preached his last sermon to a congregation in McKendree Chapel, Brown county, Ohio. He returned to his home at Point Pleasant on the following Tuesday, complaining of indisposition. He, however, started on the succeeding Friday, on horseback, to a quarterly meeting at Felicity, Ohio. He rode about six miles, when he reached the house of his niece, Mrs.

---

* Sketches of Western Methodism, p. 183.

† Rev. Jonathan Stamper, in Home Circle, Vol. III., p. 211.

Richards, in usual health, and enjoying a very happy frame of mind.* "About twelve o'clock that night, he was attacked with a chill and nausea. On Saturday and Sabbath he continued quite unwell. On Monday he was much better; and, after eating his supper in the evening, he sat some time by the fire, and conversed sweetly with the family. At about seven o'clock he arose, looked at his watch, and walked out of the room toward the front door. A noise being heard in the entry, the family followed, and found he had fallen to the floor. The first supposition was that he had fainted, and they made an effort to revive him; but it was the paralyzing touch of death—his spirit had fled."†

John Watson entered the ranks as an itinerant in 1792. The first four years of his ministry were spent on the Clarksburg, Huntingdon, and Pittsburgh Circuits.‡ In 1796, he came to Kentucky, where, after remaining one year on the Salt River Circuit, he was sent to the Russell Circuit, in Virginia. The next year, he returned to Kentucky, where he remained for two years, preaching on the Hinkstone and Lexington Circuits. In the year 1800, he again left Kentucky, to enter it as an itinerant preacher no more. We, however, see him lifting the standard of the cross on the Holston and New River Circuits, in Virginia—proclaiming the unsearchable riches of Christ—from 1802 to 1805,

* Sketches of Western Methodism, pp. 183, 184.

† General Minutes M. E. Church, Vol. IV., p. 385.

‡ He traveled on the Pittsburgh Circuit two years.

throughout the vast extent of territory embraced in the Holston District. In 1805, he is the standard-bearer on the Swanino District, in South Carolina, where he declines in health until his "tired nature" is compelled to seek for rest. The following year finds him a supernumerary, with "longing desires for his early home." Restored to health, we see him once more amid the active duties of his sacred calling. In 1807, he was appointed to Washington City, in the Baltimore Conference, in the bounds of which we see him actively engaged, filling various charges, until the Conference of 1824, when his health gives way, compelling him, first, to ask for a supernumerary relation; and the subsequent year, to be placed upon the superannuated roll, where he remains until his death, which occurred in the early part of the summer of 1838, at the house of Mr. Weller, near Martinsburg, Virginia.

We regret that we are in possession of so few facts in reference to Mr. Watson. During the three years he spent in Kentucky, he contributed largely toward the building up of the Church. The first year—which he spent on the Salt River Circuit—his labors were not only abundant, but were crowned with success.

The "Level Woods Society,"* that, in the early days of Methodism, sent out such a salutary influence into all the surrounding country, and that still blesses the community within its range, was organized by him.

*In Larue county.

Henry Smith also came to Kentucky this year. Although only three years of his ministry were spent in this field, yet the prominent part that he bore as an itinerant Methodist preacher for more than two generations, the labors he performed, his great usefulness, together with his spotless life, demand more than a passing notice.

He was born near Frederick City, Maryland, April 23, 1769, and was of German parentage. He was baptized in infancy in the communion of the German Reformed Church, of which his parents were members, and under the influence of which he was brought up. In the autumn of 1790, under the ministry of the Rev. Thomas Scott, he was awakened to a sense of his sinfulness, and admitted by him into the Church as a seeker of religion. About two weeks afterward, while his father was conversing with him one day, and explaining the nature of faith as the only condition of the sinner's justification, he says: "The glorious plan of salvation opened to my mind. I believed with a heart unto righteousness, and stepped into the liberty of the children of God." *

Impressed with the conviction that he ought to preach the gospel, yet without the advantages of education, only to a very limited extent, he obtained license to preach in August, 1793. His name appears in the General Minutes, for the first time, in 1794, in connection with the Clarksburg Circuit, in Western Virginia, although, the greater portion of

* General Minutes M. E. Church, Vol. X., p. 17.

the previous year, he had labored under the direction of the Presiding Elder on the Berkeley Circuit. In 1796, he was sent as a missionary to Kentucky, and appointed to the Limestone Circuit; and in 1797, to Salt River. The following year we find him prosecuting his calling on the Green Circuit, in East Tennessee.

At the Conference of 1799, he was appointed to the Miami Circuit, in the North-western Territory; and the following two years, to the Scioto and Miami, combined. In 1802, he returned to Kentucky, and was stationed on the Limestone Circuit; in 1803, on the Nollichuckie. In 1804, he was transferred to the Baltimore Conference, in connection with which he continued until his death.

For twenty-four years after his return to the Baltimore Conference, he bore an active part as a faithful herald of the cross. In whatever position he was placed, whether as a pastor or as the Presiding Elder of a District, he labored with untiring energy, and made "good proof of his ministry." During a ministry of *seventy* years—forty-two of which he was actively employed in the itinerant work—he labored with a zeal that knew no limit, except his own wasting strength.* The performance of his work during the three years that he labored in the North-western Territory, was sufficient not only to have exhausted the strength, but to have prostrated the energies, of any man. In entering upon this work, he crossed the Ohio River

---

*General Minutes M. E. Church, Vol. X., pp. 17, 18.

at the mouth of the Little Miami, on the 11th day of September; and on the following Sabbath, the 14th of the month, "for the first time, he sounded the peaceful gospel of Jesus Christ to a listening few on the pleasant banks of the Miami." *

Uniting his field of labor with the Scioto, and forming a six-weeks' circuit, he directed his course up the Ohio River, and "found some families friendly to religion." At the mouth of the Scioto he found several Methodist families "from Redstone and Kentucky," and organized them into a class. On the 15th of October, he preached in Chillicothe, "for the first time, to a considerable congregation," but met with no success. His circuit embraced a large territory, over which he traveled regularly every six weeks, organizing societies, and performing all the work of a minister of Christ.†

It is a melancholy hour for a faithful minister who had spent the morning and the noon of his life in the effective field—who had cheerfully made sacrifices, suffered privations, and met hardships, without complaint, that he might aid in the advancement of the noble cause of gospel truth—when his waning strength compels him to seek such a change in his relation to the work as deprives him of a pastoral charge. For nearly forty years, Henry Smith had gone in and out among his brethren, a representative man. In the mountains of Western Virginia; in the sparsely settled State of Kentucky; in East

---

* Methodist Magazine, Vol. IV., p. 271.

† Ibid., p. 273.

Tennessee; along the waters of the Nollichuckie; and across the "beautiful Ohio," in advance of the rapid tide of emigration; and then amid the scenes of his early childhood, he had, in the forefront of the battle, "lifted the consecrated cross." Nothing daunted by the perils to which he was exposed from the Indians, nor discouraged by the privations he endured, nor the want of support, he had ever been true to the trust confided to him by his brethren. In 1828, his name is stricken, for the first time, from the effective roll, and he is returned as *superannuated.* In the following year, with his strength slightly renewed, he reënters the list, and for six years prosecutes his labors as an itinerant; and then, at the Conference of 1835, he yields to advancing age, and, as a superannuated preacher, retires from the effective list, to be placed upon it no more.

He settled at Hookstown, Baltimore county, Maryland. In referring to this event, he says: "On reflecting that the Lord had provided a home for me, after many years' wandering without house or home, and just at the very time when I must change my relation to the Conference—for I plainly saw that I could no longer do effective work—I felt grateful to him for all his tender mercies over me, and called my house 'Pilgrim's Rest.' Perhaps 'Pilgrim's Lodge' would have been a more suitable name, for this is not yet my rest." *

---

*General Minutes M. E. Church, for 1863, p. 18.

For about thirty years he sustained this relation to the Baltimore Conference—so bright an example of meekness, patience, and of all the adornments of Christian character, that he was called "good Henry Smith."

"As he drew near his end, and was no longer able to speak, he made signs to those who sat watching by him of a desire to be placed in his usual attitude of prayer. After remaining on his knees about two minutes, he was gently laid upon his bed again, where he lingered for a short time, and then expired, in the ninety-fourth year of his age, and sixty-ninth of his ministry." *

Mr. Smith, although a delicately framed man, outlived all his cotemporaries.

By order of the Baltimore Conference, held March 4, 1863, it was resolved that his remains should be removed from Hookstown, where he was buried, to Mount Olivet Cemetery, there to repose with the dust of Bishops Asbury, George, Waugh, and Emory. †

The successful termination of the expedition under Gen. Wayne brought with it the most beneficial results to Kentucky. Not only did hundreds of persons return to the homes which they had left for safety, but a tide of emigration from Virginia and Maryland, and other States, set in, that increased the population with remarkable rapidity.

Among those who this year sought a home in

---

*General Minutes M. E. Church, for 1863, p. 17.

†Ibid., p. 18.

Kentucky, was the Rev. John Baird. He had been for several years a traveling preacher in Maryland. In 1791, he was admitted into the itinerancy, and traveled successively the Cecil, the Somerset, and Talbot Circuits. In the itinerant ministry he had been successful in the great work of doing good. In 1795, he located, and immediately emigrated to Kentucky. He passed by the Falls of the Ohio, and declined a settlement on the fertile lands at the mouth of Beargrass Creek, in consequence of their unhealthy location; and, finding a home more congenial to his views of health, he settled in Nelson county, (now Larue,) at what is known as the "Level Woods." Distinguished for his ability in the pulpit, as well as for his devotion to the Church, he determined to sow the seeds of Methodism in the neighborhood in which he resided. The first sermon ever preached in that neighborhood was delivered by Mr. Baird, on the 7th of August, 1796, at the house of Philip Reed, Esq. A short time afterward, a small society—consisting of the Rev. John Baird, Elizabeth Baird, William and Matthew Mellander, James and Ann Murphy—was organized by the Rev. John Watson, which gradually increased until it numbered about *seventy* members.* The influence exerted by the

*A letter from the Rev. J. F. Redford, the present pastor, informs us that "out of this class several societies have subsequently been formed. At one time it dwindled to twenty-five members. At the commencement of the Conference-year for 1838 and 1839, it again increased to *forty-two* members. At the present time, (January, 1868,) this society numbers *seventy-four*."

life and labors of John Baird is felt to the present time, not only in his family, but in the community in which he lived and died. In all the surrounding country, he, as an able expounder of the word of God, proclaimed its heaven-born truths. For fifty years his walk and conversation exemplified the doctrines of the gospel, and in death their hallowed principles afforded him sweet consolation.

On a marble slab, in the garden, close by where he lived and breathed his last, is the inscription:

Sacred
to the memory of
THE REV. JOHN BAIRD,
who departed this life,
April 17, 1846,
in the 78th year of his age,
54 years of which he spent
in the Methodist Episcopal Church,
calling sinners to repentance.
He was an acceptable preacher,
an affectionate husband,
a kind father,
and faithful friend.

We report this year an increase of *forty-seven* in the membership. The causes of the small increase in the membership about this period will be accounted for in a separate chapter.

At this Conference the Shelby Circuit was formed, or rather detached from the Salt River—making six circuits in Kentucky.

CHAPTER IX.

FROM THE CONFERENCE OF 1797 TO THE CONFERENCE OF 1799.

The Conference of 1797 held at Bethel Academy—Bishop Asbury—Thomas Allen—Francis Poythress—Williams Kavanaugh—John Kobler—Decrease in membership—The Conference of 1798 held on Holston—Robert Wilkerson—Valentine Cook—Increase in membership—John Kobler, the first missionary to Ohio.

THE Conference for 1797 was held at Bethel Academy, and met on the 1st day of May. Bishop Asbury was present, and presided.* In his journal he informs us that, "from the 9th of April to the 27th of May," he kept no written account of his travels; that, during this period, (which embraced his visit to Kentucky,) he had "traveled about six hundred miles, with an inflammatory fever and fixed pain in his breast." His diet was "chiefly tea, potatoes, Indian-meal gruel, and chicken broth." His "only reading" was "the Bible." Why, under such severe afflictions, did he not seek for rest? Thoughts of the "charge" confided to his trust, "of the Conferences, and the Church," pressed him on. "I must," said he, "be made perfect through sufferings." "Cheerful" all the while, yet sometimes "forced by weakness to stop" for a short time, he expresses his gratitude for the distinguished

*Judge Scott.

kindness "shown him by families" with whom he made a brief sojourn. Truly, he was "made perfect through sufferings"—an evangelist, in the highest sense of that term.

In the Minutes of the Conference, the names of three preachers, not previously mentioned in connection with the work in Kentucky, appear in the list of Appointments: Thomas Allen, John Kobler, and Williams Kavanaugh.

Of Thomas Allen we have no information, only such as we derive from the General Minutes. The present year he was admitted on trial, and appointed to the Danville Circuit. The following year, he was sent to the New River Circuit, in Virginia. At the subsequent Conference, he was returned to Kentucky, and appointed to the Salt River and Shelby Circuit; and in 1800, to the Lexington. This year closed his itinerant labors. At the following Conference, he located.

The health of the Rev. Francis Poythress—who, since the Conference of 1787, had held the responsible position of Presiding Elder over the District in Kentucky—had, through incessant labors, so far declined as to render it impracticable for him to perform any longer the onerous duties of the office. In the Minutes of this year, he is returned as a supernumerary, and John Kobler is reported as his successor on the District.

Williams Kavanaugh,* whose name is this year

*He was the father of Bishop Hubbard Hinde Kavanaugh, Benjamin T., Leroy H., and Williams B. Kavanaugh—all Methodist ministers.

mentioned in the list of Appointments for Kentucky, was born August 3, 1775. In a family Bible now in the possession of the family, there is the following record, in his own hand-writing:

"My grandfather in the paternal line was named Philemon. He was descended from an ancient Irish family, (I have understood,) much devoted to the Stuart interest. About A. D. 1705, he and one other brother came to Virginia, and first settled in Essex county, though my grandfather's final settlement was in Culpepper. He was twice married. His last wife's maiden name was Williams. She was from Wales. My grandfather had several children by each marriage. My father was (by the last marriage) a posthumous child, and was called by his mother's maiden name.

"My grandfather in the maternal line, (whose name was Harrison,) was born, I believe, in England, though he came from New England to Virginia. He and two brothers, who came with him, all lived to very great ages. His wife's maiden name was Johnson, or Johnston, of a Scotch family. My father and mother were both born in February, 1744, Old Style. When they were married, I do not know."

His father, Williams Kavanaugh, came to Kentucky at a very early period, and settled in Madison county. A member of the Methodist Episcopal Church, and a warm-hearted, zealous Christian, he impressed upon the tender heart of his son the importance of Christianity, and the doctrine of the new birth. Converted in early life, Williams Kavanaugh, Jr., at nineteen years of age, entered upon the labors and duties of an itinerant preacher. In 1794, at the Conference held at Lewis's Chapel, in Jessamine county, his name was placed upon the Conference roll. His first appointment was to the Green Circuit, in East Tennessee, with Lewis Garrett as his colleague. Mr. Garrett says: "Williams Kavanaugh and myself proceeded to Green Circuit. This circuit was a frontier circuit. It lay along the Holston and French Broad Rivers. There were few settlers south of French Broad, and what there were either lived in forts, cooped up in dread, or lived in strongly built houses, with puncheon doors, barred up strongly when night approached. The Cherokee Indians, who were their near neighbors, were in a state of hostility. We visited those forts and scattered settlers, in quest of perishing souls." To reach this remote field, he had to pass "through the wilderness, which was both difficult and dangerous." In company with "about sixty men, six of whom were traveling preachers"—among whom were John Ray and Lewis Garrett—he left the Crab Orchard, the place where the company met, and set out upon his journey. The first night he encamped in the vicinity of a fort in the woods, with no covering but the clear blue sky. Around their camp-fires they worshiped God—"the intrepid, fearless, zealous Ray" leading in the devotions.

The next day, the company "passed the gloomy spot where, a short time before," several persons "had been massacred by the Indians, two of whom were Baptist preachers;" and again, at night, they slept in the woods.

The third day, they "crossed the Cumberland Mountains, and reached the settlement on Clinch River, where" they "rested until the next day."*

Although only a youth, he was not insensible to the responsibilities of the holy office to which he had been called. He prosecuted with a commendable zeal the duties imposed upon him, and won a warm place in the confidence and affections, not only of the people, but of his colleague, Mr. Garrett, by whom he was always kindly remembered.

In 1795, he was sent to the Brunswick Circuit; in 1796, to the Cumberland—both lying in the State of Virginia. In the Minutes of 1797, his name appears in connection with *two* circuits—the Franklin, in Virginia, and the Salt River, in Kentucky. It is probable that he spent the first six months on the Franklin, and the latter in Kentucky.

On the 29th of March, 1798, he was married to Miss Hannah H., daughter of Dr. Thomas Hinde; and at the ensuing Conference, he asked for and obtained a location.

While we deeply regret that a minister who promised so much usefulness to the Church as did Mr. Kavanaugh, should have retired from the itinerant field, yet we cannot be insensible to the reasons that decided him in this purpose. The vast extent of territory embraced in a single circuit, separating a minister from his family nearly all the time, to-

* Recollections of the West.

gether with the difficulty of obtaining the most meager support, influenced him to this step.*

In his local relation, however, he was not idle. His name stands recorded as one of the eight persons who formed the first class at Ebenezer,† in Clarke county. Spending the principal portion of the week in teaching school, he devoted his Sabbaths to the work of the ministry, in which he had already attained eminence. His mind, however, had no rest. He was then an ordained Deacon. He felt the incongruity of such an office in the Church, without a pastoral relation; and the more he pondered the duties devolving upon a minister of the gospel, the more unpleasant he felt to hold the office without an opportunity to discharge the duties involved. He was not willing to be what was but a little more than a nominal minister of the gospel; and this gave him much disquietude of mind. Some gentlemen of the bar urged him to study law and enter upon the practice, stating that his talents—analytical and strongly discriminative—

---

* Among the preachers who were traveling in this division of the work, Messrs. Burke and Page were the only married men who had been able to continue in the itinerancy.

† Bishop Kavanaugh writes us from Lexington, Kentucky, March 11, 1868: "I learn from my mother, that he gave the Church the name it bears, or rather has borne, in the various edifices which the society there has erected, and which the remaining members and their friends are about to erect, for Ebenezer, this spring and summer, under the auspices of our young and enterprising brother, W. T. Poynter, so recently taken into the Kentucky Conference, and so new in the ministry, and now the stationed preacher at Winchester, Kentucky."

eminently fitted him for that profession; but his convictions were that it was his duty to preach the gospel of the grace of God, and that he dare not compromise this duty. Believing that he could, without the compromise of principle, become a minister of the gospel in the Protestant Episcopal Church, and sustain the relation of pastor, he determined to do so, made his application, and was received.

After entering the Protestant Episcopal Church, he spent a short time in the city of Louisville, but afterward settled in Henderson, as the rector of that parish, where, on the 16th of October, 1806, he ended his labors and his life.

Reared under Methodist influences, blessed with the example and the instruction of pious parents from his childhood, converted, and having entered the ministry when only a youth, during the entire period of his connection with the Methodist Episcopal Church, his piety shone with resplendent luster. As a preacher, "he was not boisterous, but fluent, ready, and his sermons smoothly delivered; his style perspicuous, and every word expressive of the idea intended."

However much we may regret that he was influenced to make any change in his Church-relations, it is gratifying to know that he carried into the Communion which he entered, the deep piety and devotion to the work of the ministry that distinguished him as an evangelist in the Church of his father. Judge Scott says: "He sustained an excellent character until he died."

We close this sketch with the following letter, received by us from the Rev. B. B. Smith, D.D., the Senior Bishop of the Protestant Episcopal Church in the United States:

"Some years after I entered upon the office of the first Bishop of the Protestant Episcopal Church in the Diocese of Kentucky, it occurred to me that it might become a matter of some interest to those who should come after me, if I were at some pains to collect such fragmentary notices as I could obtain of those early clergy who accompanied the first colonies which came to Kentucky, chiefly from Virginia. Some of these notices were not at all creditable to the characters of some of the colonial clergy. For example: Dr. Chambers, of Nelson county, fell in a duel with the celebrated Judge Rowan; and the distinguished Judge Sebastian, who escaped impeachment by resigning—on the accusation, which proved susceptible of a favorable interpretation, of receiving a pension from the Spanish Governor of Louisiana. The letters of orders of both these, and of that amiable and blameless Swedenborgian, Dr. Gant, of Louisville, by Bishops in England, were submitted to my inspection.

"The most favorable impression made by any of them upon my mind, was made, by all that I could learn, by the Rev. Williams Kavanaugh, of Henderson, who, however, was not ordained in England, but either by Bishop White, of Pennsylvania, or by Bishop Madison, of Virginia, if I remember aright.

"Amongst my first acquaintances in Henderson were several who distinctly remembered to have heard him preach; and some, I think, who had received baptism at his hands. His memory was cherished as that of a good man, an instructive and interesting preacher, and of one 'who adorned the doctrine of God our Saviour,' by a blameless and holy life. He adorned his sacred profession in all things."

John Kobler was born in Culpepper county, Virginia, August 29, 1768. Through the example and teachings of a pious mother, he was early impressed with the importance of religion, and on the evening of the 24th of December, 1787—then in the nineteenth year of his age—was happily converted to God. In 1790,* he entered upon the itinerant work, and was appointed to Amelia Circuit. His second year was on the Bedford; his third, on the Greenbrier—all in the State of Virginia. In 1793, though only twenty-five years of age, he was placed in charge of the District, as Presiding Elder, embracing New River, Green, and Holston Circuits, where he remained until 1797, when he succeeded Mr. Poythress in Kentucky.

After the termination of the Indian war, the North-western Territory began to settle rapidly. That portion of it, lying in the State of Ohio,

---

* The probabilities are that he was admitted in 1789, as it is so stated in the memoir of him in the General Minutes, as the Minutes of 1790 recognize him as "remaining on trial." This is confirmed by his appointment to a District as Presiding Elder, in 1793. The Minutes of 1789, however, have no notice of his name.

known as the Mad River country, was first settled by emigrants from Kentucky, while numbers from the same State settled on the Big and Little Miamis.* Among those who had gone from Kentucky, were many members of the Methodist Church. The emigration from the State was so great that "many of the societies were broken up." † It was only natural that Methodists from Kentucky should look to the State whence they had emigrated for ministerial aid.

Mr. Kobler, then in the flower and strength of manhood—possessed of a constitution naturally robust; deeply alive to a sense of his responsibility to the Church and to God; familiar with the dangers of frontier life, and well prepared to meet its privations and hardships—cheerfully volunteered to be the first missionary to cross the Ohio. In the year 1798, he enters on the duty of forming a circuit in the North-western Territory.‡ In entering upon that field of ministerial labor, "he found the country almost in its native rude and uncultivated state."

---

* Methodist Magazine, Vol. IV., p. 311.

† Western Methodism, p. 74.

‡ The Rev. Mr. Hinde, in the Methodist Magazine, Vol. V., p. 270, fixes the date of Mr. Kobler's entrance on his work in the North-western Territory at 1799; but Mr. Kobler himself, in an account furnished by him for the Western Historical Society, in 1841, and published in Finley's Sketches of Western Methodism, p. 169, says: "In the year 1798, I was sent by Bishop Asbury, as a missionary, to form a new circuit in what was then called the North-western Territory." His name, for 1798, stands in the Minutes in connection with the Cumberland Circuit. Judge Scott informs us that Bishop Asbury withdrew him from the Cumberland, and appointed Lewis Hunt in his place.

As yet, "no sound of the everlasting gospel had broken upon their ears, or gladdened their hearts." It is true, that the General Minutes, as early as 1787, report a circuit under the name of Ohio, but this circuit did not enter any portion of what is now that State, but "stretched along the frontier settlements of the Ohio River, in Western Pennsylvania and Virginia." *

He remained in Ohio until the ensuing Conference, having formed the Miami Circuit, and returned *ninety-eight* white members, and *one* colored. In 1799, we find him in charge of the Hinkstone Circuit, in Kentucky; and in 1800, on the Orange, in Virginia. The privations, toils, and exposures incident to frontier missionary life, "gave to his constitution a shock, from which it never recovered." Prostrated in health, at the Conference of 1801, he located, and "settled in the neighborhood in which he was born." In 1836, the Baltimore Conference, without any solicitation on his part, reädmitted him, and placed his name on the superannuated list, where it remained during the rest of his life.

Possessed of preaching abilities above mediocrity, in every relation he sustained to the Church—whether in the itinerant field, or in a local sphere—he prosecuted with untiring zeal the great work to which he had been called.

During the period of his connection with the Church in Kentucky, he gave entire satisfaction to

---

*Extract from proceedings of the Ross County (Chillicothe) Bar, on the occasion of the death of Judge Scott.

both preachers and people. During the year in which he presided over the Kentucky District, with such men under his supervision as Page, Lakin, Williams Kavanaugh, and Henry Smith, he exhibited those high qualifications, both as a preacher and an officer, in the Church, that rendered him a universal favorite, and crowned his ministry with great success. Everywhere he went, listening crowds gathered around him, and communities where no Methodist Churches had been organized invited his ministrations. At that period, no Church had been planted in the town of Washington, then the county-seat of Mason, and no Methodist preacher had probably ever preached in the place. Through the efforts of a few of the most influential citizens, the use of the court-house was obtained, and Mr. Kobler was invited to preach. "All the respectable citizens attended, and listened to his sermon with profound attention." When the public services were over, the people insisted that he was wrongly named—that he was no cobbler, but a complete workman.*

It always affords us pleasure to know that one, the morning and noon of whose life have been devoted to the service of the Church, retains his influence for good in its "sere and yellow leaf." "Fond of meeting with the redeemed of the Lord, to worship the Most High, as age grew upon him, and his ability to transport himself to the distant circuit appointments declined, he sought for a residence in

*Judge Scott.

a place where he could assemble with the people of God, and be useful. The highly favored spot of his selection was Fredericksburg, Virginia. The saint-like spirit, the Christian conversation, the dignified and ministerial bearing, and the untiring labors in preaching, exhorting, praying, visiting the sick and imprisoned, of John Kobler, have done more, under God, to give permanency to Methodism in Fredericksburg than any other instrumentality ever employed."*

Amongst the last active labors of Mr. Kobler was a tour to the West, in his seventy-fourth year, to solicit aid in the erection of a more comfortable church in Fredericksburg than the one in which they worshiped. Appealing to those to whose fathers he had preached the gospel, he placed more than one thousand dollars in the hands of the building committee. He lived to behold the completion and dedication of this house to the worship of God, and to see in it the most interesting revival of religion that the Church in Fredericksburg had ever witnessed. "Hardly had the work of God abated, when disease laid its destroying hand upon him. While upon his bed of affliction, he was perfectly happy; his countenance always wore a smile that seemed heavenly. Without murmuring or complaining, and with lamb-like patience, he suffered his Master's will. The following are some of the remarks he made during his affliction: 'Living or dying, so God is glorified, and I,

*General Minutes, Vol. III., p. 465.

a poor sinner, saved, is all I want.' Calling on his friends to engage in prayer, he was asked, 'Is there any thing special for which you wish us to pray?' 'Pray,' said he, 'for the Church, that God would pour out his Spirit abundantly upon it, and take it into close keeping with himself.' And again: 'I have dug deep, and brought all the evidence to bear, and I find I have a strong confidence, which nothing can shake, but all is through our Lord Jesus Christ. Brother, I wish it to be known that the principles I have believed, and taught, and practiced in life, I hold in death, and I find that they sustain me. I have tried all my life to make my ministry and life consistent.' About half an hour before he expired, he was asked, 'Is Jesus precious?' 'O yes,' said he, 'very precious, very precious!' and then added, 'Come, Lord Jesus! Come, Lord Jesus, in power! Come quickly!' and then in a few minutes breathed his last, in the seventy-fifth year of his age, on July 26, 1843."

Although the Church had prosperity in many portions of the State, we are called upon to report a decrease in the membership of *one hundred and ninety-six.*

The Shelby and Salt River Circuits were again united, and constituted one field of labor.

In the arrangement of the work, there was no farther change previous to the Conference of 1800.

The Conference for Kentucky, for 1798, met on the 1st day of May, on Holston.* Mr. Burke, in

*Judge Scott. We also learn from the General Minutes that the appointment of the Conference was for the date and place we have given.

his Autobiography, says: "In the spring of 1798, Bishop Asbury met the Conference on Holston." Mr. Burke, however, is evidently mistaken as to Bishop Asbury being present at this Conference. On the 2d day of May, according to his journal, we find him opening the Baltimore Conference, in reference to which he says: "*Wednesday, May* 2. Our Conference began. It was *half-yearly*, to bring an equality to the change from fall to spring."

The name of Robert Wilkerson appears this year among the Appointments in Kentucky. In 1797, he was admitted on trial, and appointed to the Green Circuit. He was sent to the Danville Circuit in 1798. He remained in Kentucky only one year. In the Appointments for 1799, his name stands connected with the Guilford Circuit, and in 1800, with the Haw River—both in North Carolina. In 1801, he located.

Valentine Cook, the energetic leader for the present year of the valiant corps of preachers who were devoting their strength in this Western field to the promotion of religious truth, had already labored successfully for several years in the East. As early as 1788, he became an itinerant, and was appointed to the Calvert Circuit, in Maryland. The three following years he traveled in Virginia, on the Gloucester, Lancaster, and Berkeley Circuits. In 1792, he had charge of the Pittsburgh Circuit, in the bounds of which he held his famous debate with the Rev. Mr. Jamieson, a Scotch Seceder clergyman—his denomination being prevalent in that community. The points involved in the controversy embraced those doctrines upon which Calvinists and Arminians so widely differ. Mr. Cook had ventured into the bounds of the congregation of the Rev. Mr. Porter, a Presbyterian minister, in Westmoreland county, Pennsylvania, and preached the doctrines of Free Grace and Sanctification, and compared them with those of Unconditional Election and Reprobation. Mr. Porter, regarding himself insulted, and his rights invaded, addressed a letter to the Methodist preacher, in which he informed him that he "wanted none of his friendly visits or help," and "charged him with propagating false doctrines in several particulars." Mr. Cook, by no means abashed, replied, vindicating the truth of the principles he held, and avowed his purpose to impress them upon the minds and hearts of the people. Several communications passed between them, when Mr. Porter was informed that no farther time could be wasted in a "paper controversy," but, if he was "not satisfied, he would meet him in public," and discuss the points at issue between them. It was thought by the friends of Mr. Porter that it would be best to withdraw him from the field, and to substitute in his place the Rev. Mr. Jamieson. Entering the lists under the conviction that an easy task lay before him, Mr. Jamieson addressed a letter to Mr. Cook, in which he informed him that he had spent many "years at college," had "studied theology" and "the art of logical reasoning;" that he had been many "years a preacher of the gospel;" and that he "must be," by this time, "deeply imbedded in the mire of Calvinism;" and to extricate him from which, he asked of Mr. Cook his favorable assistance, and assured him that he was "ready to meet" him. Mr. Cook, in reply, requested Mr. Jamieson "to appoint the time and the place" for the debate, and asked him to make the appointment before he "would leave the country, and cross the mountains to Conference," as he had "no certainty that" he should "return again."

The time was appointed, and the place was promptly fixed at Mr. Porter's church, the stronghold of Calvinism, within five miles of which, probably, not a Methodist family resided. The hour was nine o'clock.

Mr. Cook, accompanied by his friend, Mr. Banning, reached the place before the hour arrived, and took his seat in the woods.*

Bishop Roberts, at that time a young member of the Church, resided in the bounds of Mr. Cook's circuit, and was present at the debate; and to him, as detailed by the Rev. Dr. Stevenson, in his Biographical Sketch of Valentine Cook, we are indebted for the following account of the scene:

"On reaching the ground, he found that ample preparations had been made for the accommodation of all concerned. A lofty wooden pulpit had been erected in the midst of a dense forest, and surrounded with a vast number of seats for the convenience of the immense concourse that was evidently

*Contributions to the Western Historical Society, by A. Banning, published in the South-western Christian Advocate, of November 7, 1840.

expected on the occasion. These extensive arrangements appeared to have been exclusively prepared by the friends and votaries of the old Scotch minister. In truth, he saw no one who appeared to be at all inclined to favor Mr. Cook, or his cause. As the people began to assemble, he occasionally heard the name of *Cook* pronounced, and being anxious to know all that was going on, he passed round from group to group, and heard much that was being said. Here, Cook was represented as a mere ignoramus—that, if he should chance to appear on the ground, there would be but little of him or his Methodism left by the time Mr. ——— had done with him. Upon the whole, it was perfectly clear, from all that he could see and hear, that a great victory, in the estimation of the dominant party, was that day to be achieved on the side of Calvinism. By this time his fears had become so aroused, he was strongly inclined to wish that Mr. Cook might not attend. But it was soon announced that the Methodist preacher had arrived. He found him a little beyond the limits of the congregation, quietly seated on the trunk of a fallen tree. But two or three individuals approached him, or gave him the hand of friendship. His presence, however, appeared to put a quietus for the time being on the rampant spirit of the opposition, especially as their champion had not yet made his appearance. At length the old Scotchman drove up, as large as life; nor did he rein up his noble steed until he had well-nigh reached the center of the crowd. He was a well-set, broad-shouldered, venerable-looking man, of about sixty. His features were strongly marked, and indicated a due proportion of *iron* as well as intellect. When interrogated by one of his friends as to the cause of his delay, he promptly replied, with a heavy Scotch brogue: 'I'm here in ample time to gi'e the youngster a dose from which he'll not soon recover.' The parties had never seen each other, and, of course, had no personal acquaintance. When introduced, as they soon were, though in a very awkward manner, Mr. Cook was treated with marked incivility and rudeness.

"'What!' said the old Scotchman, 'is this the young mon who has had the impertinance to assail the doctrines of grace?'

"'No, sir,' was the prompt reply of Mr. Cook, 'I have never assailed the doctrines of grace, though I have entered my protest to the prominent peculiarities of the Calvinistic system, believing, as I do, that they cannot be sustained by the word of God.'

"An effort was then made to adjust the propositions to be discussed, as well as rules of order for the debate; to all of which, however, the old Scotchman peremptorily demurred. He would agree to nothing proposed by Mr. Cook. It was his purpose to occupy the stand as long as he might think proper; and then, if the stripling had any thing to say, he might say on. With an air of self-confidence he ascended the pulpit, and, without prayer, explanation, or any thing of the sort, he commenced a most furious attack on Mr. Wesley and Methodism in general. He soon became greatly excited—raved, stamped, and literally foamed at the mouth. By the time he entered on the support of Calvinism properly so called, his voice was well-nigh gone. He, however, screwed himself up as best he could, and held on for a considerable length of time, relying almost exclusively on the opinions of distinguished men and learned bodies of ecclesiastics for the support of the prominent features of his theology. At the close of about two hours, he brought his weak and very exceptionable remarks to a close, and sat down greatly exhausted.

"Mr. Cook then rose in the pulpit, and after a most solemn and fervent appeal to Almighty God, for wisdom and help from on high, to maintain and defend the truth, he commenced, though evidently laboring under much embarrassment. His hand trembled, his tongue faltered, and at times it was with difficulty he could articulate with sufficient clearness to be heard on the outskirts of the assembly. He first took up in order, and refuted with great power and effect, the allegations that had been made against Wesley and Methodism. By this time his embarrassment had passed off, his voice became clear and distinct, and, withal, there was a strange sweetness in his delivery, that seemed to put a spell on the whole assembly. He then entered his solemn protest to the exceptionable features of the Calvinistic theory. He opposed to the opinions of reputedly great and learned men, on which his opponent had mainly relied, the plain and positive teachings of Moses and the prophets, of Christ and his apostles; and in conclusion, presented an outline view of the great gospel scheme of human salvation, as believed and taught by Wesley and his followers, both in Europe and America; not in its theory only, but in its experimental and practical bearings on the present and future destiny of the world. At an early period in his discourse, the venerable champion of Geneva rose to his feet, and exclaimed, with all the voice he had left, 'Wolf! wolf! wolf in sheep's clothing!' Mr. Cook, however, had become so perfectly self-possessed, and so thoroughly occupied with his subject, that this excessive rudeness on the part of the old Scotchman had no effect whatever upon him. As he advanced in the discussion, he appeared to acquire additional strength, physical, mental, and spiritual. The fixed attention of the vast multitude seemed to inspire him with new powers of investigation, argument, and eloquence. His voice, though soft and soothing, rolled on, in thunder-tones, over the vast concourse, and echoed far away in the depths of the forest; while his countenance lighted up, kindled, and glowed, as if newly commissioned from on high to proclaim the salvation of God to a perishing race. The poor old Scotchman could endure it no longer; he again sprang to his feet, and bawled out at the top of his shattered voice: 'Follow me, follow me, and leave the babbler to himself!' Only some two or three obeyed his mandate. Mr. Cook was engaged in too important a work to pay the slightest attention to the ravings or flight of his opponent. He pressed directly forward with his argument, dealing out at every step the most startling demonstrations against error in Christian faith and practice. Long before the mighty effort was brought to a close, the whole assembly were on their feet, all eagerly listening, and insensibly pressing toward the speaker. Every eye was fixed, every ear was opened, and every heart was tremblingly alive to the importance of the theme. When Mr. Cook took his seat, all faces were upturned, and, for the most part, bathed in tears. The great multitude stood for some time like statues, no one appearing disposed to move, utter a word, or leave the place. All seemed to be overwhelmed, astonished, and captivated. When the crowd began to disperse, the Bishop said, he started down to the spring, in company with many others. For some time all was as silent as a funeral procession. At length a good-looking old gentleman turned to his companion, and said: 'Did you ever hear such a man?' 'Never,' was the prompt reply. A free conversation ensued. It was readily admitted that he must be a very great and learned man, and that they had never wept so much under a discourse in all their lives before. It was perfectly evident that they were strongly inclined to set him down as a good as well as a great man. In the midst of their conversation, another elderly gentleman—all of Scotch descent, and evidently of the same persuasion—spoke up, and said, with a good deal of apparent excitement and solicitude: 'Sirs, I perceive that ye are in great danger of being led captive by the de'il at his will. Ha'e ye never reed how that Satan can transform himsel' into an angel of light, that he may deceive the very elect, if it were possible? I tell ye, sirs, he's a dangerous mon, and the less we ha'e to do wi' him the better for us a'.' Soon after this, young Roberts left the place, and returned to his father's, greatly delighted with the result of the discussion.

"It is well known to those who are acquainted with the early history of Methodism in Western Pennsylvania, that this controversy was the means of opening to her ministry a 'great and effectual door' of usefulness. From that day forward the Methodist Church, in all that mountain range of country, has been rapidly advancing in numbers and influence."

The result of this discussion was not only a triumph for Methodism in the vindication of its great gospel truths, but it also conferred on Mr. Cook a reputation that placed him by the side of the ablest ministers of the Church.

The following year we find him among the mountains of Western Virginia, on the Clarksburg Circuit. In 1794, his appointment is to the District embracing Bristol, Chester, Philadelphia, Lancaster, Northumberland, and Wyoming Circuits, lying almost entirely in Pennsylvania; and in 1795, his District comprises the Northumberland, Wyoming, Tioga, and Seneca Circuits. In 1796 and 1797, he leads the band of itinerants, who, amid privations and sacrifices, traverse the mountains over which the Clarksburg, Ohio, Redstone, Pittsburgh, and Greenfield Circuits spread. A faithful messenger of truth, he passed through his District, scattering the rays of Divine light, proclaiming the everlasting gospel, encouraging the preachers by his untiring zeal, and everywhere calling the people to repentance. In 1798, he came to Kentucky, and, as the successor to John Kobler, was placed in charge of the District, as Presiding Elder. His immense labors had broken down his health, and at the Conference of 1800, he located. "Such, however, were his extraordinary endowments, mental, moral, and evangelical—such the strength of his faith, the fervency of his zeal, and the efficiency of his ministry—that no seclusion of place or obscurity of position could prevent the Church or the world from recognizing him as a great and good man, as well as an able, laborious, and eminently successful minister of the cross of Christ." *

The Bethel Academy, to which we alluded in a former chapter, was still in an unfinished state. It was the second institution of learning established by the Methodist Church in America.†

The educational advantages of Valentine Cook—his great popularity in the pulpit, as well as adaptedness to such a position—pointed him out as well qualified to take charge of this academy. He, however, remained at Bethel but a few years. He subsequently took charge of an academy at Harrodsburg, and finally removed to Logan county, three miles north of Russellville, where he resided until his death.

---

* Sketch of Valentine Cook, by Dr. Stevenson, p. 10.

† Cokesbury College was the first.

In 1798, "he was married to Miss Tabitha Slaughter, the niece of the ex-Governor of that name." In his local sphere, he made "good proof of his ministry." Regarding Methodism as perfectly daguerreotyped in the Holy Bible, to defend its doctrines, to enforce its precepts, and proclaim its truths, was the most fondly cherished wish of his heart. As an able champion placed for the defense "of the faith," Kentucky will always hold him in admiration and reverence. The controversies in which he engaged, and their successful termination in behalf of the Church of which he was so able a minister, would, by tradition, transmit his name to future generations, though no sketch of him had ever been written. But while his controversial powers were of the highest order, the great theme on which he loved to dwell was *experimental religion.* Not only in the pulpit, but in the social circle—where the urbanity of his manners, and his bright Christian example, made him a welcome guest—he always turned the conversation on the subject of religion. He was truly a man of deep piety.

During the winter of 1811–12, Kentucky was visited by a succession of earthquakes, that produced great alarm among the people. The most violent concussion was felt on a certain dark night, at an untimely hour, when men were wrapped in slumber. It was enough to make the stoutest heart tremble. Brother Cook, suddenly roused from sleep, made for the door, exclaiming, "I believe Jesus is coming."

His wife was alarmed, and said, "Will you wait

for me?" Said he, "If my Jesus is coming, I will wait for nobody!"*

The same writer says:

"My personal acquaintance with Brother Cook commenced in his own house, near Russellville, Kentucky, in the summer of 1815, and was renewed when I became a member of the Kentucky Conference, by transfer, in 1821. From that time till his death, my fields of labor being somewhat contiguous to his residence, I saw something of his movements, and heard much more. He was then an old man, and honored as a father in the Church, but still possessed of strong physical and mental powers. His aid was anxiously sought after on all important occasions in the west part of the State; and wherever he appeared in a religious assembly, he was hailed as a harbinger of mercy. Whole multitudes of people, on popular occasions, were moved by the Spirit of grace, under his preaching, as the trees of the forest were moved by the winds of heaven. His last public effort, as I was informed by those who were present, made at Yellow Creek camp-meeting, in Dixon county, Tennessee, was a signal triumph. While preaching on the Sabbath, such a power came down on the people, and produced such an excitement, that he was obliged to desist till order was partially restored. Shortly after he resumed speaking, he was stopped from the same cause. A third attempt produced the same result. He then sat down amidst a glorious

*Morris's Miscellany, pp. 175, 176.

shower of grace, and wept, saying, 'If the Lord sends rain, we will stop the plow, and let it rain.'" *

Impressed with the belief that his work was well-nigh done, in the autumn of 1819, he consummated a fondly cherished desire of his heart, in visiting his old friends in Pennsylvania, Maryland, and Virginia. He "felt a wish to kneel by the graves of his departed parents, and to take a last look, as well as a last leave, of the memorable spot where first the light of Heaven broke upon his soul." In his route, he passed through Lexington, Kentucky, Cincinnati, Ohio, and Pittsburgh, Pennsylvania, where he preached "the unsearchable riches of Christ." He then proceeded to Philadelphia, New York, and Baltimore, where "vast crowds of people flocked to hear him," and "scores and hundreds were awakened and converted to God through his instrumentality." Returning home, he passed through the Greenbrier country, seeing "many of his relatives and early friends;" looking upon "the scenes of his childhood," and kneeling "at the spot" where slept the dust of his parents. Then, bidding adieu to his friends, he wended his way to his own home, from which he had been absent for several weeks. Passing around his little farm, the well-known sound of his sweetly toned voice was heard, as he sang:

'Salvation, O the joyful sound!
'T is pleasure to our ears:
A sov'reign balm for every wound,
A cordial for our fears."

---

*Morris's Miscellany, p. 177.

His whole tour through the East resembled the triumph of a conqueror. Wherever he went, he says, "the power of the Spirit of the Lord was with me." Thousands hung in breathless silence around him, and caught the words of mercy as they warmly fell from his burning lips. Contemplating death, he says: "My labors in the ministry are drawing to a close. I shall soon have performed my last day's work on earth. Thank God, I am ready, all ready, through his abundant mercy and grace, to depart and be with Christ!"*

In less than a year after he returned from this tour, he was dead.

"A short time previous to his death, he attended a camp-meeting, some eight or ten miles from home. As usual, he labored with great zeal and success. He preached on the Sabbath to a vast crowd, from these words: 'For our light affliction, which is but for a moment, worketh for us a far more exceeding and eternal weight of glory.'—2 Corinthians iv. 17. After a solemn and very impressive pause, he lifted his eyes to heaven, and said: 'What! our *afflictions* work for us a *weight of glory!—a far more exceeding* and *eternal weight of glory!*' and added, 'I believe it with all my heart, because thou, O God, hast revealed it in this blessed volume.' The effect upon the congregation is said to have been very remarkable, and the discourse throughout has been represented as among the most able and effective that he ever delivered. This was

* Dr. Stevenson.

the last sermon he preached, as I was informed by his weeping widow, a few months after his death.

"On his return home from this meeting, he was violently attacked with bilious fever. His case, from the first, was considered doubtful, and finally hopeless. Conscious of his approaching dissolution, he called his wife and children to his bedside, and, after taking a last earthly leave of his family, he committed them, with many expressions of confidence, to the guidance and protection of Almighty Goodness. When asked by one of his neighbors, a few moments before his death, how he felt, he answered, 'I scarcely know,' and then added, 'When I think of Jesus, and of living with him for ever, I am so filled with the love of God, that I scarcely know whether I am in the body or out of the body.' These were the last words that ever fell from his lips. He died as he had lived, 'strong in faith, giving glory to God.'" *

The year 1798 was distinguished for the introduction of Methodism into that portion of the Northwestern Territory now known as the State of Ohio. Kentucky was already the great center of Methodism in the West. The rapid tide of emigration to the vast fields beyond the Ohio, not only from Kentucky, but also from other States, very properly invited the attention of Bishop Asbury to the importance of sending a missionary to them, and John Kobler was selected for that enterprising yet arduous field.

---

* Sketch of Cook, by Dr. Stevenson, pp. 75, 76.

Francis McCormack, a local preacher of piety and zeal, who immigrated to Kentucky in 1795, and settled in Bourbon county, not pleased with the State, had preceded Mr. Kobler to the North-western Territory, and settled "on the Little Miami, near where Milford now stands." Up to the time of the entrance of Mr. Kobler on this missionary field, "no sound of the everlasting gospel had as yet broken upon their ears; no house of worship was erected wherein Jehovah's name was recorded; no joining the assembly of the saints, or those who keep the holy-day; but the whole might with strict propriety be called a land of darkness and the shadow of death." *

Mr. Kobler "spread the first table for the sacrament of the Lord's Supper that was spread northwest of the Ohio," when only "twenty-five or thirty—the sum total of all that were in the country"—communed.

At the following Conference, he reported the Miami Circuit with *ninety-eight* white members and *one* colored—and to which Henry Smith was appointed the succeeding year.

At the close of this year, we have the pleasure to report an increase of *thirty-seven* members, which, though small, indicates that the downward tendency is checked.

---

* Finley's Sketches of Western Methodism, p. 170.

CHAPTER X.

FROM THE CONFERENCE OF 1799 TO THE CONFERENCE HELD IN APRIL, 1800.

The Conference held at Bethel Academy—Daniel Gossage—Farther increase in membership—The decline in membership between the years 1792 and 1800, and the causes—Emigration from the State—The O'Kelly schism—Legislation on the subject of slavery—Prevalent infidelity—Erroneous Doctrines—John and William McGee—The great revival—Red River Church—Muddy River—The Ridge meeting—Desha's Creek—Letter from the Rev. John McGee.

THE Conference of 1799 was held on the 1st day of May, at Bethel Academy. In reference to the session we have but little information, except such as we find in the General Minutes.

The name of Daniel Gossage is the only one in the list of Appointments in Kentucky, of whom previous mention had not been made. He, however, only entered the Conference this year, and was appointed, with Thomas Allen, to the Salt River and Shelby Circuit. At the next Conference his name disappears from the roll, and all trace of him is lost.

At the close of this year, we have the pleasure of reporting again an increase of members, amounting to *one hundred and three*—an improvement on the report of the previous year.

It is a pleasant task to trace the history of the

Church amid scenes of revival, when the achievements of Christianity, "like the rushing of a mighty wind," arrest the attention of entire communities; or when, in its more gentle influence, it gradually adds to the number of its conquests from the ranks of sin. But when, in the midst of tireless efforts on the part of chosen instruments, we discover any decay of its power, or any diminution of its sway, it is proper that we pause to inquire into the causes by which its prosperity has been impaired.

Between the years 1792 and 1800, the men who occupied the field in the West, if equaled, have not been surpassed, for their zeal, their abundant labors, and their self-sacrificing spirit, in any age of the Church; yet, during this period, while the State of Kentucky increased in population from less than one hundred thousand to two hundred and sixty-four thousand three hundred and three, including whites and colored, the Methodist Episcopal Church decreased in membership from *one thousand eight hundred and eight* to *one thousand seven hundred and forty-one.*

Why this result? It certainly cannot be ascribed to any want of fidelity to the Church on the part of the preachers of that period; nor can it be traced to any defect in the doctrines they preached—for these, if not found in the Confessions of Faith of other evangelical Churches, have met with almost universal adoption by the orthodox pulpit.

The Rev. D. R. McAnally, in his "Life and Times of the Rev. Samuel Patton," in referring to the Conference for 1800, says: "The settlements in Kentucky were rapidly enlarging and being filled up, and all the Western preachers that could be spared were taken for that work; so that only three were left for all the Holston country. New River, Holston, and Russell Circuits were united, under the care of John Watson and John Page, while James Hunter was sent to Green. One preacher only (William Lambeth) was all that could be, or that was, afforded to the Cumberland or West Tennessee country, while there were seven in Kentucky. Regarding the facts connected with the early history of the Church in these different sections, and seeing the manifest advantages given to the Kentucky settlements, the reader would naturally expect to find Methodism there greatly in advance of what it was in the other sections. And this was the case for many years; but the precedence thus gained was not well sustained, and in process of time, the others not only overtook, but, in many important respects, outstripped their early favored sister. A close inquiry into the reason of this, prosecuted with a cool, philosophic pen, could reveal facts, and the operation of principles, important to Methodists everywhere, and through all time."

We may not be able to discover the partiality shown to Kentucky, to which allusion is made in the extract we have quoted. We have always accepted the opinion that the comparative wants of the work in each Episcopal District were duly considered by those who had the oversight, and that the best distribution was made of the talents and laborers to be employed; nor does it belong to our purpose to institute comparisons between the Church in Kentucky and any other portion of our priceless heritage. We rejoice in the success of Methodism anywhere. It is our common inheritance; and in Holston, Tennessee, and Kentucky, it claims, under God, a common parentage, and has been bequeathed to us by the same noble men. The names of Haw, Ogden, Poythress, McHenry, Burke, Page, Wilkerson, Ward, Ray, Kobler, and others, are equally dear to them and to us; and if, in the Holston Conference, Methodism has met with fewer antagonisms than in Kentucky, and been more successful, it shall be our glory and joy.

The decrease in the membership, to which we have referred, cannot be justly attributed to any single cause, but to a combination of causes. The generally received opinion, that the decrease during this period may be traced to the emigration from the State, is not sustained by the facts. Between the years 1792 and 1795, we had no material increase in membership; and yet, during this period, we had no emigration from Kentucky. The expedition of Gen. Wayne into the Indian country was not made until the summer of 1794, nor was the treaty of peace made until the following year; and hence the North-western Territory was not opened to emigration previous to that date. Whatever influence emigration from the State may have exerted on the welfare and numerical strength of the Church, subsequent to 1795—and we readily concede that, between that year and 1800, as well as at later periods, it was sufficient, in the midst of extensive revivals of religion, to produce a declension of numbers—certainly the apparent want of success, while largely indebted to this cause, cannot be confined to it. We also readily admit that, before the close of the past century, in some places, large societies were entirely broken up, and in others, only portions were left, by removals from the State. We have already seen large bodies of Methodists from Kentucky settled in what is now the State of Ohio, in the Mad River country, "and also on the Big and Little Miamis;" * so that, notwithstanding the success that crowned the labors of the preachers, and the hundreds that were brought to the saving knowledge of the truth, through their instrumentality, yet, in their annual exhibits, they often showed a decrease of membership in their respective fields of labor.

In Marion county, in the neighborhood known as Thomas's Meeting-house, we had one of the most flourishing societies in the State. The land around it was fertile, and many influential families from Virginia had settled in the vicinity, and became members of the Methodist Episcopal Church.

From a letter we received from the Hon. Charles A. Wickliffe, we learn that, "about the year 1800, a considerable emigration of Roman Catholics from Maryland came into this neighborhood, and bought out the residences of many members of the Church, who sought homes in other portions of the State,

* Methodist Magazine, Vol. IV., p. 311.

and in Indiana." By this means, a large extent of territory, where Methodism had been fostered and flourished, passed from our hands; and, at the present date, is one of the strongholds of Roman Catholicism; while Protestant Christianity, in any of its forms, though favored with a ministry distinguished for their zeal and devotion, and a membership, though small, yet influential, has found it difficult, in the same community, to do more than maintain a feeble existence.

To the Church in Kentucky it was a source of unspeakable pleasure, that, while their societies at home were being thus depleted, they were sending forth into the vast field beyond the Ohio hundreds from their Communion, by whom Methodism would be planted, and beneath whose fostering care it would flourish, and put forth "its leaves for the healing of the nations."

Another cause of the decrease in our membership during this period, is to be found in the influence exerted by Mr. O'Kelly. While the injurious effects of the step that he had so unfortunately taken, for a while arrested the prosperity of the Church in Virginia and North Carolina, the evil that he wrought was not confined to these sections, in which he had previously attained such popularity as an evangelist: its pernicious results reached the farthest limits of the Church in America, immediately following his secession. For several years, a decrease in the aggregate membership is reported in the General Minutes. In 1795, when his power was at its height, and he was spreading desolation throughout the Church, the decrease reached *six thousand three hundred and seventeen*—which was more than one-tenth the entire membership of the Church. Kentucky had chiefly been settled by emigrants from Virginia, and the infant Church in the West became involved in the controversy. Some of the prominent preachers were beguiled by its teachings. We have already seen James Haw—one of the first two missionaries—embracing the views of Mr. O'Kelly, and carrying with him almost the entire corps of preachers, and many of the members in the Cumberland Circuit, which lay partly in Kentucky. The infection reached the central and northern portions of the State, and threw many of the societies into confusion and strife.

Whatever may be the beneficial results of religious controversy, when it involves the vindication of the doctrines of the Bible, certainly no good can follow from a discussion between religionists who accept the same great axioms of Bible truth, and differ only upon questions of minor importance. In controversies of this kind, the passions are much more likely to become inflamed than where the issue is in reference to great evangelical questions. The strife in which many of the societies became involved very naturally produced ill-feeling, and turned away from our Communion hundreds who had been blessed by the teachings of our fathers.

There is still, however, another cause for our want of success during this period: the legislation of the Church on the subject of slavery. Previous to the Christmas Conference—at which time the "Methodist Episcopal Church in America" was organized—the Annual Conferences had enacted laws on this question. At the Conference of 1780—realizing the delicacy of the subject—we find an expression of "disapprobation on all" Methodists who held slaves, and "their freedom" advised. In the Conference of 1783—emboldened by their former step—the question is asked: "What shall be done with our local preachers who hold slaves, contrary to the laws which authorize their freedom, in any of the United States?" The answer is: "We will try them another year. In the meantime, let every assistant deal faithfully and plainly with every one, and report to the next Conference. It may then be necessary to suspend them." The action of the Conference of 1783 produced some disturbance in the State of Virginia, and at the Conference of 1784, while a more rigid discipline was adopted for the laity, final action was suspended for another year against the preachers in Virginia; and at the same time, more stringent measures were to be enforced against our local brethren in Maryland, Delaware, Pennsylvania, and New Jersey. The traveling preachers, also, who might own slaves, were to be suspended.

The enactments of this Conference are:

"*Question* 12. What shall we do with our friends that will buy and sell slaves?

"*Answer*. If they buy with no other design than to hold them as slaves, and have been previously warned, they shall be expelled, and permitted to sell on no consideration.

"*Question* 13. What shall we do with our local preachers who will not emancipate their slaves in the States where the laws admit it?

"*Answer*. Try those in Virginia another year, and suspend the preachers in Maryland, Delaware, Pennsylvania, and New Jersey.

"*Question* 22. What shall be done with our traveling preachers that now are, or hereafter shall be, possessed of slaves, and refuse to manumit where the law permits?

"*Answer*. Employ them no more."

These several actions were previous to the organization of the Church.

At the Christmas Conference, held in the city of Baltimore—at which the "Methodist Episcopal Church in America" was organized—in answer to the question, "What methods can we take to extirpate slavery?" we have the following:

"*Question* 42. What methods can we take to extirpate slavery?

"*Answer*. We are deeply conscious of the impropriety of making new terms of communion for a religious society already established, excepting on the most pressing occasion; and such we esteem the practice of holding our fellow-creatures in slavery. We view it as contrary to the golden law of God, on which hang all the law and the prophets, and the unalienable rights of mankind, as well as every principle of the revolution, to hold in the deepest debasement, in a more abject slavery than is perhaps to be found in any part of the world except America, so many souls that are all capable of the image of God.

"We therefore think it our most bounden duty to take immediately some effectual method to extirpate this abomination from among us; and for that purpose we add the following to the rules of our society, viz.:

"1. Every member of our society who has slaves in his possession, shall, within twelve months after notice given to him by the assistant, (which notice the assistants are required immediately, and without any delay, to give in their respective circuits,) legally execute and record an instrument, whereby he emancipates and sets free every slave in his possession, who is between the ages of forty and forty-five, immediately, or at farthest when they arrive at the age of forty-five.

"And every slave who is between the ages of twenty-five and forty immediately, or at farthest at the expiration of five years from the date of the said instrument.

"And every slave who is between the ages of twenty and twenty-five immediately, or at farthest when they arrive at the age of thirty.

"And every slave under the age of twenty, as soon as they arrive at the age of twenty-five at farthest.

"And every infant born in slavery after the above-mentioned rules are complied with, immediately on its birth.

"2. Every assistant shall keep a journal, in which

he shall regularly minute down the names and ages of all the slaves belonging to all the masters in his respective circuit, and also the date of every instrument executed and recorded for the manumission of the slaves, with the name of the court, book, and folio, in which the said instruments respectively shall have been recorded; which journal shall be handed down in each circuit to the succeeding assistants.

"3. In consideration that these rules form a new term of communion, every person concerned, who will not comply with them, shall have liberty quietly to withdraw himself from our society within the twelve months succeeding the notice given as aforesaid; otherwise the assistant shall exclude him in the society.

"4. No person so voluntarily withdrawn, or so excluded, shall ever partake of the Supper of the Lord with the Methodists, till he complies with the above requisitions.

"5. No person holding slaves shall, in future, be admitted into society or to the Lord's Supper, till he previously complies with these rules concerning slavery.

"*N. B.* These rules are to affect the members of our society no farther than as they are consistent with the laws of the States in which they reside.

"And respecting our brethren in Virginia that are concerned, and after due consideration of their peculiar circumstances, we allow them two years from the notice given, to consider the expedience of compliance or non-compliance with these rules.

"*Question* 43. What shall be done with those who buy or sell slaves, or give them away?

"*Answer.* They are immediately to be expelled, unless they buy them on purpose to free them."*

"At the Annual Conferences for 1785, it was concluded that the rule on slavery, adopted at the Christmas Conference, would do harm. It was therefore resolved to suspend its execution for the present, and a note to that effect was added to the Annual Minutes for that year. The Conferences, however, still expressed the deepest abhorrence of the practice, and a determination to seek its destruction by all wise and prudent means."†

It is not our purpose, in this place, to discuss this question. We only desire to show that it retarded the progress of the Church at this early period. The climate of Kentucky, as well as the fertility of the soil, not only invited immigration after the cessation of Indian hostilities, but also previous to this period, when even life and safety were in constant peril from the tomahawk and the stake, the dangers of the journey were braved, and settlements formed throughout the northern and central portions of the District. We have already said that "it was not the dull, the unambitious, the idle," who came first to Kentucky. The early settlers were, in the main, fair representatives of the communities in which they had resided, with the exception, that only those who possessed bold and adventurous

---

* Emory's History of the Discipline, pp. 43, 44. † Ibid., p. 80.

spirits dared to remove to a country not yet given up by the Indians. The District of Kentucky having originally been a part of Virginia, that State was more largely represented upon its soil than any other. Entering the Confederacy as a slave State in 1792, many families of wealth and influence, who were slave-holders in Virginia, as well as other States, were induced to seek a home within its rich domain. It is true, the action of the Christmas Conference upon the question of slavery was, to a great extent, inoperative; nor will it be denied, that, with scarcely an exception, the preachers of Kentucky confined themselves to their legitimate calling—the preaching of the gospel—so that no fault could be found with their conduct; yet, in the statute-book of the Church, prominently stood the declaration, that "*no person holding slaves shall, in future, be admitted into society or to the Lord's Supper, till he previously complies with these rules concerning slavery.*" And in many communities this law was enforced. In the Hartford Circuit, although organized at a later date, the records of their Quarterly Conferences, from 1804 to 1825, show the continual agitation of the question, in the examination of the characters of official members, who, by any means, had become connected with slavery—thereby producing prejudice in the entire community against the Church.

This interference of the Church with an institution purely civil, and, by consequence, its departure from primitive and apostolic Christianity, was too obvious not to attract the attention of even a casual observer. Slavery, in the early ages of the Christian Church, existed in the Roman Empire in the worst imaginable forms. The master had power over the life of his slave; and the Church, without interfering with the relation, only defined and enjoined the mutual duties and obligations resulting from it.

In Kentucky, while many families of high social position, in view of the inoperativeness of the rule on slavery, connected themselves with the Methodist Church, a very large proportion, among the most influential—while admiring the zeal of its preachers, the simplicity of its worship, and the truth of its doctrines—sought other Communions; so that many of our forms of worship, as well as the doctrines once peculiar to Methodism, and that had been assailed with tireless energy by sectarian bigots, were adopted by hundreds and thousands in other Christian Communions, while they turned away from the Church to which they were so largely indebted.

In the attacks so frequently made upon Methodism at this early day, it was by no means uncommon for our opponents to charge upon our preachers a wish to interfere with the civil institutions of the State; from which allegation, however false, there was no means of escape, since they were the representatives of a Church that, in its statute-book, had placed itself in antagonism to an institution which was recognized by the Confederated Government as right.

In addition to the causes we have already assigned, it is proper to notice the prevalence of infidelity at this period.

"Early in the spring of 1793, circumstances occurred which fanned the passions of the people into a perfect flame. The French Revolution had sounded a tocsin which reverberated throughout the whole civilized world. The worn-out despotisms of Europe, after standing aghast for a moment, in doubtful inactivity, had awakened at length into ill-concerted combinations against the young Republic, and France was engaged in a life-and-death struggle against Britain, Spain, Prussia, Austria, and the German Principalities. The terrible energy which the French Republic displayed against such fearful odds, the haughty crest with which she confronted her enemies, and repelled them from her frontier at every point, presented a spectacle well calculated to dazzle the friends of democracy throughout the world.

"The American people loved France as their ally in the Revolution, and now regarded her as a sister Republic contending for freedom against banded despots." *

The wide-spread sympathy of this country with France was natural. But France had embraced infidelity. The Bible there had undergone a total eclipse; its hallowed teachings despised and spurned; "death declared to be an eternal sleep;" while Atheism—the very worst form of infidelity—was openly professed by all classes of society. We

*Collins's Kentucky, p. 46.

too had just emerged from a long and bloody war, and were not free from the vices and demoralization always consequent upon a protracted, sanguinary strife. Vice, in hideous form, in the light of noonday, walked through the land. The writings of Paine, Voltaire, and others, intended to sap the foundations of Christianity, and, at the same time, offering no other "balm to the wounded spirit," were sown broadcast throughout the land. Not only were their sentiments embraced by the masses of the American people, but many, holding high positions of public trust, and belonging to the more influential walks of life, imbibed these doctrines, and openly avowed their disbelief in the word of God.

"To add to the darkness of the moral horizon, most of the Churches had sunk into mere formality, so that the doctrine of the new birth—implying that radical change of heart which brings with it the evidence of pardon and adoption—was quite ignored or totally repudiated. The dogmas of election and reprobation, predestination and decrees, were the themes of the pulpit; and they rather confirmed than weakened the popular disposition to reject revelation. The masses considered such doctrines a slander upon God's justice, as well as his goodness, and concluded that, if the Bible afforded such views of Jehovah, it could not be true." *

If, under these circumstances, there is an apparent

---

* Rev. Jonathan Stamper, in Home Circle, Vol. I., p. 61.

lull in the moral and religious atmosphere, we need express no surprise. Christianity was preparing for a mighty contest. The doctrines revealed in the word of God had been faithfully preached by our fathers in the ministry, as well as by pious men of other denominations, during the period we have just had under review. Occasionally manifestations of Divine power were seen and felt, under the preaching of the word, and at times remarkable revivals blessed the Church. Persons in different portions of the State, and of all classes of society, from the most humble to the most refined and enlightened, had become the subjects of converting grace, though, in the midst of the general apathy and vice, they were like scattered lights along the sky. A bright day, however, was just at hand.

The occasional revivals of religion in Tennessee and Kentucky, with which these States had been favored toward the close of the century, and which had resulted in so much good, not only in keeping alive the faith of the Church, but also in extending its borders, were the precursors of displays of Divine power, more signal than had been known in this country. Glorious as they were, and freighted with so many blessings, they were as the unpretending cloud preceding the abundant rain. The future was full of hope to the Church. Infidelity, that long had stood up with brazen front, must stand abashed; false and erroneous doctrines yield to the power of truth, and men who had spurned the Bible must recognize its authority and its claims.

The year 1799 was remarkable for the beginning of the revival of religion in the West, since known as "the great revival." It commenced under the labors of the Rev. John and William McGee, two brothers—the former a local preacher in the Methodist Episcopal Church, and the latter a Presbyterian minister in charge of a congregation in Sumner county, Tennessee. They had formerly resided in North Carolina, but had removed to Tennessee.

Most ardently attached to each other, they frequently held meetings together, and labored side by side for the promotion of a common Christianity. Starting upon a preaching tour toward the Ohio River, they concluded to attend a sacramental meeting on Red River, in Logan county, Kentucky, in the congregation of the Rev. Mr. McGready, a minister in the Presbyterian Church. The opening sermon was preached by John McGee, with more than his usual liberty. The pulpit was also filled by his brother William, and the Rev. Mr. Hodge, also a Presbyterian minister, who "preached with much animation and liberty."

Although a deep religious feeling pervaded the assembly, there was no remarkable stir until Monday, the last day of the meeting. Under the preaching of Mr. Hodge, a lady obtained "an uncommon blessing," and "shouted" the praises of God. The Rev. Messrs. Rankin and McGready, Presbyterian ministers, who were also present with Mr. Hodge, left the house, while the two brothers McGee sat still—the people also remaining in their seats. John McGee was appointed to preach, but a Divine power filled the house, and he could only exhort, and following his exhortation were cries from penitent hearts, and many passed "from death unto life."

The meeting on Muddy River, three miles east of Russellville, which was the next popular meeting held by the McGees, was attended by a large concourse of people from far and near. They came on foot, on horseback, and in wagons, and camped on the ground.

This meeting was the origin of camp-meetings in the United States. About forty souls were converted to God.

Their next appointment was ten miles west of Gallatin, Tennessee, in Sumner county, a little south-east of the Cumberland Ridge. The attendance at this meeting was more numerous than at either of those previously held. Ministers of the Presbyterian and Baptist Churches, as well as Methodists, in large numbers, were in attendance. The work generally met with opposition from the preachers of the Baptist Church. For intensity of feeling, for extraordinary displays of Divine power, for the amount of good accomplished, this meeting surpassed the former two.

The most remarkable meeting, however, that was held by these faithful ministers of Christ, was the one on Desha's Creek, near Cumberland River. Thousands attended. Under the preaching of the word, hundreds were convicted, and converted to God. All ranks of society, all classes of people—persons of every age, from gentle youth to those trembling with the weight of years—were the subjects of the work.

The following letter, dated June 23, 1820, written by John McGee to the Rev. Thomas L. Douglass—at that time the Presiding Elder of the Nashville District—will be read with interest:*

"DEAR SIR:—In compliance with your request, I have endeavored to recollect some of the most noted circumstances which occurred at the commencement of the work of God in the States of Kentucky and Tennessee, and which came under my observation in 1799 and the two following years.

"I suppose I am one of the two brothers referred to in 'Theophilus Arminius's account of the work of God in the Western country.' My brother William McGee is fallen asleep in the bosom of his beloved Master. We were much attached to each other from our infancy, but much more so when we both experienced the uniting love of Jesus Christ. I was the oldest, and by the mercy and grace of God, sought and experienced religion first. With great anxiety of mind, he heard me preach the unsearchable riches of Christ, before he felt or enjoyed peace with God. After he obtained religion, he thought proper to receive Holy Orders in the Presbyterian Church; and, after preaching some time in North Carolina and in the Holston country, he came to Cumberland, (now West Tennessee,) about the year 1796 or 1797, and settled in a con-

*Methodist Magazine, Vol. IV., pp. 189, 190, 191.

gregation in Sumner county, about the year 1798. Several reasons induced me to remove, with my family, from North Carolina to the Western country; and in the year 1798, settled in Sumner (now Smith) county. The difference of doctrines professed by the Presbyterian and Methodist Churches were not sufficient to dissolve those ties of love and affection which we both felt. We loved, and prayed, and preached together; and God was pleased to own and bless us and our labors. In the year 1799, we agreed to make a tour through the Barrens, toward Ohio, and concluded to attend a sacramental solemnity in the Rev. Mr. McGready's congregation, on Red River, in our way. When we came there, I was introduced by my brother, and received an invitation to address the congregation from the pulpit, and I know not that ever God favored me with more light and liberty than he did each day, while I endeavored to convince the people they were sinners, and urged the necessity of repentance, and of a change from nature to grace; and held up to their view the greatness, freeness, and fullness of salvation, which was in Christ Jesus, for lost, guilty, condemned sinners. My brother and the Rev. Mr. Hodge preached with much animation and liberty. The people felt the force of truth, and tears ran down their cheeks, but all was silent until Monday, the last day of the feast. Mr. Hodge gave a useful discourse; an intermission was given, and I was appointed to preach. While Mr. Hodge was preaching, a woman in the east end of the house got an uncommon blessing, broke through order, and shouted for some time, and then sat down in silence. At the close of the sermon, Messrs. Hodge, McGready, and Rankin went out of the house; my brother and myself sat still; the people seemed to have no disposition to leave their seats. My brother felt such a power come on him, that he quit his seat, and sat down on the floor of the pulpit, (I suppose, not knowing what he did.) A power which caused me to tremble was upon me. There was a solemn weeping all over the house. Having a wish to preach, I strove against my feelings; at length I rose up and told the people I was appointed to preach, but there was a greater than I preaching, and exhorted them to let the Lord God Omnipotent reign in their hearts, and to submit to him, and their souls should live. Many broke silence; the woman in the east end of the house shouted tremendously. I left the pulpit to go to her, and as I went along through the people, it was suggested to me: 'You know these people are much for order; they will not bear this confusion; go back, and be quiet.' I turned to go back, and was near falling. The power of God was strong upon me; I turned again, and, losing sight of the fear of man, I went through the house, shouting and exhorting with all possible ecstasy and energy, and the floor was soon covered with the slain; their screams for mercy pierced the heavens, and mercy came down. Some found forgiveness, and many went away from that meeting, feeling unutterable agonies of soul for redemption in the blood of Jesus. This was the beginning of that glorious revival of religion in this country, which was so great a blessing to thousands; and from this meeting camp-meetings took their rise. One man, for the want of horses for all his family to ride and attend the meeting, fixed up his wagon, in which he took them and his provisions, and lived on the ground throughout the meeting. He had left his worldly cares behind him, and had nothing to do but attend on Divine service.

"The next popular meeting was on Muddy River, and this was a camp-meeting: a number of wagons loaded with people came together, and camped on the ground; and the Lord was present, and approved of their zeal by sealing a pardon to about forty souls. The next camp-meeting was on the Ridge, where there was an increase of people, and carriages of different descriptions, and a great many preachers of the Presbyterian and Methodist orders, and some of the Baptist; but the latter were generally opposed to the work. Preaching commenced, and the people prayed, and the power of God attended. There was a great cry for mercy. The nights were truly awful; the camp-ground was well illuminated; the people were differently exercised all over the ground—some exhorting, some shouting, some praying, and some crying for mercy, while others lay as dead men on the ground. Some of the spiritually wounded fled to the woods, and their groans could be heard all through the surrounding groves, as the groans of dying men. From thence many came into the camp, rejoicing and praising God for having found redemption in the blood of the Lamb. At this meeting, it was computed that one hundred souls were converted from nature to grace. But perhaps the greatest meeting we ever witnessed in this country, took place shortly after, on Desha's Creek, near Cumberland River. Many thousands of people attended. The mighty power and mercy of God were manifested. The people fell before the word, like corn before a storm of wind, and many rose from the dust with Divine glory shining in their countenances, and gave glory to God in such strains as made the hearts of stubborn sinners to tremble; and after the first gust of praise, they would break forth in volleys of exhortation. Amongst these were many small, home-bred boys, who spoke with the tongue, wisdom and eloquence of the learned—and truly they were learned, for they were all taught of God, who had taken their feet out of the mire and clay, and put a new song in their mouths. Although there were converts of different ages under this work, it was remarkable, they were generally the children of praying parents. Here John A. Granade, the Western poet, who composed the Pilgrim's songs—after being many months in almost entire desperation, till he was worn down, and appeared like a walking skeleton—found pardon and mercy from God, and began to preach a risen Jesus. Some of the Pharisees cried *disorder* and *confusion*, but in disorderly assemblies there are generally dislocated and broken bones, and bruised flesh; but here, the women laid their sleeping children at the roots of the trees, while hundreds, of all ages and colors, were stretched on the ground in the agonies of conviction, and as dead men, while thousands, day and night, were crowding round them, and passing to and fro, yet there was nobody hurt;* which shows that the people were perfectly in their senses; and on this chaos of apparent confusion, God said, Let there be light, and there was light! and many emerged out of darkness into it. We have hardly ever had a camp-meeting since, without his presence and power to convert souls. Glory to God and the Lamb, for ever and ever!

"Yours respectfully,

"JOHN McGEE."

The revivals that thus began, under the labors of these two brothers, soon spread over the entire of Southern Kentucky, and what is now known as Middle Tennessee. Their sacred influence was carried into every community, and felt in almost every home. The Church was inspired with a new zeal, and the truth was proclaimed with an energy and pathos that impressed it on the hearts of the people.

---

* "There was a man at the Ridge meeting, who got mad, cursed the people, and said he would go home; but before he got out of sight of the camp-ground, a tree fell on him, and he was carried home dead."

CHAPTER XI.

FROM THE CONFERENCE OF 1800, HELD AT DUNWORTH, ON HOLSTON, ON THE FIRST FRIDAY IN APRIL, TO THE CONFERENCE HELD AT BETHEL ACADEMY, KENTUCKY, COMMENCING ON THE SIXTH DAY OF THE FOLLOWING OCTOBER.

Local preachers—John Nelson—Robert Strawbridge—Francis Clark—Gabriel and Daniel Woodfield—John Baird—Benjamin Northcutt—Nathanael Harris—Philip W. Taylor—Henry Ogburn—William Forman—Joseph Ferguson—The Conference in the spring of 1800—The General Conference—William Burke—Thomas Shelton—Controversy with the Baptists—William Burke chosen Presiding Elder—The Revival—Sandusky Station—William Algood—Hezekiah Harriman—John Sale—Jonathan Kidwell.

WE have now reached a period in the history of Methodism in Kentucky from which we may survey the chief instruments by whose influence it attained its position at the close of the last century.

For several years previous to the appointment of Messrs. Haw and Ogden to the District, Kentucky had been constantly receiving accessions from the older settlements, some of whom had been members of the Methodist Church in the States whence they came. They had, with reluctance, left the altars around which they had worshiped, and had come to the West, cherishing the hope that, at no distant day, their new homes would be visited by the ministers of Christ, of their own denomination. The Revolutionary war, which had been protracted beyond the expectations of the infant Republic, had greatly retarded the enterprises of the Church, and prevented, at an earlier period, the occupancy of this distant field. Indeed, the societies that, under the auspices of the preachers sent out by Mr. Wesley, and those who joined them, had grown up in New York, New Jersey, Pennsylvania, Maryland, Virginia, Delaware, and North Carolina, had, during the American struggle, maintained their existence and increased in strength, amid opposition and under difficulties, before which the standard-bearers of a cause less worthy would have yielded. "Persecuted, but not forsaken," they had lifted their colors, never to strike them; and, from the Conference held in Baltimore, May 21, 1776, to the one "begun at Ellis's Preaching-house, Virginia, April 30, 1784, and ended at Baltimore, May 28, following—covering a period of eight years, during which ten Conferences were held—the societies had increased from *four thousand nine hundred and twenty-one* to *fourteen thousand nine hundred and eighty-eight*, and the number of preachers from *twenty-four* to *eighty-three;* and during the same period the number of circuits had grown from *eleven* to *forty-six*"—this, too, while the nation was in commotion, and struggling to be free. It is but seldom that the Church, under such circumstances, has been permitted to record triumphs superior to those achieved by Methodism during this period. The war had closed favorably to the colonies, and, closely identified with its termination, and in the same year, the Christmas Conference was held at which the "Methodist Episcopal Church in America" was organized. Kentucky, in the meantime, when we consider the dangers to which the settlers were exposed, had rapidly increased in population, and presented to the Church, if not an inviting field, at least one having claims upon their consideration. In 1786, we have seen two men, severing the ties that had bound them to friends and home, pursuing their solitary journey over unfrequented paths, meeting dangers, and exposed to sufferings and sacrifices, such as few men had previously encountered. We pause to inquire for the motive that influenced them. Why did they leave homes surrounded, at least, by the comforts of life, and embark in such an enterprise—exchanging ease for hardship, and safety for peril? In the humble cabin of Thomas Stevenson, as we see Benjamin Ogden kneel and offer up to God the first public prayer that ever fell from an itinerant's lips in Kentucky, pleading for the blessings of Heaven upon the cause he had come to establish, and upon the generous family whose hospitality he was enjoying, and around whose altar he was kneeling, we find an answer to the inquiry. We have seen the success that crowned their labors. The little Church organized in the cottage-home of Mr. Stevenson was seed sown in good ground, while the teachings of Mr. Ogden was "bread cast upon the waters, to be seen after many days." Unpromising as was this commencement, it was the opening of a new era in the wilds of the West; it was the introduction of a system that—whether rapid in its growth, or slow in its development—should gladden the hearts and bless the homes of thousands. To the brightest dreams of the imagination it could scarcely have occurred, that, before the close of the century, from the Church in Kentucky, the gospel, in the form of Methodism, would not only have permeated every section of Kentucky, but would extend its lines into Middle Tennessee, and beyond the Ohio into the North-western Territory. No such bright hopes opened up before the minds of the pioneer preachers in this District. True, they expected good results from their labors. For this they preached, and prayed, and suffered. We have followed them and their coadjutors in their hardships, their toils, and their triumphs. We have traveled with them from fort to fort, until we have traversed the entire State, permeating every settlement, and listened to the truths they proclaimed. Looking to the interest of the rising generation and the future of the Church, we have seen them projecting schemes of education, and laying the foundation of sanctified learning. We have seen houses of worship erected in different portions of the State—not costly edifices, it is true, but plain structures, adapted to the times, and to the wants of the people—where hundreds were accustomed to assemble and worship God. We have seen the Church triumphing over obstacles, and assuming a permanent form. And now, we inquire, what instrumentalities, besides the itinerant ministry, have been employed, under the blessings of Heaven, by which such results have been achieved? To the careful observer of the events we have recorded, and the times through which we have passed, there is no difficulty in answering the inquiry.

We have already noticed that, previous to the appointment of James Haw and Benjamin Ogden to Kentucky, a few local preachers had settled in the District. With whatever opposition the introduction of a lay ministry had met in the councils of the Church, the utility of this element of strength was developed, in the early days of Methodism, both in Europe and America. The force of circumstances compelled many of the first preachers to assume this relation. Ministers who had entered the itinerant field expecting to close their labors only with the termination of life, after a few years of active service, were compelled to retire from the ranks. Worn out by the arduous duties they performed, and unable longer to meet the responsibilities of pastoral work, they yielded to the stern decree of necessity, and in the shades of the local ranks they sought for quietude and rest. Carrying with them to their retirement constitutions impaired by incessant toil, and, in many cases, the germs of disease which too plainly indicated that they were martyrs to the work to which their strength had been devoted, and that theirs would be an early grave, yet feeling no abatement in their interest in the cause to which they had pledged their all, we find them unwilling to loiter in the vineyard of the Lord.

Others, however, who had been soundly converted to God, and feeling divinely impressed with the conviction that they ought to preach the gospel, yet unable, from domestic cares and responsibilities, to devote themselves exclusively to the work of the ministry, were to be found in the Church. Of undoubted piety, possessing gifts that qualified them for usefulness, and capable of exerting an influence for good, with the approval of the Church, they were inclined to participate in the services of the sanctuary.

Such was the introduction of a lay ministry into the Church.

The faithful stone-mason of Birstal was scarcely surpassed in zeal by Mr. Wesley himself; and the labors of the eccentric and devoted Strawbridge compare favorably with those of Watters and of Garretson. If, in the early days of Methodism, the lay ministers were not so successful in planting Churches, by their faithful labors they watered the good seed that had been sown by the itinerant, and, in many instances, with parental care, watched the growth of the infant societies.

Into newly settled countries, not only as pioneer settlers, but as pioneers of their faith, they have frequently gone, and, in advance of the itinerant preacher, have organized societies, to be transferred afterward to his pastoral care.

In the older and more populous settlements, they have enjoyed the high distinction of seeking communities which the circuit-preacher could not embrace in his field of labor, because of the amount of work he already had to perform. When, through their instrumentality, communities have been converted and brought under their teachings, with a cheerfulness that evinced their devotion to the Church, they have invited the itinerant preacher to take them under his pastoral charge, and then they have turned their attention to other and untried fields. Thus have new circuits been formed, and the borders of the Church enlarged. In the communities in which they have resided, their influence has been salutary, rendering the Church healthful and prosperous, without the promise of any remuneration for their services, except that derived from a consciousness of the performance of duty, and the hope of being instrumental in the salvation of sinners. Many of them have passed weeks together from home on tours of preaching, laboring with a zeal commensurate with the wants of the Church and the interests of those whom they served. Without the responsibilities of the pastoral office, they have exercised its functions and performed its labors. In the homes of poverty; by the bedside of the sick; in places of bereavement and sorrow, as well as at the altars of the Church, they have successfully rivaled the zealous and indefatigable evangelist in offering hope to the despairing, salvation to the lost, and life to the dead.

Allusion has already been made to Francis Clark, a local preacher of fervent piety, of untiring zeal, and of considerable ability, who settled in Kentucky three years before the appointment of Haw and Ogden.

The year following his settlement in the District, under his ministrations, a few persons in Mercer county associated themselves in a class, and thus formed the first society of Methodists in Kentucky. This society was the nucleus around which was formed the Danville Circuit, recorded at so early a period in the printed Minutes. Other local preachers, whose names we have mentioned, had labored assiduously in their respective communities, either as the precursors of the missionaries, or in coöperation with them, in the establishment of Christianity, and in pushing forward the victories of the cross.

Several of the preachers who had been compelled to retire from the itinerant field because of the failure of their strength, and whose labors had been greatly blessed, had settled among those who had been brought to Christ through their instrumentality, and continued to watch over their spiritual interest with the same vigilance that had previously distinguished them, though in a more circumscribed sphere.

Among these the name of Benjamin Northcutt—of whose life and labors we gave an account in a previous chapter—stands preëminent. Failing in health after a few years in the itinerant field, he became more prominent than any other minister in the local ranks. Not only in the vindication of the great truths of Christianity, but in those revivals that occasionally shed their light upon the Church near the close of the past, and especially in the great revival that spread throughout Kentucky about the commencement of the present century, he was remarkably prominent and useful.

Previous to the year 1800, Nathanael Harris, Philip W. Taylor, Joseph Ferguson, William Forman, and Henry Ogburn, from Virginia; Gabriel and Daniel Woodfield, from Pennsylvania; William J. Thompson, from North Carolina, and John Baird, from Maryland, settled in Kentucky. Messrs. Harris and Taylor located in Jessamine; William Forman in Bourbon; Henry Ogburn in what is now Carroll; the Woodfields in Fayette; William J. Thompson in Mercer; Joseph Ferguson in Nelson, and John Baird in the same county (now Larue.)

These men, scattered through different portions of the State, by their zeal and their piety, contributed much to the planting and growth of the Church.

Nathanael Harris was a very superior man. Having enjoyed the advantages of a liberal education, and possessing a fine native intellect—his whole life an exemplification of the truth of Christianity—he brought all his powers to the foot of the cross, and consecrated them upon the altars of the Church. We will, however, meet with him again, in the itinerant ranks, dispensing the blessings of Christianity, and shedding upon the people the light of a holy life.

Philip W. Taylor was among the most indefatigable and useful of the early local preachers. He was born in Eastern Virginia about the year 1764, and entered the Continental army, and was present at the siege of Yorktown and the surrender of Cornwallis.

About 1793, he came to Kentucky. While descending the Ohio River, he was fired on by the Indians, and had one arm shattered by a ball.* His wound confined him for six months at the Falls of the Ohio.

In 1795, he was married to Miss Elizabeth Poor, and, a short time afterward, they were both converted, and joined the Methodist Episcopal Church. Impressed with the conviction that he ought to preach, he was soon authorized to exercise his gifts as a licentiate.

At the Conference held in October, in the year 1800, he was ordained a deacon by Bishop Asbury, and subsequently was elected to Elders' orders, but was refused ordination, in consequence of his connection with slavery.

Dissatisfied with this interference on the part of the Church with a civil institution, he permitted himself to become estranged from its communion; and when the Methodist Protestant Church extended its influence into Kentucky, he became a leading minister in that denomination.

Of a bold and fearless disposition, he was one of the number who, on two different occasions, accompanied Bishop Asbury through the wilderness, on his early Episcopal visits to Kentucky.

In his alienation from the Methodist Episcopal Church, he requested his wife to enter with him the Methodist Protestant Church, which she steadily refused. Her reply was: "When you find a Church

---

*Methodist Magazine, for 1819, p. 185.

in which I can enjoy more religion, and do more good, than the one I first joined, I will go with you; but not before." She died in triumph, March 17, 1845, in the eighty-fourth year of her age. Her name should be held in everlasting remembrance.

Mr. Taylor was a good Bible-preacher, perfectly familiar with its doctrines, the duties it inculcates, and the blessed experience it gives the Christian.

Until he was eighty-five years of age, he continued to preach, with his mental faculties unimpaired, when by an accidental fall he broke his hip-bone, after which he was never able to walk. From this misfortune until the time of his death, in his private conversations, his constant theme was the love of God in providing salvation for a lost race, and the happiness of those who by faith were made partakers of the blessing of pardoned sin. He continued to witness, to all who visited him, the truth of religion, as well as the comfort and happiness it brought to his own soul, in view of approaching dissolution. In this happy frame of mind he continued until death released him from his sufferings.

In the month of February, 1856, at about ninety years of age, at the residence of his son-in-law, John Wright, he entered upon the reward of the blessed.*

Among the first-fruits of Virginia Methodism was Henry Ogburn. He was born in Mecklenburg, Virginia, November 26, 1754, and, in the twenty-

* Letter from John Cochran, Esq., of Spencer county, Kentucky, to the author.

first year of his age, joined the Methodist Episcopal Church.

In 1779, he entered upon the itinerant work, and, until the Conference of 1790, when he located, labored extensively and usefully in Virginia, North Carolina, and Pennsylvania.

In the spring of 1794, with his wife, he came to Kentucky, to make it his future home. For a short time he located in Lexington, but in 1795, he removed to the mouth of the Kentucky River, and, a year or two subsequently, purchased a tract of land, two miles above, on the banks of the Ohio, where he spent the remnant of his days.

As a preacher, he was above mediocrity. While a member of the Conference, he was remarkable for his zeal; and in a local sphere, he was distinguished for the energy and fidelity with which he prosecuted his high and holy calling. During the period of his connection with the Church in Kentucky, he was the honored instrument of turning "many to righteousness;" and in his death left behind him the fragrance of a good name. He calmly passed away in the month of August, 1831.

William Forman came "to Kentucky as early as 1790, and settled in Bourbon county, where he remained until his death, which took place in February, 1814. He never belonged to the traveling connection, but was one of the most industrious and useful local preachers I ever knew. His life was a practical comment on the gospel he preached; and when the people were speaking of a good man, it was their habit to say, 'He is almost as good a man as Billy Forman.' Such a life could have but one termination. When the midnight cry came, he arose, and, with his lamp trimmed, and oil in his vessel, went forth with joy to meet his Lord." *

Daniel Woodfield, though not so able or efficient a preacher as his brother, was instrumental in doing much good.

Of Joseph Ferguson we have already made mention in a former chapter, but such a man deserves more than a passing notice. The following interesting sketch was furnished us by the Rev. George T. Gould, of the Kentucky Conference:

"The Rev. Joseph Ferguson was born in Virginia, some time in the year 1760; served through the greater part of the Revolutionary war; moved to Kentucky, and settled in Nelson county, in 1784, where he died, November 28, 1828.

"Previous to the time of his conversion, and of his being licensed to preach, we have utterly failed to obtain any information, except that he was an authorized minister of the gospel at the time of his emigration to Kentucky.

"His mind was of that evenly balanced, unimpassioned order, which lifted him above mediocrity, but yet kept him back from marked superiority. He was a man of few books, but those, especially his Bible, were well read. Hence his sermons, though they lacked that polish and general fund of information which extensive reading gives, were yet marked by strong good sense, and a practical adap-

---

*Rev. Jonathan Stamper, in Home Circle, Vol. II., p. 73.

tation to the wants of his audience, while they contained a very noticeable abundance of Scripture words and Scripture sentiment. In labors he was 'more abundant,' preaching far and near, and was thus greatly instrumental in the introduction and spread of Methodism in that part of Kentucky. Though living at the distance of twelve or fifteen miles from Chaplin, yet he had a regular monthly appointment at that place, and some of the oldest and most useful of the members who now live to bless that Church, or have gone from the Church below to the Church above, were brought into the fold through his instrumentality. So kind and debonair was he in his manners, that he was a great favorite with the young, who sent for him, both far and near, that he might perform for them the ceremony of marriage, until it was reckoned by some that he had officiated on such occasions more frequently than any other man in Kentucky.

"Nor did Father Ferguson confine the manifestations of his love for Methodism to these, his personal efforts, but we find him one of the strongest friends, advisers, and supporters of the preacher in charge to be met with in those days. An instance of this, as illustrating the condition, manner of life, and sacrifices of those same preachers in charge, we have gathered from the personal recollections of his son:

"The Rev. Adjet McGuire, being appointed to the Salt River Circuit, was unable to secure, throughout its entire extent of several hundred miles, a house for the accommodation of his family. Father

Ferguson had just erected a new loom-house in his yard, and into this Mr. McGuire's family were received, and in it they lived during the year; while their removal, together with their effects, from Crab Orchard to their new home, was accomplished upon the backs of two horses, one of which was sent by Mr. Ferguson.

"On a certain occasion, Ferguson and Taylor happened at Buck Creek Baptist Meeting-house, in Shelby county. Ferguson being invited to preach, took occasion to come over the expression, '*Sanctum sanctorum*,' when one of the Baptist brethren very eagerly inquired of Taylor if the preacher were not a Bishop. From that day, 'Bishop' was the *sobriquet* by which he went.

"In the sixty-eighth year of his age, on the 28th of November, as above stated, he closed his life of usefulness and Christian hope, seated in a chair, as the dropsical affection from which he suffered prevented him from lying upon his bed. 'Come, Lord Jesus! come quickly!' were the last words that fell from his lips, as he stretched out his hands as though feeling for his Saviour, while he raised to heaven the eyes from which death had already stolen the power of vision. 'How blest the righteous when he dies!'"

Besides those already mentioned, other local preachers had emigrated to Kentucky, or been raised up from the revivals in the State, who devoted their energies to the advancement of truth.

The Conference for the West, for 1800, was held at Dunworth, on Holston, commencing the first

Friday in April. The General Conference was to convene on the sixth day of May, in the same year, in the city of Baltimore. Bishop Asbury requested that all the preachers who had labored in the West for any considerable time, should attend the General Conference, and "receive their appointments in the old States; and a new set be sent to this division of the work." * The journey to Baltimore had to be performed on horseback. It was impracticable for preachers who were entitled to seats in the General Conference to be present at Dunworth, and then reach Baltimore in time for the General Conference; and hence the Conference on Holston was attended by only a few.†

The Kentucky District, over which the Rev. Francis Poythress had presided the previous year, was left at this Conference without a Presiding Elder. We have, however, several new men introduced into the ministry in the West: William Algood, Hezekiah Harriman, John Sale, and Jonathan Kidwell were appointed, with others previously mentioned, to the division of the work in which Kentucky was included.

It was the purpose of Bishop Asbury to appoint a Presiding Elder to take charge of "Kentucky, Tennessee, and all that part of Virginia west of New River, and the North-western Territory, including the Miami and Scioto Valleys," in one District. During the General Conference, "he used his utmost endeavors" to accomplish his purpose,

* Rev. William Burke. † Judge Scott.

but failed. The vast extent of territory over which the Presiding Elder would have to travel was more than equal to the strength of almost any man.

Before the adjournment of the Conference, he applied to the indefatigable and gifted William Burke, and requested him to return to Kentucky, and to take with him "all the papers appertaining to the Annual Conference and Bethel Academy, and do the best" he "could for the work in that part of the field."* The previous year had been one of signal triumph to Mr. Burke in Kentucky.

Kentucky had been originally settled chiefly by the Baptists, and they were at this date the largest and most influential denomination in the State.

Any attempt to set forth the peculiar views of the Methodist Episcopal Church—especially so far as the issue between the two denominations on the subjects and mode of baptism was involved—was regarded by the former as an invasion of their rights; and hence they watched with a jealous eye the rising star of Methodism. The teachings of our Church upon these questions met with most violent opposition, and was rudely assailed by the most able ministers of the Baptist denomination.

In the vindication of our views, Mr. Burke had stood up, not only as the bold and fearless, but also as the successful advocate. The prosperity that had attended his ministry, together with the frequency with which he administered the ordinance of baptism to infants, had induced an opposition,

---

* Western Methodism, p. 55.

which culminated in a challenge to a debate, from the Rev. Thomas Shelton, at that time the most influential minister in the Baptist Church in Kentucky. The challenge was promptly accepted by Mr. Burke, the time appointed, and the place fixed at Irvin's Lick, in Madison county. The debate lasted about four hours, the speeches occupying about fifteen minutes each, alternately. At the close of the discussion, Mr. Shelton said to the vast assembly that he "believed Mr. Burke to be an honest but mistaken man;" after which he stood by and witnessed the administration of the ordinance by Mr. Burke. The controversy thus begun continued through many years.*

At the Conference held at Dunworth in April, it is probable that none of the Appointments were made, as Bishop Asbury held the selection of the men for the West in reserve until the General Conference. This view is sustained by the statement of Mr. Burke, who, after referring to the request of Bishop Asbury, that he should return to Kentucky, says: "I consented, and he appointed to go with me, John Sale, Hezekiah Harriman, William Algood, and Henry Smith; for the Holston country, James Hunter, John Watson, and John Page; and for Cumberland, William Lambeth."

Mr. Burke was appointed to the Hinkstone Circuit—the same charge he had, for a few months in 1794, so usefully filled.

The absence of a Presiding Elder from the Dis-

---

* Western Methodism, p. 54.

trict was calculated to produce some embarrassment in the work; and the preachers, therefore, immediately on their return from the General Conference, met in council, and elected Mr. Burke to take charge of the District, which he did.* This, too, was in accordance with the expressed wish of Bishop Asbury, who "appointed him to superintend the quarterly meetings, where there was no Elder." †

It was proper, in an eminent degree, that Mr. Burke should be the leader of the host in the West. He had been identified with the sacrifices, the sufferings, and the triumphs of the Church in this department, since his admission into the itinerancy in 1792. In the various conflicts through which the Church had passed, whether our foes were from among those of our own household, or from other religionists, he had stood in the forefront of the battle, and repelled every assault. Under such a standard-bearer, failure could never be written.

The summer of 1800 was distinguished for the continuance and spread of that extraordinary revival of religion, of which we spoke in a former chapter. It had not yet, to any great extent, affected the northern and central portions of the State; but, like the sweep of the hurricane, bearing every thing before it, spread throughout Southern Kentucky and Middle Tennessee, pouring its benign blessings on hamlet and village, in every community. The fires that it enkindled will never be extinguished. We shall, in another chapter, follow it through

---

* Judge Scott.

† Western Methodism, p. 55.

Northern and Central Kentucky, and stand astonished at its mighty achievements.

True, the northern portion of the State was not without its seasons of revival. In many communities the Church had prosperity. At Sandusky Station, (now Pleasant Run,) more than one hundred persons, at a single meeting, were converted to God.*

In other portions of the State displays of Divine power were felt. The Church was putting "on her beautiful garments," and preparing for the glory and triumph awaiting her.

We have already referred to the names of four preachers who were this year appointed to the work in Kentucky, not mentioned before. William Algood, who was appointed by Bishop Asbury to Kentucky, and placed in charge of the Limestone Circuit, never came to the West.

Jeremiah Lawson, who had located the previous year, was employed by Mr. Burke to supply his place, while Lewis Hunt took the place of Mr. Burke on the Hinkstone Circuit; Mr. Burke, at the same time, traveling on the District, and devoting his energies chiefly to the interest of the Church in the bounds of the Lexington, Hinkstone, and Limestone Circuits.

Mr. Harriman was admitted on trial in 1796, and appointed to Bath Circuit, in Virginia. The two following years, he traveled the Stafford Circuit, in

---

* We are indebted to the Hon. Charles A. Wickliffe, who was then a youth, and was present, for this information.

the same State, after which he was changed to the Frederick Circuit, in the State of Maryland.

At the General Conference of 1800, he volunteered for the work in the West, and, with John Sale, accompanied Mr. Burke from that Conference to Kentucky. He spent the years 1800 and 1801 on the Danville Circuit; 1802 on the Salt River, and 1803 on the Hinkstone.

At the Conference of 1804, he was sent to Natchez, with the Rev. Moses Floyd, A. Amos, and Tobias Gibson. His exposure to a Southern climate, together with the privations he endured, and the arduous labors he performed, so impaired his once vigorous constitution, that he was compelled to seek a transfer from that field.

It is natural for a minister, when his health is broken, to turn his thoughts to his childhood's home, and the scenes of his early ministry. The name of Mr. Harriman, for the next year, is in connection with the Harford Circuit, in Maryland. The following year, he is at Frederick and Annapolis, and in 1807, he is appointed to the Baltimore Circuit, on which he closes his labors as an effective minister. The remaining eleven years of his life, he sustained a superannuated relation.

During the four years of his connection with the Church in Kentucky, he was in labors abundant, and his ministry greatly blessed. He participated in the glorious revivals that spread over the State during that period.

The precise date of his death is not given. It occurred in 1818. His biographer says, in 1807, while he was traveling on the Baltimore Circuit, "he was suddenly seized with a paralytic stroke, under the following circumstances: When on his way from a friend's house to one of his appointments, he met a boy, of whom he attempted to ask the way to his appointment, and found his tongue refused obedience to his volition, whereby he was rendered incapable of speech. The progress of the disease was farther evinced by his glove falling from his hand, contrary to his wishes, into a stream of water, while his horse was drinking; to prevent the final loss of which, he dismounted, with a view to stop its farther progress down the stream; to effect which, he attempted to leap across a small rivulet, and fell into it, whose banks concealed him from the observation of travelers on the road, and which, but for the presence of his horse exciting curiosity, would probably have been the spot of his dissolution—from which attack he never fully recovered. This, with a combination of other diseases, terminated in his dissolution.

"Through the whole period of his last illness, he testified that he had no fear of death.

"His wife and family lay with considerable weight on his mind, but he was soon enabled to resign them into the hands of his Heavenly Father. A few days previous to his dissolution, when visited by a friend, he found his mind serene and tranquil; and a few moments before his death, he gave to a relation the most satisfactory evidence of his preparation for the important change, and bade the world a final adieu.

"Hezekiah Harriman was sound in the faith, and a good and useful minister of Jesus Christ."*

John Sale, who also accompanied Mr. Burke to Kentucky this year, was born in the State of Virginia, on the 24th of April, 1769. When about twenty years of age, he was awakened and converted to God.

In 1796, he was licensed to preach, and entered the itinerant field.

From the Conference of 1796, he was appointed to the Swanino Circuit, lying in the sparsely populated settlements of Virginia. His second circuit was the Bertie, and the following year he traveled on the Mattamuskeet Circuit—both in North Carolina; and in 1799, he is placed in charge of the Holston and Russell Circuit, in Virginia.

In the spring of 1800, he enters upon his work in Kentucky, in charge of the Salt River and Shelby Circuit, to which he was appointed at the Conference held in October.

At the Conference of 1801, he was placed on the Danville Circuit, where he remained until the Conference of 1802.

At the close of his labors on the Danville Circuit, he was sent to the North-western Territory, and stationed on the Scioto Circuit, and the following year on the Miami.

In 1804, he was returned to Kentucky, and appointed to the Lexington Circuit. From 1805 to

*General Minutes, Vol. I., p. 309. It will be perceived that we do not follow the Minutes, in the biographical sketch they contain, in giving a list of his appointments, as they are certainly inaccurate.

1808—three years—we find him on the Ohio District, and in charge of the Miami District in 1808 and 1809.

The following four years, he presides over the Kentucky District, having associated with him such men as Charles Holiday, Henry McDaniel, John Johnson, Marcus Lindsey, Thomas D. Porter, Jonathan Stamper, William McMahon, and Benjamin Lakin—whose names are a tower of strength, and around whose labors gather so many pleasant memories, as will more fully appear in our next volume.

At the Conference of 1814, we find him again on the Miami District, on which he remains two years. Unable to perform the labors of a District, at the Conference of 1816 he was appointed to the Union Circuit, and the following year to the Mad River—both in Ohio.

In 1818, he again has charge of the Miami District. Worn down by the excessive labors he had performed, through twenty years of incessant toil, on fields remarkable for the vastness of the territory over which they spread, in 1820 he was compelled to ask for a superannuated relation to the Conference. In this relation he served the Church, as his health would permit, until 1824, when he was again placed on the effective roll, and appointed to the Wilmington Circuit.

In 1825, he traveled the Union, and in 1826, the Piqua Circuit, where he closed his useful and laborious life.

The Hon. John McLean, of Ohio, says, in reference to him:

"He was a man of fine presence, of erect and manly form, and of great personal dignity. He was naturally of a social turn, and had excellent powers of conversation, though nothing ever fell from his lips that even approached to levity. He always conversed on subjects of interest and utility, and very frequently on matters connected with his ministerial labors. I was always struck with the excellent judgment and accurate discrimination which he evinced in his social intercourse.

"His mind could not be said to be brilliant, and yet he sometimes produced a very powerful effect by his preaching. His distinct enunciation, earnest manner, and appropriate and well-digested thoughts, always secured to him the attention of his audience; but I have sometimes heard him when, rising with the dignity and in the fullness of his subject, he seemed to me one of the noblest personifications of the eloquence of the pulpit. His words were never hurried—they were always uttered calmly and deliberately. Without the least tendency to extravagance or undue excitement, there was still a luster in his eye, and a general lighting up of his features, that revealed the workings of the spirit within. In some of his more felicitous efforts, I think I have heard him with as much interest as I have heard any other man; and I never heard him without being deeply impressed with the conviction that, among all the men known to me at that early period, I should have selected him as the man to fill up, under all circumstances, the measure of his duty.

"Mr. Sale's life was an eminently useful one, and he adorned every relation that he sustained, and every sphere that he occupied. Whether as preacher or pastor, as minister in charge or Presiding Elder, he was always intent upon the faithful discharge of his duty, and always approved himself to those among whom he ministered as 'a workman that needeth not to be ashamed.' His character was so pure that every one felt that it was formed by a close conformity to the Divine Model. His mission on earth was emphatically a mission of benevolence to the world which his Master came to save; and when that mission was accomplished, he finished his course with joy." *

"On the 15th of January, 1827, while on the Piqua Circuit, at the house of his friend and brother, Mr. French, he was called to yield up his spirit into the hands of God. We visited him a day or two before his death, and although his sufferings were intense, yet he had great peace in believing. His faith enabled him to behold the land that was afar off, and to rejoice in the sight of his distant heavenly home. He was frequently heard to say, 'I am nearing my home. My last battle is fought, and the victory sure! Hallelujah! My Saviour reigneth over heaven and earth most glorious! Praise the Lord!' On my second visit, we were accompanied by Col. William McLean, one of his warm personal friends. We found him very happy—just on the verge of heaven. When, on

* Sprague's Annals of the American Methodist Pulpit, pp. 257, 258.

rising to leave, we took his hand, and bade him farewell, he said, 'My son, be faithful, and you shall have a crown of life.' We left the dying herald of the cross strong in faith, giving glory to God for a religion that

"'Can make a dying-bed
Feel soft as downy pillows are,
While on his breast he leaned his head,
And breathed his life out sweetly there.'

"Worn down with the toils and sufferings, as the necessary and always concomitant attendants of an itinerant life, he was ready and prepared to enter into the rest of heaven.

"'Servant of God, well done,
Rest from thy loved employ;
The battle 's fought, the vict'ry won,
Enter thy Master's joy.'

"Brother Sale was about five feet ten inches high, of great symmetry of form, dignified and courteous in his manners. He had a dark eye, which, when lighted up with the gospel themes, would flash its fires of holy passion, and melt at the recital of a Saviour's love. But he has gone where anxiety, and toil, and tears come not." *

We love to linger around the memory of such a man as John Sale. During the eight years in which he labored in Kentucky, by the urbanity of his manners, and his devotion to his calling, he won,

---

* Sketches of Western Methodism, pp. 190, 191.

not only upon the affections of the Church, but the admiration of the people. The four years in which he had charge of the Kentucky District, he exhibited those high executive qualities so essential to usefulness and success in the office of Presiding Elder. In the early part of his connection with Methodism in Kentucky, he took an active part in the great revivals.

He was among the first preachers from Kentucky who bore the tidings of a Redeemer's love across the beautiful Ohio. He organized the first society of Methodists in Cincinnati, while traveling the Miami Circuit, "consisting of the following eight members, namely, Mr. and Mrs. Carter, their son and daughter, Mr. and Mrs. Gibson, and Mr. and Mrs. St. Clair. Mr. Gibson was appointed the leader." *

The Rev. Mr. Hinde, in speaking of Mr. Sale, and his preaching in Cincinnati, says: "It was as late as the month of August, 1803, that I had the satisfaction of hearing the first sermon ever preached by a Methodist preacher in the now flourishing town of Cincinnati, in Ohio—with, perhaps, the exception of a sermon in the vicinity preached by Mr. Kobler. The sermon to which I allude was preached by Mr. John Sale. His circuit then embraced what now comprehends nearly three Presiding Elders' Districts in extent of territory." †

The name of Jonathan Kidwell only appears in

---

* Sketches of Western Methodism, p. 108.

† Methodist Magazine, Vol. II., p. 396.

the list of Appointments for this session of the Conference. He is appointed, with John Sale, to the Salt River and Shelby Circuit. No memento is left us, from which we can learn when he was admitted on trial, or when he ceased his labors as an itinerant.

It will be perceived that, up to this date, we have taken no account of any membership we may have had in the southern portion of the State.

From 1787 to the Conference of 1796, the only identity Methodism could claim in Southern Kentucky was in connection with the Cumberland Circuit, which included the settlements of Logan and what is now Simpson counties.

In 1796, the Logan Circuit was formed, to which Aquila Sugg was appointed; but, at the ensuing Conference, there was no report of the membership it embraced, and it was again thrown into the Cumberland Circuit, in which it remained until the formation of the Red River Circuit, in 1802.

No change in the membership in Kentucky is reported in the Minutes for this year. The statistics had not been furnished for record.

CHAPTER XII.

FROM THE CONFERENCE HELD AT BETHEL ACADEMY, OCTOBER 6, 1800, TO THE CONFERENCE OF 1801.

Representative women—Mrs. Lydia Wickliffe—Mrs. Sally Helm—Mrs. Sarah Stevenson—Mrs. Mary Davis—Mrs. Elizabeth Durbin—Mrs. Jane Hardin—Mrs. Jane Stamper—Mrs. Mary T. Hinde—Conference held October 6, 1800, the second in Kentucky for this year—Bishops Asbury and Whatcoat present—The Conference Journal—William McKendree—Lewis Hunt—William Marsh—The spread of the great revival—Ilai Nunn—Major John Martin—Dr. Hinde—Increase of membership.

In the former chapter we have referred to the efficient aid that was rendered by the local preachers in planting and nourishing the Church.

Another element that contributed largely to give it permanence in Kentucky, was the accession to its communion of many of the most remarkable women of that period.

As has been beautifully said, Woman was last at the cross, and first at the sepulcher; and in every age, in most communities where the truths of the Christian religion have been presented, she has been the first to embrace them. Indebted as she is for her social elevation to the teachings of the Bible, woman has, in all countries where the opportunity has offered, shown her high appreciation of the doctrines of the cross, by bowing in reverence before it, and acknowledging the supremacy of the Saviour.

It was so in the introduction of Methodism into Kentucky. While many of the finest intellects among the men in the District had become connected with the Methodist Church, yet, in the organization of the societies, they were generally preceded by the women. If the men of that period were hardy, chivalrous, and brave, they did not surpass their wives in those noble qualities of endurance, of patience, and of intrepidity. While woman's sphere entailed upon her the holy duties of home, it was not unfrequent that her safety levied contributions upon her valor, and placed her side by side with her gallant husband or father, with gun in hand, against the white man's foe. The page of history nowhere records deeds of daring more noble than those performed by the pioneer women of Kentucky.

It is, however, in her character as a Christian, that she shines with the brightest luster. The Christian woman is to her husband and her children the softener of their sorrows and the soother of their cares, the guardian angel that keeps unceasing vigils over the interests of her home; in the community in which she resides, shedding a holy influence, that checks the vanities of the gay, and administers sweet consolation to the sorrowing and the sad.

Among the early women of Kentucky, Methodism numbered many who were remarkable for all those excellent traits of character that have, in all

Christian countries, ennobled their sex. Patient in suffering, encountering dangers undaunted, submitting to the privations of pioneer life without a murmur, unswervingly devoted to the cause of Christianity, "adorned in modest apparel—not with broidered hair, or gold, or pearls, or costly array—but, which becometh women professing godliness, with good works," they set before the community examples of piety, and used every proper exertion to elevate the standard of religion. While hundreds of men had become seduced from the doctrines of the Bible, and been led away from the only Rock of salvation, by the teachings of infidelity, those Christian women adhered more closely to the cause of the Redeemer—the only hope of the world. They exhibited in their "daily walk and conversation" the sincerity of their profession, and in their death reposed their hope of immortality upon the many "exceeding great and precious promises" of the word of God.

They left, too, their impress on society, not only by restraining vice, but by the promotion of virtue and religion; and, in the quietude of their own homes, trained for future usefulness their sons—many of whom have filled prominent positions in Church and State; and their daughters, who have adorned society by their charms, and blessed it by the beauties and graces of Christianity.

Their names and their memories ought not to be forgotten.

Among the many whose memory is too dear to Kentucky Methodism to be allowed to fade away, we take pleasure in mentioning the name of Mrs. Lydia Wickliffe.*

Mrs. Wickliffe was the daughter of Martin Hardin, of Fauquier county, Virginia, and the sister of Col. John Hardin, to whose tragical fate we have already referred.

In 1784, Mr. Charles Wickliffe, (her husband,) with his wife and five children, removed from Virginia to Kentucky, and settled in that part of Nelson county now in the county of Marion.

In early life Mrs. Wickliffe became impressed upon the subject of religion, and, before leaving Virginia, attached herself to the Church of England. A few years after her removal to Kentucky, under the labors of the early preachers, a society—one of the first established in the District—was organized in the neighborhood in which her husband had settled, and a log church erected, known for many years afterward as Thomas's Meeting-house.

Entertaining a high regard for the Church she had joined in Virginia, she nevertheless felt unwilling to be deprived of the privileges of Christian communion, and hence she was among the first to become connected with that society, in which she lived in Christian fellowship until she was transferred to the Church above.

Ardent in her piety, the peculiar doctrines of Divine influence, and the witness of the Spirit, ac-

* Mrs. Lydia Wickliffe was the mother of the Hon. Charles A. Wickliffe, ex-Governor of Kentucky; and the grandmother of the Hon. Robert C. Wickliffe, ex-Governor of Louisiana.

cording, as they did, with her own religious experience, embalmed in her affections "the Church in the wilderness," and endeared to her heart that system of Christianity so consonant with religious truth. Her attachment to the Church continued to increase with every succeeding year of her life, while her Christian character developed new beauties, and her holy walk shed a luster on the profession she had made, until the period arrived for the termination of the battle in which she was engaged, and then, in Christian triumph, she passed away to the home of the redeemed.

The personal appearance of Mrs. Wickliffe was good, her height above ordinary. Possessed of fine common sense, without the advantages of superior education, yet favored with the best the country afforded, her mind stored with useful knowledge, she often performed the duties of physician to the sick. Benevolent to the poor, kind and liberal to all, she was frequently found in the homes of sorrow and of suffering. One practice from which she never deviated, was the strict religious observance of old Christmas-day. Beneath her hospitable roof the weary itinerant always found a welcome and a shelter. Ogden, Wilson Lee, and McKendree knew her well.

In her own home, however, her Christian character shone more brightly than anywhere else. Industrious and frugal, she impressed these virtues on the minds of her children. A sincere Christian and a strict observer of the Sabbath, it was the great aim of her life to persuade them to follow her example. She lived to see her children grown, and prosperous, and happy, and the most of them converted to God.

Her last interview with her youngest son* was deeply affecting. It was in 1828, when he was about to leave for Washington City. He visited her, that he might bid her farewell. Always attentive to her interest, he desired the blessing once more of so good a mother. The time for parting came. She held him by the hand, and bequeathed to him the last blessing of a dying Christian mother.

She lived but a short time after this interview. In a few weeks she died in the full enjoyment of that faith which she had professed during a long life, trusting implicitly in the teachings of the Bible, which was her great book, and which she constantly read.

Mrs. Sally Helm, who was born about the year 1773, was the adopted daughter of Bazil and Mary Brown, of Nelson (now Marion) county, Kentucky.

On the 22d of March, 1787, she was happily married to John Helm, in Haycraft's Fort, adjoining Elizabethtown.

In the year 1788, she attached herself to the Methodist Church, at Thomas's Meeting-house, when there were only about ninety members in the District of Kentucky.

Her husband was born in Prince William county, Virginia, and had emigrated to Kentucky in the fall of 1779. He had passed through those thrilling

---

* Hon. Charles A. Wickliffe.

scenes of anguish and of blood, in Indian warfare, the bare recital of which, even at the present time, is so heart-rending.

In 1791, he bore a conspicuous part in St. Clair's memorable and disastrous campaign, in which he received a severe wound, shattering one of the bones in the left arm, from the wrist to the elbow. In this condition he clung to his faithful rifle with the true feelings and spirit of a backwoodsman—a treasure to be parted with only in death—and kept up with his retreating comrades, making the distance of more than thirty miles a day.

Living in these perilous times, and with a population in Kentucky insufficient to protect the frontier, continually exposed to danger from the ruthless savage, Mrs. Helm, in early life, evinced that Spartan courage that so eminently distinguished the pioneer women of Kentucky.

Having joined the Church when only fifteen years of age, and becoming familiar with its doctrines and its polity, with all the earnestness of a warm heart sanctified by grace, she fully embraced the former, and approved of the latter. As well educated in early life as was practicable, and availing herself of all the facilities within her grasp, she made all her advantages subservient to the cause of truth. For sixty-five years she bore the Christian's cross, openly and everywhere professing an interest in the Redeemer, and on all proper occasions presenting the claims and the hopes of Christianity to others. She was a burning and a shining light, reflecting upon others the savor of a holy life.

In the year 1824, her husband settled in Elizabethtown, Kentucky, where she immediately associated herself with the small class, then in its infancy, in that place. Her agreeable manners, added to her fervent piety, contributed much to the growth and prosperity of the Church where she resided.

Her husband was not a member of the Church. Having in his home so bright an example of Christianity, he nevertheless ignored the claims of religion, and rested apparently contented with external conformity to the teachings of the moral law. Descended from two of the best families in the State, participating extensively in those wars which recovered Kentucky from Indian depredations, the possessor of an ample fortune, and, in an important sense, the friend of mankind, he seemed indifferent to the sanctions of the Bible.

The heart of his pious wife was deeply touched at this neglect of an interest so vital. The continual falling of a rain-drop on the flinty rock will finally leave its impression. The sincere prayers and holy life of Mrs. Helm could not fail to exert a salutary influence on her husband. In the seventy-second year of his age, he joined the Church with his wife, having professed religion a short time previously. Their children, too—six in number—had embraced the Saviour. The cup of her joy was now full.

Seven years later, the arm which had protected and sustained her was palsied in death. His end was peaceful.

On Wednesday, the 19th of January, 1853, she breathed her last, in the eightieth year of her age. For the last seventeen years of her life she was a cripple, from the effects of a fall, yet her remarkably fine sense and buoyant disposition, united with her ardent piety, drew around her a host of friends and admirers.

Having sustained in the most exemplary manner the various relations of wife, mother, neighbor, and servant of God, and filled her well-appointed time, like a shock fully ripe, she was gathered to her people in peace. She has left a numerous band of descendants, in the second, third, and fourth generations, many of whom are members of the Church.

Among the representative women of Methodism in Kentucky, at this early period, we record the name of Mrs. Sarah Stevenson, the wife of Thomas Stevenson.

She was born in Frederick county, in Maryland, in 1756, and, in the twelfth year of her age, under the preaching of Robert Strawbridge, was awakened and converted to God.

In advance of the first missionaries, her husband emigrated to the District of Kentucky, and was here to offer to those men of God the first welcome to the hospitalities of their home. They located in Mason county, at what was called Kenton's Station, about six miles south-west of Maysville. In consequence of the frequency of the Indian massacres, they remained inside this fortress for some time. No family settlements could yet be made. Thus confined and exposed to danger, the hardships they endured can scarcely be imagined.

Mr. Stevenson, though a member of the Church, and a strict observer of its rules, made no open profession of religion until near the close of his life. Devoted, however, to its interests, he threw open the doors of his hospitable home; and from the arrival of Messrs. Haw and Ogden, in 1786, until his death, his house was a regular preaching-place for the traveling ministers of the Methodist Connection. Beneath their roof McKendree, Burke, Northcutt, Ray, O'Cull, Sale, and others, often found a place of rest.

During the period of a long life, the piety and zeal of Mrs. Stevenson shone with undiminished luster. In her home, amongst her neighbors, and in the house of God, everywhere, as a Christian she had but few equals. Her love to the Church was only equaled by the sweetness of her temper and her interest in the religious welfare of her children. On the 27th of May, 1828, she breathed her last. "Amid the tears and lamentations of friends and relations, her remains were deposited in the family burying-ground." Upon the marble slab that stands at the head of her grave, is the following epitaph, inscribed by her son, the Rev. Edward Stevenson, D.D.: "Sacred to the memory of Sarah Stevenson, who was born October 7, 1756; embraced religion and joined the Methodist Church in 1768; and after having lived the gospel for more than half a century, died in peace, May 27, 1828. The righteous shall shine as the sun in the firmament." Among her descendants the Church has been blessed with several enterprising and useful ministers.

Mrs. Mary Davis was among the first to connect herself with the Methodist Church in Kentucky. She was the daughter of Stephen and Molly Fisher, who emigrated from Virginia to Kentucky about the year 1776, and established a fort, about one mile from Danville, which, for many years, was known as "Fisher's Station." In 1783, under the preaching of Francis Clark, she became awakened, and immediately connected herself with the first society organized in the District. Early in the present century, with her husband, she removed to Union county, where she continued to reside until a short time previous to her death. The last few months of her life were spent at the residence of her son-in-law, Lazarus Powell, senior, in Henderson county, where, on the 2d of January, 1859, she passed away from earth, in the ninety-seventh year of her age, and having been for seventy-five years a member of the Church. At the time of her death, she was the oldest Methodist in Kentucky.

Along the entire pathway of life, from the hour of her conversion, her interest for the welfare of the Church, and the success of Christianity, continually increased. Favored with an intellect remarkable for its strength—with her mind well cultivated, unimpaired by age, and richly stored with the events of nearly a hundred years, the intimate friend of Asbury, McKendree, and other early preachers—perfectly familiar with the thrilling events of the Revolution, and reared amid the dangers of frontier life—an active participant in those great revivals that favored the Church at different periods—and entirely free from that childishness so often the accompaniment of age—her conversation, both to the old and the young, was of a most instructive and entertaining character. No subject, however, engrossed her thoughts as did that of religion. It had guided her steps in early life, was the companion of her more mature years, and the staff on which she was leaning, now the "almond-tree was flourishing," and her years were being numbered.

A few weeks previous to her death, in apparent good health, after a free conversation on the subject of religion, she informed a granddaughter that she should die in a short time, and requested her to prepare her clothing for her burial. So soon as the preparations she requested were made, she retired to her bed, from which she never arose. In a few days her spirit was with God.

She retained her senses, and conversed freely, to the last moment, speaking of death as the harbinger of a bright and happy eternity.*

* In the summer of 1847, while in charge of the Smithland District, we held a quarterly meeting in the Morganfield Circuit, of which the Rev. J. W. Cunningham had charge. Mrs. Davis was sitting in her carriage, on the skirt of the congregation, (the service being in a grove,) with her daughter, Mrs. Elizabeth Yeager, a pious member of the Baptist Church. When the sacrament of the Lord's Supper was administered, the elements were carried to Mrs. Davis, she not being able to get from her carriage. After administering to her, Mr. Cunningham remarked to Mrs. Yeager that he would not offer the elements to her, as for her to partake of them would be in violation of the rules of her Church. She promptly replied that no rules could prevent her from partaking of the sacrament with her aged

The name of Elizabeth Durbin deserves a conspicuous place among the representative women of Methodism in Kentucky. She was not only familiar with the early struggles of the Church, but for more than fifty-six years she was identified with its fortunes.

She was the daughter of Ilai Nunn, and was born in the State of Georgia, October 12, 1781. In 1783, her father emigrated to Kentucky, and settled in Bourbon county.

Before he came to Kentucky, Mr. Nunn attached himself to the Methodist Episcopal Church, and, in his devotion to its welfare and prosperity, displayed a remarkable zeal. Impressing upon the minds of his children the obligations of religion, his daughter Elizabeth, when only about fifteen years of age, was awakened and converted to God.

In her eighteenth year, she was married to Mr. Hosier Durbin, who left her, at his death, with five children, two of whom became distinguished ministers of the Methodist Episcopal Church.

In 1817, she was married to Mr. Clement Theobald, and removed to Grant county, Kentucky, where, after a long and useful life, she quietly breathed her last on the 20th of April, 1852.

---

and Christian mother; and then she partook of the elements. On the following Saturday, she was arraigned before the Baptist Church for the offense; and not being able to perceive any wrong in what she had done, and refusing to make any acknowledgments, she was allowed four weeks for consideration. During the interim, she had an opportunity of communing with the Cumberland Presbyterians, and availing herself of the privilege, no farther complaint was made by her Church.

Among the distinguished women of the Methodist Church in Kentucky, no one presented a brighter Christian example than Mrs. Durbin. Devoted to the Church of her choice, as well as to the common cause of Christianity, she contributed the influence of a holy life and a liberal hand to promote the great ends of religion. Endowed with an intellect of a superior cast, with a heart sanctified by grace, and with an inflexible purpose to accomplish the highest aims and ends of life—whether by the bedside of affliction, or in her own family circle, or pouring out the devotions of her heart around the altars of the Church—she was everywhere an angel of mercy. Through many years her house was consecrated to God, and beneath her hospitable roof the faithful minister of Christ found a welcome and a place of rest.

In a brief biography, written by her pastor soon after her death, he says: "Many there are who bless God that she ever lived. Her place in the Church and family circle cannot be easily filled. In her death a pillar of Christianity has been broken, and a moral, guiding light extinguished. Her children and society have sustained a loss that time cannot repair. She in an eminent degree trained up her children in the way they should go, and had the high satisfaction of seeing them all soundly converted, and exemplary members of the Church, while two of them became eloquent ministers of the gospel of Christ." *

* Nashville Christian Advocate, July 15, 1852.

For several years she suffered from severe affliction, yet her last attack, a disease of the throat, was brief. After a few days' illness, calmly and easily she passed away.

We need not the dying testimony of the servants of God, however gratifying it may be to catch the last words of triumph that may fall from their expiring lips—or however fondly we may treasure them in our hearts—to satisfy us of their safe entrance into eternal rest. Unable to converse during her illness, her entire life having shed a luster on her profession, her death could not be otherwise than one of victory. She passed away like the sun which sinks behind the western hills, "giving a sure hope of rising in brighter array."

The following extract from a letter received from her son, the Rev. John P. Durbin, D.D., dated March 5, 1868, in answer to a letter of inquiry which we sent him, will be read with interest:

"I have no family records within my reach, and cannot therefore be precise in regard to any point. My mother was the daughter of Ilai Nunn, of Bourbon county, Kentucky. He was originally from Georgia, at a very early day, when the Indians were in some parts of Kentucky. My mother was born quite as early as 1781, perhaps earlier. Her father's house was the church for their neighborhood. My mother early became pious. By her first husband she had five children, all sons, of whom I was the eldest. Myself and my brother William (third son) are the only ones living. Her first husband died about 1814; and, two or three years thereafter, she was married to Mr. Theobald, of Grant county, Kentucky. A son and a daughter were the fruit of that marriage. The son is dead, but the daughter—now Mrs. Sayres, of Grant county—is still living, and is the mother of a large family of children. My youngest brother, Hosier J. Durbin, after whom you inquire, was a traveling preacher at his death, which happened more than twenty years ago, in Indiana. He was killed in a storm, by the limb of a tree falling on him, as he rode homeward. He was in the service of the American Bible Society at the time, and was an energetic man, and, I have been told, a powerful preacher. His widow and children (three girls and two boys) still survive.

"I forgot to say, my mother's house was a church, where the ministers preached, and found a home, when passing or resting, during her second marriage. I wish I could write more satisfactorily about a mother whom I reverenced and loved so dearly."

Another name that bore a conspicuous part in planting Methodism in Kentucky, and in watching its growth in the years of its infancy, is that of Mrs. Jane Hardin, the wife of Col. John Hardin, to whom we have made previous reference. She was the daughter of Nathanael Davies, was born in 1750, and brought up in Western Pennsylvania, on the Monongahela. Her grandparents were from Wales. On reaching Kentucky, in 1786, Col. Hardin settled near Sandusky Station, a few miles from Springfield. In Pennsylvania, Mrs. Hardin had been a member of the Presbyterian Church.

Amongst the early societies planted in Kentucky, there was one at Josiah Wilson's, on Pleasant Run, and another at John Springer's, about two and a half miles from the former place. Very soon after their settlement in Kentucky, Col. Hardin and his wife both joined the Methodist Episcopal Church at Sandusky Station, now Pleasant Run.

When at home, from the time he connected himself with the Church, until the hour of his departure on the mission which made his wife a widow and his children orphans, at morning and at night, he regularly called his family around the altar of prayer, and commended them to the care of Jehovah. In his absence, while living, and after his death, Mrs. Hardin knelt, with her children, as had her husband, around the same altar, for worship. On all the public means of grace she faithfully attended. In the places of public worship, the prayer-meeting, and the class, she was always found, unless providentially hindered. In her private devotions, she was accompanied by her children, where she invoked the blessings of Heaven upon them, while they listened to her soft, sweet voice, lifted in supplication, and beheld the tears that trickled down her cheeks, as she pleaded before God for those deprived of a father's care, but now doubly entrusted to her own. Her every-day life was that of a true Christian, and each day was a day of communion with God. Her life, shadowed by the stroke that had fallen on her heart in the death of her husband, was consecrated every hour to God.

About the year 1799, she was married to

Capt. Christopher Irvine, of Madison county, near Richmond; and, after his death, she resided with her youngest daughter, Mrs. Rosanna Field, adjoining Richmond, where, in 1829, she died in great peace.*

Highly gifted by nature, possessed of indomitable energy, and with a heart sanctified by grace, she was well prepared to impart an influence to the Church, that could be claimed but by few of her time. Through the whole period of her life, zealous for the cause of Christ, in her own family, in the community in which she resided, and in the Church of which she was a member, she was "a burning and a shining light." Among her descendants have been men, some of whom, by the power of their eloquence and the greater power of an upright life, have graced the halls of legislation, while others have won distinction in the learned professions; and women who, as the wives of ministers of the gospel, who have been prominent in the Church, or filling other spheres, have been useful members of society, gracing it with their charms, and shedding upon it the glorious example of a holy life.

One of the earliest families to join the Methodist Church in Kentucky, was that of Joshua Stamper. His wife, Mrs. Jane Stamper, preceded him in entering the Church. They were the parents of the Rev. Jonathan Stamper. Whatever responsibility

* We have been favored with these facts by her son, Mark Hardin, Esq., of Shelbyville, Kentucky.

may belong to the father in the religious training of his children—and no language can estimate it—yet certainly the first impressions are made by the mother on the infant mind. The moral and religious character of Mrs. Stamper cannot be overdrawn. Of a meek and quiet spirit, within the sphere of her own home she exerted an influence that has been felt in the Church to the present time. Her daughter, Mrs. Danley, the mother of the Rev. Leroy C. Danley, once said "that of all the members of the several branches of the family of her parents, including those who had married into the family, about fifty or sixty in number, who have grown to mature years, there were but two who were not professors of religion." * Deeply pious, and devoted to the Church, as was her husband, yet to the influence and religious counsel of Mrs. Stamper was her family chiefly indebted for these blessed results.

The following sketch of her character, furnished at our request, by Mrs. W. M. Grubbs, the daughter of the Rev. Jonathan Stamper, and wife of the Rev. William M. Grubbs, of Russellville, Kentucky, is so excellent a portraiture of Mrs. Stamper, that we give it to our readers without any alteration:

"My grandparents were among the very early settlers of Kentucky, coming to this State from Virginia about the year 1778. For more than twelve years they were compelled to live in forts, and endure all the hardships of frontier life. They lived

---

* Letter to the author from J. M. Brawner, of Louisville, Kentucky.

first at Boonesborough, and afterward at Strode's Station. Long after they ventured outside of the walls of a fort, they were exposed to Indian depredations. During all these tedious years they lived almost entirely on the wild game procured by my grandfather's rifle—much of the time without bread or salt. To get even this scanty fare, he had many thrilling adventures and hair-breadth escapes. My childish heart has almost stood still with terror as I have heard it told how the Indians, with uplifted tomahawks, ran him into the fort, while his poor, agonized wife, from her lookout, saw the fearful race, until some kind friend, who would not have her witness the murder of her husband, drew her away. It is true, he escaped, and was spared to his family; but often had she been called to look upon such scenes among her friends. Being naturally a very delicate woman, the many privations, the fearful uncertainty and excitement of pioneer life, told heavily upon her health in all after life.

"My grandmother was born in Bedford county, Virginia. Her maiden name was Jane Woodrough. In her early home she was nurtured in the Presbyterian Church, and being of an extremely sensitive and conscientious turn of mind, she was often in great fear lest she was not among the elect. The first Methodist sermon she ever heard was preached in her new home: under it she was converted, and joined the Methodist Episcopal Church; and for nearly forty years she lived a faithful, consistent Christian.

"Her house was not only the home of the weary

itinerant, but was for many years a preaching-place.

"Her record is not found among the notable women, whose deeds, like great rivers, have blessed many lands: her sphere was humble; but in the quiet seclusion of her own home, she led a godly life; and the world is better that she lived, for she trained and sent forth a Christian family of sons and daughters, who loved and labored for the cause she prized.

"I saw her many times, yet one scene only remains with me. It was a bright summer day, and as I stood in the door, she sat by her low bed, earnestly regarding me. She wore the plain dress of her day, with the white muslin kerchief folded around her in the style used by the old Methodist ladies. Much is now said of magnetic faces. Why it is that this one picture of her is so vividly impressed on my mind, I cannot tell, unless her face, with its steady blue eye, can come under this class.

"She was a very firm woman, but most tender and affectionate. My father was very young when he joined the itinerant ministry, and of course had his share of hardship. When he came home to her, after a hard year's work, worn and *ragged*, she wept over him, but comforted him with many cheering words, and soon, with her own hands, made him ready for his mission again. Many instances of this kind might be spoken of; but to show that she was not weakly sympathetic and tender, when, at another time, he came to her discouraged by the unkindness and harshness of his seniors in the ministry, determined to abide at home, she cared for him most lovingly; but when the time came for him to start, she said to him, (and any loving mother may imagine what it cost her,) 'Young man, get your horse and go; you can't stay here.'

"One other trait much to be admired, was the perfect freedom of her religious intercourse with her family. They talked, prayed, and rejoiced together in their own home. She taught her children to bear the cross in the beginning of their religious life. When my father came home from the camp-meeting at which he was converted, my grandfather being absent, although an elder brother was present, she made him lead the family devotions.

"She died in 1825, and my father thus writes of her death:

"'My mother lingered about four months after the death of my father, and then sweetly fell asleep in Jesus. I was permitted to be present and close her eyes, when the happy spirit left its clay tabernacle. We had been anticipating this event for months, yet when it came we were unprepared to give her up. My own feelings were almost beyond control when I saw those calm, blue eyes, which had so often beamed upon me with all a mother's love, close for ever in the darkness of death. A sense of orphanage pervaded my spirit; and though I had been a husband and father for years, I felt that in some way I was left alone when my dear old mother died.

"'My mother possessed a very tender heart, and could see nothing suffer without great pain. She was an example of shining piety to her children; and to this hour I am thankful for the gift of such a mother—one who cared for my soul, and taught my youthful feet the way to the house of God. I am now an old man; but her look, her counsels, her prayers, her tears, are all fresh in my memory; and I rejoice in the hope of meeting her in heaven, and once more calling her by the precious name of mother.

"'I think that a cold and cheerless doctrine which teaches we shall be wholly unknown to each other in the future world, or that the bonds of earthly affection shall be so severed that we shall lose all kindred nearness to each other. It seems to me that it will constitute a portion of heaven's perfect happiness to sit down under the bending branches of the tree of life,

With those so dear
While lingering here,

and tell over, again and again, our experience of God's dealings with us in this world of enemies and conflicts. O I should feel sorry if I thought it would not be permitted me to lay my head on my precious mother's lap once more, as I used to do when a little white-headed boy, and hear her sweet song, or her soothing voice saying, My precious son!'"

In the early history of Methodism in Kentucky, Mrs. Mary Todd Hinde* bore a prominent part. She

* As many as nine of her descendants have taken rank in the ministry of the Methodist Church, to wit: Thomas S. Hinde, her son,

was the daughter of Benjamin Hubbard, an English merchant. On the 24th of September, 1764, she was married to Dr. Thomas Hinde, an eminent physician and surgeon, who had settled in Virginia. Descended from an excellent family, favored with the best educational advantages of her times, her mind well cultivated, easy and graceful in her manners, charitable in her views of the words and deeds of others, and occupying a high social position, she imparted happiness to the society in whose circle she moved.

For many years after her marriage, she lived without the comforts of religion. The great aversion of her husband to Christianity was a hindrance to the cultivation of any religious emotions that may have impressed her heart.

One of her daughters became impressed upon the subject of religion, and in an interview with her mother, the latter also became awakened. A short time afterward, preaching was introduced into the neighborhood in which she resided, by Methodist

---

Leroy H. Kavanaugh, and Edward L. Southgate, Sen., her grandsons, all of whom died in peace some years since. There are still living, Hubbard Hinde Kavanaugh, Bishop of the M. E. Church, South, Benjamin Taylor Kavanaugh, pastor of the M. E. Church, South, Houston, Texas, and Williams Barbour Kavanaugh, preacher in charge of Alexandria Circuit, Kentucky Conference, her grandsons; Peter E. Kavanaugh, preacher in charge of Orangeburg Circuit, Kentucky Conference, Hubbard Hinde Kavanaugh, Jr., preacher in charge of Oddville Circuit, Kentucky Conference, and Edward L. Southgate, Jr., preacher in charge of Richmond and Providence Station, Kentucky Conference, her great-grandsons. Two of her daughters, moreover, married Methodist ministers, to wit: Williams Kavanaugh and Leroy Cole.

preachers, and, under their preaching, she was more fully instructed in the way of salvation, and was converted to God.

In her early efforts to become religious, she was met by the opposition of her husband. Refusing to furnish her with a horse to ride to church, she walked regularly to the house of God. Unwilling to yield her purpose to become a Christian, no argument could induce her to abandon it. Declaring his belief that his wife was losing her mind, he applied a blister to her neck to bring her to her senses. In this condition she went to the place of prayer. The sufferings she bore, together with the patience she evinced under them, had an effect contrary to the expectations of her husband. It terminated in his awakening, but not in the curing of his wife.

We copy the following from a letter we received from her grandson, Bishop H. H. Kavanaugh, dated Lexington, Kentucky, April 14, 1868:

"Faith in the promises of God, and the efficacy of the blood of the atoning Lamb, was much more efficient to the removal of her distracting grief and burdened soul. How long she was seeking the pardon of her sins, until she obtained peace with God through our Lord Jesus Christ, I am not informed; but having obtained the pearl of great price, she beautifully illustrated its value by a godly conversation — walking 'worthy of the vocation wherewith she was called.'

"After Mrs. Hinde and her husband were fully enlisted in the service of the Captain of their salvation, they removed to Kentucky, and settled in Clarke county. Here she became instrumental in the organization of a class, afterward known as the Ebenezer Church. In this neighborhood, the purity of her life, the sweetness of her spirit, together with the clearness of her mind, were all elements of usefulness.

"Under the influence of the French infidelity of the day, there was at that time a good deal of that form of infidelity which was styled Deism. Its adherents admitted the existence of one God, denied the doctrine of the Trinity, the divinity of Jesus Christ, and the inspiration of the Scriptures. One of her neighbors, Major John Martin, who was an adherent of this doctrine, was indulging in a little pleasant raillery, ridiculing her religion as being untrue, irrational, and not worthy of belief. In a kind and gentle tone of voice, she said to him: 'Major Martin, the Christian religion *may* be true.' The expression fastened strongly upon the Major. He said afterward, that, on his way home, the thought was constantly revolving in his mind, *The Christian religion may be true.* The manner of the Major was rather blunt and pointed; so he said to himself, 'If the Christian religion is true, it is an awful truth to me.' And as he pondered the great facts of religion, before he reached his home he said to himself, 'The Christian religion is true, and I am a sinner, and on the way to hell.' He hastened home, called for the Testament, and betook himself to prayer, in which he persisted until he had the knowledge of salvation by the remission of sins.

From that time he was the uncompromising soldier of the cross and follower of the Lamb, until he closed his life in peace.

"Mrs. Hinde had a singularly clear and distinct memory of the events of her life and observation. Unlike the Doctor, her memory never failed her. When in advanced age, she became apprehensive that she should lose her eye-sight, as her eyes were weak and failing: she thought that one of the most gloomy features of that calamity would be the deprivation of the pleasure and profit of reading the good books that had so often cheered her heart and edified her mind.

"To relieve, in some measure, the calamity she saw coming upon her, she committed to memory a large portion of Baxter's Saint's Rest, and an astonishing amount of the practical remarks of Scott's Commentary, some of the sermons of Wesley most admired by her, and some other authors that I cannot now remember, and forty hymns. I have held the book and heard her recite for an hour at a time, and she but rarely miscalled a word; and those she would miss were a mere substitution of the little connective forms of speech that did not much affect the sense. The satisfaction she realized in this, she said, well rewarded her for the labor of committing. Even in her blindness she was cheerful, devoted to her Christian duties, and resigned to the will of God.

"I do not remember any detail of her dying exercises, which I may have heard. But her race is ended, the battle is fought, and the long anticipated crown has been bestowed. How glorious it is to think that her grand attainments through grace are hers for ever!"

The Annual Conferences for the western division of the work had hitherto been held in the spring. In a former chapter we noticed the Conference for this year, which convened at Dunworth, on Holston, on the first Friday in April.

During this year the Conference was changed from the spring to the fall of the year.

On the 30th of September, Bishop Asbury entered Kentucky, and on the following Saturday reached Bethel Academy, accompanied by Bishop Whatcoat and William McKendree, and on the 6th of October commenced the session of the Conference. We copy from his Journal, Vol. II., pp. 473, 474, 475:

"*Saturday, October* 4. I came to Bethel. Bishop Whatcoat and William McKendree preached: I was so dejected I could say little, but weep. *Sabbath-day* it rained, and I kept at home. Here is Bethel—Cokesbury in miniature—eighty by thirty feet, three stories, with a high roof, and finished below. Now we want a fund and an income of three hundred per year to carry it on; without which it will be useless. But it is too distant from public places; its being surrounded by the river Kentucky in part, we now find to be no benefit: thus all our excellences are turned into defects. Perhaps Brother Poythress and myself were as much overseen with this place as Dr. Coke was with the seat of Cokesbury. But all is right that works right, and all is wrong that works wrong, and we must be blamed by men of slender sense for consequences impossible to foresee —for other people's misconduct. *Sabbath-day*, *Monday*, and *Tuesday*, we were shut up in Bethel with the traveling and local ministry, and the trustees that could be called together. We ordained fourteen or fifteen local and traveling deacons. It was thought expedient to carry the first design of education into execution, and that we should employ a man of sterling qualifications, to be chosen by and under the direction of a select number of trustees and others, who should obligate themselves to see him paid, and take the profits, if any, arising from the establishment. Dr. Jennings was thought of, talked of, and written to. I visited John Lewis, who lately had his leg broken; I left him with good resolutions to take care of his soul.

"*Wednesday*, 8. We rode fifteen miles to Shawnee Run, and crossed Kentucky River at Curd's Ferry; the river was as low as a stream, and the streams are nearly dried up.

"*Thursday*, 9. I preached on Heb. iii. 12–14, at the new house at Shawnee Run. We had rich entertainment for man and beast at Robert Johnson's.

"*Friday*, 10. We rode to Pleasant Run to John Springer's: it was a very warm day for the season. I had a running blister at my side, yet I rode and walked thirty-two miles. We refreshed ourselves at Crawford's Tavern upon the way. We have visited Knox, Madison, Mercer, and Washington counties, in this State. It was strongly insisted upon by preachers and people that I should say something before I left Bethel; able or unable, willing or unwilling: accordingly, on *Tuesday*, in the academical hall, I gave a long, temperate talk upon Heb. x. 38, 39.

"*Sabbath-day*, 12. It rained excessively; we were shut up; William McKendree met the people. We have had but two Sabbaths to spend in Kentucky, and in both I was prevented by rain.

"*Monday*, 13. We left John Springer's, and came to Lewis Thomas's, fifteen miles; a deep, damp, narrow path; the underwood very wet. Crossed Cartwright and Hardin's Creeks. I gave a short sermon on Rom. viii. 9: 'If any man have not the Spirit of Christ, he is none of his.'

"*Tuesday*, 14. We began our march for Cumberland. We were told by two persons that we could not cross the Rolling Fork of Salt River; I judged we could, and as I thought, so it was—we forded it with ease. We came up a solitary path east of the Level Woods, and struck into the road to Lee's Ferry. For ten miles of the latter part of this day's journey, we rode through barrens of hickory, shrub-oak, and hazel-nut: thirty miles, if not thirty-five, is the amount of this day's work: in the morning there was a very great damp, and in the afternoon it was, I thought, as warm as the west of Georgia.

"*Wednesday*, 15. We crossed Green River, the main branch of which riseth near the Crab Orchard. We crossed at the mouth of Little Barren River. We then made a bold push for the Great Barren: dining at Mr. Morrison's, I could not eat wallet-provision; but happily for me, I was provided with a little fresh mutton at the house, made warm in a small space. Now we had unfavorable appearances of rain; we had bleak, barren hills to ride; which, although beautiful to sight, were painful to sense. The rain came in large and rapid drops for fourteen miles; we were well soaked on all sides. A little after dark we came to Mr. Hagin's, upon Big Barren River: a good house, an excellent fire to dry our clothing, good meat and milk for supper, and the cleanest beds—all this we had. I have paid for this route."

The session lasted but two days, and as the Journal is brief, we copy it entire:

"Journal of the Western Annual Conference, held at Bethel Academy, Kentucky, October 6, 1800. Members present: Francis Asbury, Richard Whatcoat, William McKendree, William Burke, John Sale, Hezekiah Harriman, Benjamin Lakin; reädmitted, Lewis Hunt, Thomas Allen, and Jeremiah Lawson.

"Who are admitted on trial?

"*Answer.* William Marsh, Benjamin Young.

"What local preachers are elected to the office of deacons?

"*Answer.* Richard Tilton, Edward Talbot, William Thompson, Isaac Pavey, Reuben Hunt, Elisha Bowman, Jacob James, A. Blackman, Jonathan Kidwell, Benjamin Northcutt, Joshua West, James Garner, Jesse Griffith, Philip Taylor.

"Who have located this year?

"*Answer.* Thomas Allen.

"Benjamin Lakin, Jeremiah Lawson, Lewis

Hunt, and Thomas Allen ordained to the office of deacons.

"The preachers' deficiencies for six months are as follows: William Burke, £2 17s 6d; Hezekiah Harriman, £7 19s 0d; John Sale, £6 16s 6d; Lewis Hunt, £0 18s 2d; Jeremiah Lawson, £5 15s 5d; Benjamin Young, £3 5s 6d; Thomas Allen, £11 2s 0d. Total, £38 14s 3d.

"Conference adjourned to meet again at Ebenezer, State of Tennessee, October 1, 1801.

"Test, F. ASBURY.

"WILLIAM BURKE, Secretary.

"From this brief Journal it appears that there were present at the Conference only ten individuals, including Bishops Asbury and Whatcoat, and the session continued only one day, and the members were off to their several Appointments, which, according to the printed Minutes, were as follows:

"KENTUCKY DISTRICT.—William McKendree, P. E.

"Scioto and Miami, Henry Smith.

"Limestone, Benjamin Lakin.

"Hinkstone and Lexington, William Burke, Thomas Wilkerson, Lewis Hunt.

"Danville, Hezekiah Harriman.

"Salt River and Shelby, John Sale, William Marsh.

"Cumberland, John Page, Benjamin Young.

"Green, Samuel Douthet, Ezekiel Burdine.

"Holston and Russell, James Hunter.

"New River, John Watson." *

---

* Nashville Christian Advocate, January 16, 1851.

The deep solicitude felt by Bishop Asbury for the success of Bethel Academy, as well as his fear for its failure, is certainly very touchingly expressed in the extract we have quoted from his journal. During his brief stay in Kentucky, he "ordains fourteen or fifteen local and traveling deacons," preaches at Bethel Academy and at several other points, traverses a large portion of the State, visits Churches, suffering all the while under deep affliction. Wonderful man!

On the 16th of October, he enters the State of Tennessee, and the 18th he preached at Parker's, where he was met by "Brothers McGee, Sugg, Jones, and Speer, local preachers," and "had a small shout in the camp of Israel." On the 19th he looked upon Nashville for the first time, and met a congregation of "not less than one thousand in and out of the Stone Church," to whom sermons were preached by "Mr. McKendree, Bishop Whatcoat, and himself, the services lasting three hours." On the following day we find him at "Drake's Creek Meeting-house, at the close of a sacramental solemnity that had been held four days by Craighead, Hodge, Rankin, McGee, and Adair, Presbyterian ministers, at which sermons were preached by McKendree, Whatcoat, and himself." On that day and night following, he enjoyed the privilege of mingling "with scenes of deepest interest." The great revival, to which we have so frequently referred, was now in its zenith, in Tennessee and Southern Kentucky. The vast assemblies that attended the preaching of the gospel could not be accommodated in any of the churches. At this meeting "the stand was in the open air, embosomed in a wood of lofty beech-trees." We copy from Asbury's Journal, Vol. II., pp. 476, 477:

"*Tuesday, October* 21. Yesterday, and especially during the night, were witnessed scenes of deep interest. In the intervals between preaching, the people refreshed themselves and horses, and returned upon the ground. The *stand* was in the open air, embosomed in a wood of lofty beech-trees. The ministers of God, Methodists and Presbyterians, united their labors, and mingled with the child-like simplicity of primitive times. Fires blazing here and there, dispelled the darkness, and the shouts of the redeemed captives, and the cries of precious souls struggling into life, broke the silence of midnight. The weather was delightful; as if heaven smiled, whilst mercy flowed in abundant streams of salvation to perishing sinners. We suppose there were at least thirty souls converted at this meeting. I rejoice that God is visiting the sons of the Puritans, who are candid enough to acknowledge their obligations to the Methodists."

The name of William McKendree, identified this year for the first time with the history of the Church in Kentucky, not only from the position he subsequently occupied, as one of the chief pastors of the entire Church, but from his commanding talents, his fervent piety, his deep devotion to the cause of Christ, and great usefulness, will always be cherished with fond remembrance. He "was born in King William county, Virginia, July 5, 1757. Of his early history we know but little, farther than that he was of worthy and pious parents, who were in moderate circumstances, and was brought up to the pursuits common to the sons of a medium farmer in those days. His early education was imperfect; but in the course of years, by close attention to study, he became a learned man." *

He was a soldier in the Revolutionary war, having entered the service as a private, but was in a short time made adjutant, and afterward in consequence of his great energy, "and fine business qualifications, was placed in the commissary department."† In this position he exhibited those traits of character, of probity, and enterprise, that afterward distinguished him as a minister of Jesus Christ. In the position he filled in the army, he contributed much "to sustain the allied armies of Washington and Rochambeau, at the siege of Cornwallis at Yorktown.

"He was about five feet ten inches in height, weighing, on an average, through life, after grown up to manhood, about one hundred and sixty pounds. He had fair skin, dark hair, and blue eyes. He increased in flesh between the years of forty and sixty, and at one time he weighed about one hundred and eighty pounds; but as he grew old he declined in flesh, and for the last ten years of his life did not exceed one hundred and forty pounds. When in his prime, his form was almost faultless,

* Rev. A. L. P. Green, D.D., in Biographical Sketches of Eminent Itinerant Ministers, p. 43.

† Ibid., p. 44.

possessing extraordinary action and great physical strength. His features, taken as a whole, were decidedly good; rather handsome than otherwise. When *calm* and *silent*, there was the expression of deep thought upon his countenance, sometimes approaching even to that of care; but whenever he spoke, his eyes would kindle up, and a smile like that of pleasant recognition would cover his face, which was the outcropping of a kind and benevolent heart. His constitution was no doubt naturally a good one, but he was so much overtaxed through life with labor, hardships, and exposure, that his old age was burdened with infirmities, being for many years under the influence of asthma and neuralgia." *

Impressed with the importance of religion from early childhood, he, however, was not converted † until about thirty years of age. Under the preaching of John Easter he was awakened and brought to Christ. In 1787, he connected himself with the Methodist Episcopal Church, "and the following year obtained license to preach, and joined the traveling connection on trial. The Conference at which he was admitted was held in Amelia county, Virginia, June 17, 1788. His first appointment was to Norfolk and Portsmouth. His next was to

---

* Rev. A. L. P. Green, D.D., in Biographical Sketches of Eminent Itinerant Ministers, pp. 44, 45.

† John and Thomas Easter both became traveling preachers. The former was one of the most successful preachers the Methodists ever had. Bishops McKendree and George were both awakened under him, and thousands of others.—*Lednum*, p. 185.

Petersburg: after the first quarter, he was removed to Union Circuit, in the bounds of the South Carolina Conference. The following year he was sent to the Bedford Circuit, Virginia Conference; the third quarter he was removed to the Greenbrier Circuit; the fourth quarter he was removed to the Little Levels, on the Western waters. The next year he was appointed to four circuits, to travel each one quarter. At the end of this year he was appointed to the Richmond District. The following year he was sent to a mountainous District in the Baltimore Conference. From this District he was returned at the end of the year to the Richmond District, from which he was taken after one round, by the Bishops, to what was then called Kentucky, and left in charge of what was then the Western Conference, which embraced Ohio, Kentucky, Tennessee, and all Virginia west of New River, and also one Circuit in the State of Illinois. The foregoing account of his labors is from the Bishop's own hand." *

Mr. McKendree entered upon the work in the West at a most propitious period. The "Great Revival" in Kentucky and Tennessee had commenced previous to his appointment to this District; and at the time he entered upon his labors, "throughout this whole region a religious excitement was spreading and prevailing." † After attending the session of the Conference at Bethel, he passed through a

* Rev. A. L. P. Green, D.D., in Biographical Sketches of Eminent Itinerant Ministers, p. 47.

† Recollections of the West, p. 33.

considerable portion of Kentucky, in company with Bishops Asbury and Whatcoat, reviewing this section of his field of labor, preaching with extraordinary fervor, and bringing the wealth of his princely intellect, and of his tireless energy, and laying all upon the altar of the Church.

The printed Minutes report his appointments somewhat different from the extract quoted above. In 1788, his name stands connected with the Mecklenburg Circuit; in 1789, with the Cumberland; in 1790, with the Portsmouth; in 1791, with the Amelia; in 1792, with the Greensville; in 1793, with Norfolk and Portsmouth; in 1794, with the Union; in 1795, with the Bedford, to change with Thomas Wilkerson in six months; in 1796, as Presiding Elder over Orange, Amherst, Hanover, Williamsburg, and Gloucester—his name also stands in connection with the Williamsburg Circuit; in 1797 and 1798, as Presiding Elder over New River, Bottetourt, Bedford, Orange, Hanover, and Williamsburg and Gloucester; in 1799, as Presiding Elder over Fairfax, Alexandria, Stafford, Lancaster, Berkeley, Alleghany, Rockingham, Pendleton, and Winchester; and in 1800, he was placed in charge of the District embracing the Greenbrier and Bottetourt, the Bedford, Orange, Amherst, Williamsburg and Hanover, and Gloucester Circuits, from which he was removed during the same year to Kentucky.

We soon find him in attendance at a Presbyterian meeting "at Drake's Creek Meeting-house," in Tennessee, where a revival was in progress, and preaching from Jeremiah iv. 14: "O Jerusalem, wash thine heart from wickedness, that thou mayest be saved. How long shall thy vain thoughts lodge within thee?" In company with Bishops Asbury and Whatcoat, and those faithful evangelists, John and William McGee, he wends his way toward East Tennessee, "preaching" and "exhorting" to listening thousands, all along his route.

Traveling his vast District, he "had been but a few months on the ground till he understood perfectly his field of labor, moving day and night, visiting families, organizing societies, and holding Quarterly Conferences. It was his constant practice to travel from thirty to fifty miles a day and preach at night. All classes of people flocked to hear him. Statesmen, lawyers, doctors, and theologians, of all denominations, clustered around him, saying, as they returned home, 'Did you ever hear the like before?' Some, indeed, were so captivated, that they would say, 'Never man spake like this man.' He saw that the harvest was truly great, and the laborers few. Early in the morning and late in the evening, with streaming eyes, he prayed God, with hands and heart uplifted, that he would send forth more laborers into the harvest.

"He was actively engaged in forming new circuits, and calling out local preachers to fill them. Whenever he found a young man of piety and native talent, he led him out into the Lord's vineyard; and large as his District was, it soon became too small for him. He extended his labors to every part of South-western Virginia; then crossing the Ohio River, he carried the holy war into the State of Ohio;

and there he formed new charges, and called out young men. Like a noble general, he was always in the first ranks. Throughout the length and breadth of the West, as far as the country was settled, McKendree was first in council and first in action. If he appeared on a camp-ground, every eye was upon him, and his word was law. In private circles, in Quarterly Conferences, he was the master spirit." *

We have already referred to Mr. McKendree as being an active participant, immediately on his entrance on the labors of his District, in the revival of religion that distinguished this period. In passing through his vast District, he carried with him a holy influence, which, like a "flame of fire," spread in every direction. No difficulty could daunt this soldier of the cross. "He led his band of tried men—and a nobler band of Christian heroes never lived than those who flocked around the standard that was borne in triumph by William McKendree."† True, sometimes he was depressed, for he was mortal; but, nothing daunted, he moved with steady and resistless step, an example of labor and piety among his brethren. Deep streams could not divert him from his course; high mountains presented no barrier; the rains of summer and the snows of winter alike unmoved him. Often he swam the turbid stream to reach the appointments he had made. And many a time, after a long day's

---

* Autobiography of the Rev. Jacob Young, pp. 61, 62.

† Rev. A. L. P. Green, D.D.

travel, he lay out in the woods at night, hungry and cold, with no other covering than his clothes and saddle-blanket, except the blue sky above him.

The first to bear to the northern and central portions of Kentucky the intelligence of the revivals in the southern part of the State, he mingled freely in them. In the pulpit, in the altar, in the family circle, by his counsel and bright Christian example, he exerted an influence for good that cannot now be estimated. We find him side by side with the pious Burke "in the contests" he had with the ministry of the Baptist Church; and in the defense of the great cardinal doctrines and principles of Methodism, he stood forth the unflinching advocate. Under his supervision many of the early church-edifices were erected;* and under his ministry the Kentucky District enjoyed continual prosperity.

We next find him on the Cumberland District, embracing "nine circuits, one of which was in Missouri. He traveled from Nashville, Tennessee, through Kentucky and Illinois, to Missouri, a distance of fifteen hundred miles, in order to pass round and through his District. Into this new and extensive field of labor he entered spiritedly, and was everywhere hailed as an able minister of the New Testament. Here he was the honored instrument, in connection with the worthy men who labored side by side with him, though under his superintendency, of laying, as a wise master-builder,

* The Brick Chapel, four miles north-east of Shelbyville, was erected under his direction. It was the second brick church in Kentucky.

the foundation of the Church which has since so gloriously prospered in this country." *

The same success that crowned his ministry on the Kentucky District, followed his labors in this inviting field. Dangers, however, often threatened him, and difficulties that could only be overcome by inflexibility of purpose, often opposed him.

"In the year 1807, Brother Walker was sent to Illinois, there being at that time but one circuit in that State; and a young man by the name of Travis was sent to Missouri. In the summer of this year, William McKendree, who was then in charge of what was called the Cumberland District, which extended to Illinois and Missouri, took with him James Gwin and A. Goddard, (Gwin was then a local preacher, and Goddard was traveling what was then called Barren Circuit,) and set out to visit Walker and Travis. They crossed over the Ohio, and entered into the State of Illinois, traveled all day, and finding no house to stop at, passed the night in the wilderness. Next day they shared a like fortune, camping out at night again. During this night their horses got away, and they did not find them till about noon the next day; but that night they found a lone settlement, and tarried with a poor family who were living in a temporary hut or camp. Next night they reached the house of a Mr. B., who received them kindly. The Mississippi was not far off; and there being no way to get their horses

* Rev. W. W. Redman, in Nashville Christian Advocate, February 26, 1847.

across it at that point, they left them with Mr. B., took their baggage on their shoulders, and went on foot to the river, which they crossed in a canoe, and after walking twelve miles, they came to the house of a Mr. Johnson. Here they met young Travis, who had gotten up a little camp-meeting in the wilderness. At this meeting their labors were greatly blessed. When it closed, they returned again to Mr. B., and went to a camp-meeting in the bounds of Brother Walker's work, called the Three Springs.

"Here they found a few faithful members of the Church, but hosts of enemies. One individual in particular, who was a leader of a band of persecutors, had called a council among them, to form a plan to drive the preachers off. He stated to his clan, that if the preachers were permitted to remain, and could have their way, they would break up all the gambling and racing in the country, and that they would have no more pleasure, or fun, as he called it. So the determination among them was to arm themselves, go to the camp-meeting *en masse*, take the preachers and conduct them to the Ohio River, carry them over, and let them know that they were to keep on their own side, and never trouble them again. This purpose was made known to the preachers in advance of their appearance on the encampment. On Sunday, while Mr. McKendree was in the midst of his discourse, preaching to a large and interested congregation, on the text, 'Come now, and let us reason together,' etc., the Major, as he was called, and his company, rode up, and halted near the congregation. The Major told his men that he would not do any thing until the man had done preaching. Mr. McKendree was then in the prime of life, his voice loud and commanding, his bearing that of undaunted courage, while a supernatural defiance seemed to shoot forth from his speaking eyes. He was sustained by the presence of Gwin, Goddard, Walker, and Travis, who sat near him. The prayers of the faithful were being sent up to heaven in his behalf; and, above all, the Divine presence was with him. Such was the power of his reasoning, that he held the Major and his party spell-bound for an hour. During his remarks, he took occasion to say that himself and the ministers that accompanied him were all citizens of the United States and freemen, and had fought for the liberty which they enjoyed; but that their visit to that place was one of mercy, their object being to do good to the souls of men in the name of Christ. As he drew his remarks to a close, awful shocks of Divine power were felt by the congregation. At length mourners were called for, and scores crowded to the altar. At this moment, the Major undertook to draw off his men and retreat in good order; but some were already gone, others had alighted, turned their horses loose, and were at the altar for prayer. He led off a few of them to the spring; and after a short consultation, none of them seemed inclined to prosecute their purpose any farther, and at once disbanded. Several of the number were converted before the meeting closed, and became members of the Church.

"On the same evening, about the going down of

the sun, a man came up to Mr. Gwin and said to him: 'Are you the man that carries the roll?' 'What roll?' said Mr. Gwin. 'The roll,' said he, 'that people put their names to that want to go to heaven.' Brother Gwin, supposing that he had reference to the class-book, referred him to Brother Walker, who took his name. The wild look and novel manner of the man indicated derangement. He left the camp-ground and fled to the woods with almost the speed of a wild beast. Nothing more was seen of him until the next morning, at which time he returned to the encampment, wet with the dew of the night, in a state of mind which was distressing beyond description; but during the day he was happily and powerfully converted to God, and was found sitting, as it were, at the feet of Jesus, clothed, and in his right mind. He afterward gave the following account of himself: He lived in what was called the American Bottom, was very wicked, and professed to be a deist. A short time before, he dreamed that the day of judgment was coming, and that three men had been sent from the East to warn him of his danger, which had distressed him greatly; and when he saw the three preachers, McKendree, Gwin, and Goddard, pass his house, he recognized them as the same persons whom he had seen in his dream, and he had followed them to the camp-meeting, and they had warned him of his danger sure enough. It was said of this man, that he possessed a large estate, was very influential in his neighborhood, and was ultimately instrumental in doing much good.

"At the close of this meeting, one hundred persons connected themselves with the Church." *

Here we take leave of Mr. McKendree for the present. We shall, however, meet him again, moving in a more responsible sphere, diffusing blessings upon the Church, as one of its chief pastors.

Lewis Hunt was admitted on trial in 1798. We, however, find no mention of his name in the General Minutes until the following year, when it is recorded, in answer to the question, 'Who remain on trial?" In the biographical sketch published of him in the Minutes, we learn that he was appointed to travel on the Salt River Circuit his first year, and that "his labors were greatly blessed."

At the Conference of 1799, he was appointed to the New River Circuit, in Virginia, on which he spent the first part of the year; † and was then sent into the North-western Territory, to take charge of the Miami Circuit, which had been formed by John Kobler. Suffering from pulmonary disease, and in consequence of his immense labors and exposures, he became prostrate, and was unable to fulfill his appointments, when Henry Smith was sent to relieve him.

Somewhat improved in health,‡ he prosecuted his ministerial labors until the spring of 1800, when, with a prostrated constitution, he returned to Kentucky, and was placed on the Hinkstone Circuit

---

* Biographical Sketches, pp. 49, 50, 51, 52.

† Judge Scott.

‡ Methodist Magazine, Vol. IV., p. 271.

by Mr. Burke, who then had charge of the District.*

At the October session of 1800, (the same Conference reported in the General Minutes for 1801,) we find him, in connection with Burke and Wilkerson, on the Hinkstone and Lexington Circuit. Spending a few months at his father's, in Fleming county, his health so improved as to enable him to enter once more on his labors in the ministry. He proceeded to Lexington, and preached during the winter, confining himself chiefly to the town, where he was greatly beloved, and where, under his labors, there was considerable religious interest. In the following March, he was completely prostrated, and, unable longer to continue in the effective work, he returned to his father's house. At the Conference of 1801, he was appointed, with Henry Smith, to the Limestone Circuit, in the bounds of which his father resided. But his work was done. "In apparent possession of an assured peace with God, and a calm and tranquil mind, on the 8th of the following December," † he rested from his labors.

Mr. Hunt was a native of Virginia, and a young man of promising abilities. Judge Scott says: "He was a tall, slender young man, with a depressed cheek. He possessed great zeal, and exerted himself beyond his natural strength. He was a very humble, sociable man, whose labors in the ministry were greatly blessed."

---

*Rev. William Burke, in Western Methodism, p. 56.

† General Minutes M. E. Church, Vol. I., p. 109.

The name of William Marsh also appears on the roll of the Appointments for Kentucky, for this year. His appointment was to the Salt River and Shelby Circuit, and the following year to the Danville, after which his name disappears from the Minutes.

To trace the progress of the revival which commenced under the labors of the two brothers, John and William McGee, in 1799, and to which we have frequently referred, belongs to this period of our history. "Extraordinary seasons of religious interest, denominated revivals of religion, have existed in the American Churches from a very early period of their history. . . . The celebrated Jonathan Edwards, author of the Treatise on the Will, states that his grandfather, who preceded him as pastor of the Church in Northampton, Massachusetts, was favored, during his ministry, with five seasons of this kind, which he called his 'harvests,' occurring at various intervals during a space of forty years. His father, he also says, had four or five similar periods of 'refreshing from on high,' among the people of his charge, and that such had been the case with many others of the early ministers. . . . The early awakenings, mentioned above, seem to have been generally of a calm and silent character, and it rarely happened that two congregations were visited at the same time. . . .

"In the year 1735, a remarkable change took place in this respect. An increased power and wider extent were given to the dispensations of the Spirit; a large tract of country became, this and the following year, the seat of numerous awakenings, which, about this time, took the name of *revivals.* The revival of 1735 commenced at Northampton, Massachusetts, under the preaching of Jonathan Edwards. The preaching of Mr. Edwards, which gave rise to this revival—like all preaching which prepares the way for extensive reformations—was doctrinal in its character. He dwelt, with great force of argument and closeness of application, on the leading doctrines of grace, which had begun to lose their power in the prevailing declension; justification by faith alone, the necessity of the Spirit's influence, and kindred topics."*

"The term 'revival,' by common consent, has been appropriated to signify a work of God, turning the attention of a considerable number in a place to the things of eternity, and bringing many in a short time to the saving knowledge of the truth as it is in Jesus. It is the ordinary effect of the gospel graciously intensified—the conversion of a large number in a short time. The conversion of one sinner gladdens the Church, and makes a new song in heaven. These emotions must be greatly heightened and enhanced by a multiplication of such cases, and these constitute what we call a 'revival.' Then the preacher sees the fruit of his labors, and, in a modified sense, Christ sees the travail of his soul, and is satisfied. For the Church to be without these visitations, is proof of worldliness, de-

---

*Baird's Religion in America, pp. 392, 395, 396.

clension, perilous backsliding. To deprecate and denounce them, as some do, involves a forfeiture of right to be considered a Christian organization.

"These religious excitements are not only the glory and rejoicing of the Church of Christ, but are her stability of life. In the darkest period of history, they have saved her from extinction. In the broadest sense, she cannot prosper without them. The history of the apostles is a history of revivals. On the day of Pentecost, the kingdom of heaven was opened to the Gentile world by a revival. This was not merely an initial fact, but a glorious type—a pattern as to mode, and a warrant to our largest hopes. The Reformation was accompanied and followed by revivals. England, Scotland, Ireland, were visited by these gracious outpourings of the Spirit in the times of the Puritans, in the days of Wesley and Whitefield. Under the ministry of Edwards, Tennent, and others, New England shared in revivals. About the close of the past century, and the beginning of the present, Kentucky and Tennessee were the scene of the most marvelous manifestations known to the Church. Among the leading denominations of the country, and those to whom we are most indebted for a pure, living religion, these events are more frequent and numerous, as years roll on. Philosophy and the history of Christianity unite to assure us that they will multiply and increase, till one general revival shall spread over the globe. What we have seen is but the first-fruits of the coming harvest. The Church should enlarge her desires upon this subject. Incidental conversions, in connection with the ordinary means of grace, are to be desired and expected, but on this plan the Church can never keep pace with the population of the world. She must have her reaping-seasons as well as her time of culture—harvests as well as seed-time. The very progress of the Church will make these ingatherings more and more necessary. Her triumph will awaken opposition, and, to maintain her ground and push her victories, she must have revivals. They are indispensable to her vigor, expansion, and final universality." *

We have previously announced that Mr. McKendree, who had been an active participant in the revivals in Southern Kentucky and Tennessee, was the first preacher to present their character to the people in the central portion of the State. Glorious as had been the displays of Divine power under the labors of the gifted McGees and their pious compeers, in the years of 1799 and 1800, and encouraging as had been the frequent revivals that, in Central Kentucky, had blessed the Church during the same period, it was reserved for the summer and autumn of 1801 to claim far grander achievements in the cause of truth—as these revivals spread into upper Kentucky—than had distinguished them in their introduction.

In 1801, "the quarterly meeting for Hinkstone Circuit was held early in June, at Owens's Meeting-house, on Four-mile Creek, commencing on Friday,

---

* Bishop Pierce, at the dedication of Broadway M. E. Church, South, Louisville, Kentucky, September 15, 1867.

and breaking up on Monday morning. At this meeting was the first appearance of that astonishing revival to which we have alluded. Several professed to get religion, and many were under deep conviction for sin, and the meeting continued from Sunday morning till Monday morning, with but little intermission. From thence Brother Lakin and myself proceeded in company, on Monday morning, to a Presbyterian sacrament at Salem Meeting-house, in the vicinity of Col. John Martin's. The Rev. Mr. Lyle was pastor of that Church. There had been during the occasion more than ordinary attention and seriousness manifested. I arrived on the ground before the first sermon was concluded, and during the interval they insisted on my preaching the next sermon; and, notwithstanding I was much fatigued from the labors of the quarterly meeting, I at length consented, and commenced about 2 o'clock P.M. I took for my text, 'To you is the word of this salvation sent;' and before I concluded there was a great trembling among the dry bones. Great numbers fell to the ground and cried for mercy, old and young. Brother Lakin followed with one of his then powerful exhortations, and the work increased. The Presbyterian ministers stood astonished, not knowing what to make of such a tumult. Brother Lakin and myself proceeded to exhort and pray with them. Some obtained peace with God before the meeting broke up. This was the first appearance of the revival in the Presbyterian Church. From these two meetings the heavenly flame spread in every direction. Preachers and people, when they assembled for meeting, always expected the Lord to meet with them. Our next quarterly meeting was for Lexington Circuit, at Jesse Griffith's, Scott county. On Saturday we had some indications of a good work. On Saturday night we had preaching in different parts of the neighborhood, which, at that time, was the custom; so that every local preacher and exhorter was employed in the work. Success attended the meetings, and on Sunday morning they came in companies, singing and shouting on the road. Love-feast was opened on Sunday morning, at 8 o'clock, and such was the power and presence of God, that the doors were thrown open, and the work became general, and continued till Monday afternoon, during which time numbers experienced justification by faith in the name of Jesus Christ. The work spread now into the several circuits. Salt River and Shelby were visited, and Danville shared in the blessing; also the Presbyterian Church caught the fire. Congregations were universally wakened up: McNamer's congregation, on Cabin Creek; Barton Stone's, at Cane Ridge; Reynolds's, near Ruddell's Station and in Paris; the Rev. Mr. Lyle, at Salem; Mr. Rankin, Walnut Hills; Mr. Blythe, at Lexington and Woodford; and the Rev. Mr. Walsh, at Cane Run; likewise in Madison county, under the ministry of the Rev. Mr. Houston. The work extended to Ohio at Lower Springfield, Hamilton county; the Rev. Mr. Thompson's congregation and Eagle Creek; the Rev. Mr. Dunlavey's congregation, Adams county. The Methodist local preachers and exhorters, and the members generally, united with them in carrying on the work, for they were at home wherever God was pleased to manifest his power; and having had some experience in such a school, were able to teach others. The Presbyterian ministers saw the advantage of such auxiliaries, and were pressing in their invitations, both for the traveling and local preachers, to attend their sacraments through the months of July and August. The Rev. Barton Stone was pastor of the Church at Cane Ridge. I had been formerly acquainted with him when he traveled as a missionary in the Holston and Cumberland country, previous to his settling at Cane Ridge; and we agreed to have a united sacrament of the Presbyterians and Methodists at the Cane Ridge Meeting-house, in August. The meeting was published, throughout the length and breadth of the country, to commence on Friday. On the first day, I arrived in the neighborhood; but it was a rainy day, and I did not attend on the ground. On Saturday morning I attended. On Friday and Friday night they held meeting in the meeting-house; and such was the power and presence of God on Friday night, that the meeting continued all night; and next morning, Saturday, they repaired to a stand erected in the woods—the work still going on in the house—which continued there till Wednesday, without intermission. On Saturday the congregation was very numerous. The Presbyterians continued to occupy the stand during Saturday and Saturday night, whenever they could get a chance to be heard, but never invited any Methodist preacher to preach. On Sunday morning Mr. Stone, with some of the Elders of the Session, waited upon me, to have a conference on the subject of the approaching sacrament, which was to be administered in the afternoon. The object in calling on me was, that I should make from the stand a public declaration how the Methodists held certain doctrines, etc. I told them we preached every day, and that our doctrines were published to the world through the press. Come and hear, go and read; and if that was the condition on which we were to unite in the sacrament, 'Every man to his tent, O Israel!' for I should require of him to make a public declaration of their belief in certain doctrines. He then replied that we had better drop the subject; that he was perfectly satisfied, but that some of his Elders were not. I observed that they might do as they thought best; but the subject got out among the Methodists, and a number did not partake of the sacrament, as none of our preachers were invited to assist in administering.

"There is a mistaken opinion with regard to this meeting. Some writers of late represent it as having been a camp-meeting. It is true, there were a number of wagons and carriages, which remained on the ground night and day; but not a single tent was to be found, neither was any such thing as camp-meetings heard of at that time. Preaching in the woods was a common thing at popular meetings, as meeting-houses in the West were not sufficient to hold the large number of people that attended on such occasions. This was the case at Cane Ridge.

"On Sunday morning, when I came on the ground, I was met by my friends, to know if I was going to preach for them on that day. I told them I had not been invited; if I was, I should certainly do so. The morning passed off, but no invitation. Between ten and eleven, I found a convenient place on the body of a fallen tree, about fifteen feet from the ground, where I fixed my stand in the open sun, with an umbrella affixed to a long pole, and held over my head by Brother Hugh Barnes. I commenced reading a hymn with an audible voice, and by the time we concluded singing and praying, we had around us, standing on their feet, by fair calculation, ten thousand people. I gave out my text in the following words: 'For we shall all stand before the judgment-seat of Christ;' and before I concluded, my voice was not to be heard for the groans of the distressed and the shouts of triumph. Hundreds fell prostrate to the ground, and the work continued on that spot till Wednesday afternoon. It was estimated by some that not less than five hundred were at one time lying on the ground in the deepest agonies of distress, and every few minutes rising in shouts of triumph. Toward the evening I pitched the only tent on the ground. Having been accustomed to travel the wilderness, I soon had a tent constructed out of poles and pawpaw bushes. Here I remained Sunday and Sunday night, and Monday night; and during that time there was not a single moment's cessation, but the work went on, and old and young, men, women, and children, were converted to God. It was estimated that on Sunday and Sunday night there were twenty thousand people on the ground. They had come from far and near, from all parts of Kentucky; some from Tennessee, and from north of the Ohio River; so that tidings of Cane Ridge Meeting was carried to almost every corner of the country, and the holy fire spread in all directions." *

We also copy the following account of these meetings from the pen of the Rev. Thomas S. Hinde, to whom we are largely indebted for much in reference to early Methodism in the West:

"The Rev. William McKendree, (now Bishop,) Presiding Elder of the District, was in the lower part of the State about the commencement of the revival, and became much engaged in it. In the latter part of 1800, or early in 1801, (if my recollection serves me,) he came up to the center of the settlement of the State, and in many places was the first to bear the tidings of these singular meetings, which had so recently commenced, and had so greatly attracted the attention of multitudes. I shall never forget the looks of the people who had assembled in a congregation composed mostly of Methodists and Presbyterians, and their adherents, when the old gentleman, after the conclusion of a very pathetic sermon, having been much animated, in the work, gave an interesting statement of the progress of it, from what he had seen, and of the meetings before described. Whilst he spoke, the very sensations of his soul glowed in his counte-

* Burke's Autobiography, in Finley's Sketches, pp. 74-79.

nance: his description of them was such as would be vain for me to attempt. He described them in their native simplicity: he told of the happy conversion of hundreds; how the people continued in their exercises of singing, praying, and preaching on the ground, surrounded by wagons and tents, for days and nights together; that many were so affected that they fell to the ground like men slain in battle. The piercing cries of the penitents, and rapture of the healed, appeared to be brought to our view; and, what was equally encouraging to the faithful, that the work, instead of declining, was progressing to the interior. After this description given by him, it was unnecessary to exhort the faithful to look for the like among themselves. Their hearts had already begun to beat in unison with his, whilst sinners were generally melted into tears. As for my own feelings, though a stranger to religion at that time, they will never be forgotten. I felt, and I wept.

"These meetings began, as the season permitted, to make their gradual approach toward the center of the State. It was truly wonderful to see what an effect their approach made upon the minds of the people. Here in the wilderness were thousands, and tens of thousands, of almost every nation; here were thousands hungry for the bread of life, and thousands thirsting for the waters of salvation. A general move was visible in the congregations previously to the arrival of these meetings. The devout Christians appeared to be filled with hope. Their hearts were greatly enlarged to pray for the prosperity of Zion. The formalists were troubled with very uneasy sensations; backsliders became terrified; the wicked in general were either greatly alarmed or struck with solemn awe; whilst curiosity was general, and raised to the highest degree, to see into these strange things. Indeed, such was the commotion, that every circle of the community appeared to have their whole attention arrested. Many were the conjectures respecting these meetings. Things, however, did not continue long to keep the attention of the people in suspense. The camp-meetings began to approach nearer and nearer to the center; when one meeting after another was soon appointed in succession, and the number that attended them is almost incredible to tell. When collected on the ground, and whilst the meetings continued, such crowds would be passing and repassing, that the roads, paths, and woods, appeared to be literally strewn with people! Whole settlements and neighborhoods would appear to be vacated; and such was the draught from them, that it was only here and there that a solitary house would contain an aged housekeeper—young and old generally pressing through every difficulty to see the camp-meeting. The Presbyterians and Methodists now united in them; hence it was that they took the name of General Camp-meetings. This union continued until circumstances hereafter mentioned produced a separation. On the 30th January, 1801, one writes, giving an account of the work as it first appeared: 'The work is still increasing in Cumberland. It has overspread the whole country.

It is in Nashville, Barren, Muddy, Gasper, Red Banks, Knoxville, etc. J. M. C—— has been there two months: he says it exceeds any thing he ever saw or heard of. Children and all seem to be engaged; but children are the most active in the work. When they speak, it appears that the Lord sends his Spirit to accompany it with power to the hearts of sinners. They all seem to be exercised in an extraordinary way—lie as though they were dead for some time, without pulse or breath; some a longer, some a shorter time. Some rise with joy triumphant, others crying for mercy. As soon as they obtain comfort, they cry to sinners, exhorting them to come to the Lord.'

"These General Camp-meetings not only came up to this description, but far exceeded it. Early this spring a work broke out in Madison county. On the 22d day of May, this year, a camp-meeting was held on Cabin Creek. The next General Camp-meeting was held at Concord, in Bourbon county, the last Monday in May, or beginning of June, and continued five days and four nights. The next General Meeting was at Point Pleasant, Kentucky. The next, at Indian Creek, Harrison county, began 24th July, and continued about five days and nights. The Great General Camp-meeting, held at Cane Ridge, seven miles from Paris, Bourbon county, began on the 6th day of August, and continued a week. This meeting will be particularly noticed hereafter. Independent of these General Meetings, the Methodists had many great and glorious meetings unconnected with their Presbyterian brethren.

Indeed, these meetings in each denomination were soon spread over the country, and this year extended over the Ohio River, into the North-west Territory, now State of Ohio.

"Having been raised in this State, the writer, then a youth, has many circumstances fresh upon his mind with regard to this great work; but in aid of this narrative he is disposed to take along whatever he finds that may be correctly given by others. 'At first appearance,' says one, 'these meetings exhibited nothing to the spectator, unacquainted with them, but a scene of confusion, such as scarce could be put into human language. They were generally opened with a sermon, at the close of which there would be an universal outcry; some bursting forth into loud ejaculations of prayer, or thanksgiving for the truth; others breaking out in emphatical sentences of exhortation; others flying to their careless friends, with tears of compassion, beseeching them to turn to the Lord; some struck with terror, and hastening through the crowd to make their escape, or pulling away their relations; others trembling, weeping, crying out for the Lord Jesus to have mercy on them; fainting and swooning away, till every appearance of life was gone, and the extremities of the body assumed the coldness of death; others surrounding them with melodious songs, or fervent prayers for their happy conversion; others, collecting into circles round this variegated scene, contending with arguments for and against the work. This scene frequently continued, without intermission, for days and nights together.' At these meetings many circumstances transpired well worth relating, and very interesting, but it would overleap our limits to narrate them — one at this time must suffice: 'At Indian Creek, a boy, from appearance about twelve years of age, retired from the stand in time of preaching, under very extraordinary impressions, and, having mounted a log at some distance, and raising his voice in a very affecting manner, he attracted the main body of the people in a very few minutes. With tears streaming from his eyes, he cried aloud to the wicked, warning them of their danger, denouncing their certain doom, if they persisted in their sins; expressing his love to their souls, and desire that they would turn to the Lord and be saved. He was held up by two men, and spoke for about an hour, with that convincing eloquence that could be inspired only from above. When his strength seemed quite exhausted, and language failed to describe the feelings of his soul, he raised his hand, and, dropping his handkerchief, wet with sweat from his little face, cried out: "Thus, O sinner! shall you drop into hell, unless you forsake your sins and turn to the Lord." At that moment, some fell like those who are shot in battle, and the work spread in a manner which human language cannot describe.'

"The numbers attending the camp-meetings at this early period, (1801,) on daily visits, whilst the meetings continued, and those attending them in their encampments, were immense. The numbers varied, according to the population of the settlements where the meetings were held, and other circumstances, from three to twenty thousand souls! At one of these meetings (Cabin Creek) the scene was awful beyond description; 'few, if any, escaped without being affected. Such as tried to run from it were frequently struck on the way, or impelled by some alarming signal to return. No circumstance at this meeting appeared more striking than the great numbers that fell on the third night; and to prevent their being trodden under foot by the multitude, they were collected together, and laid out in order, on two squares of the meeting-house, till a considerable part of the floor was covered. But the great meeting at Cane Ridge exceeded all. The number that fell at this meeting was reckoned at about three thousand, among whom were several Presbyterian ministers, who, according to their own confession, had hitherto possessed only a speculative knowledge of religion. Here the formal professor, the deist, and the intemperate, met in one common lot, and confessed with equal candor that they were destitute of the true knowledge of God, and strangers to the religion of Jesus Christ.' One of the most zealous and active Presbyterian ministers estimated the number collected on the ground at twenty thousand souls! At this meeting, as well as at all others, wherever the work broke out, the Methodists appeared to be more active and more in their element than any other people. Indeed, when it first appeared in most of the other congregations, other ministers were so alarmed, not knowing what to make of it, that they would have deserted it, and their meetings too, had they not been encouraged by the Methodists. But they soon joined, and moved forward cordially in the work. Having been thus inured and prepared, this great meeting brought on a general engagement. It was necessary that such a concourse should be scattered over a considerable extent of ground. Of course there were several congregations formed, in different parts of the encampment, for preaching and other religious exercises. In consequence of so great a collection of people, it frequently happened that several preachers would be speaking at once, to congregations as before described, generally embracing some of each denomination. Nor were they at a loss for pulpits: stumps, logs, or lops of trees served as temporary stands from which to dispense the word of life. At night, the whole scene was awfully sublime. The ranges of tents, the fires, reflecting light amidst the branches of the towering trees; the candles and lamps illuminating the encampment; hundreds moving to and fro, with lights or torches, like Gideon's army; the preaching, praying, singing, and shouting—all heard at once, rushing from different parts of the ground, like the sound of many waters, was enough to swallow up all the powers of contemplation. Sinners falling, and shrieks and cries for mercy, awakened in the mind a lively apprehension of that scene when the awful sound will be heard, 'Arise, ye dead, and come to judgment!' "*

The Rev. Learner Blackman, in his manuscript

---

*Methodist Magazine, Vol. II., pp. 221, 222, 223, 224, 272, 273.

in our possession, says: "In the time of the great revival in Cumberland, so great was the work, and so novel the exercises of many who were the subjects of the work, that it attracted the attention of the people of all ranks in society, to come out to meeting and see for themselves. They flocked together by scores, by hundreds, and by thousands, to sacramental and other meetings. Many who came out to speculate, or to gratify curiosity, stood appalled, as if thunder-struck, when they saw the exercises, and heard the groans and cries of the distressed, which were enough to rend the heavens and pierce the hardest heart. Such was the solemnity of the work, that the preachers for some time forbade singing as being too light an exercise, when there were so many solemn appearances."

In these extraordinary meetings, while the various Christian denominations bore a part, harmonizing their views, and uniting in the bonds of the gospel, preaching "repentance toward God, and faith toward our Lord Jesus Christ," it cannot be denied that by the ministry and membership of the Methodist Episcopal Church this work was promoted more than by any other instrumentality. While ministers of other Communions often stood appalled, and sometimes abandoned the field, McKendree, Burke, Northcutt, and their associates, stood firmly at their posts, laboring in the altars, and under God leading the Church to the loftier altitudes of Christianity.

We would not, however, deny to our brethren of other denominations their proper meed of praise.

Many of the ministers of the Presbyterian Church, among whom we may mention John Lyle, James McGready, Robert Marshall, and Barton W. Stone, stood side by side with our fathers in this great work.

Amongst the laity in our Church, the energy and piety of many of the members shone conspicuously, prominent among whom was Ilai Nunn, the father of William Nunn, now residing at Millersburg, Kentucky, and the grandfather of the Rev. John P. Durbin, D.D. Mr. Nunn was among the early emigrants to Kentucky, having settled in the District about 1783. "His first settlement was on the bank of a small creek, known as Clear Creek, near Lexington. Remaining there for two years, he removed; he purchased a tract of land near Millersburg, which he improved, and which was widely known as 'Nunn's Farm,' and on which he established a camp-ground, which is still remembered by all the old citizens of Bourbon county. His house, one of the best in the neighborhood, was the home of Methodist preachers, as well as those of other denominations who chose to call on him—and for many years the only preaching-place in the neighborhood. It was in the vicinity of his house that the Cane Ridge Meeting was held, in 1801, and at it occurred the most remarkable revival-meeting ever held on this continent. At this meeting he was an active lay-member."* He lived many years to bless the Church, and then entered upon "the rest that remaineth to the people of God."

* Letter to the author from the Rev. H. A. M. Henderson.

Another representative amongst the laity of the Church at this period was Major John Martin. "He was born in 1748, in Albemarle county, Virginia—was a captain, and was promoted to major at the siege of Yorktown; stayed in Virginia during the Revolutionary war, and in 1784 moved to Kentucky. He was the first sheriff in Clarke county, and was afterward for many years one of the judges of the Court of Quarter Sessions, in Clarke county." Remarkable for the influence he exerted, it was unfortunate that he had imbibed sentiments of infidelity, and regarded the Bible as a forgery and religion as a cheat.

The celebrated Dr. Hinde moved into the neighborhood in which Major Martin resided—the first and only religious family in all that community. Between Dr. Hinde and Major Martin there grew up an intimacy, in which either the religion of the one or the infidelity of the other must yield. "Upon one occasion, in 1798, during a conversation with Mrs. Hinde, in the presence of the Doctor, who had for many years been his boon companion, the good lady finally silenced his rude jests by a pointed, yet kind remark, which sped like an arrow of conviction to his heart; and there quivering, it remained, until withdrawn by the hand of the Saviour. 'T was in vain to attempt a renewal of the conversation—his confused thoughts could find no words in which to express themselves. Thus he mounted his horse, and rode briskly onward to his home, for a warning voice followed him, and as the shadows of the night fell thick around him, he was seized with a trembling and a fear as he entered the darker woods, and the very echo of his horse's hoofs seemed to repeat the words of Mrs. Hinde. The voice of conscience knocked so loudly at his heart, that he threw himself from his horse, and fell upon his knees, praying earnestly to that God whom he had hitherto refused to acknowledge. He reached his home late at night, but not being able to sleep, he wrestled, like Jacob, until the light of heaven shone all around him, and that sweet, still voice which, once heard, is never forgotten, said, in accents of mercy, 'Go, and sin no more.' There was a complete change—the whole man became a loving disciple of Jesus Christ. He never once took a backward step, and that perseverance in the cause of religion was the watch-word of his after life.

"One of the first-fruits of his conversion was to close his eyes to the flattering vision of a rich harvest of gold, which he expected from a splendid orchard of peaches, destined to be converted into brandy—he turned a drove of hogs into the orchard, and thus satisfied his awakened conscience. He was a man highly respected, loved for his amiable qualities, and admired even for his eccentricities. But up to this period he had lived without God in the world, his companionable qualities rendering him the more dangerous to a large circle of friends and acquaintances. Happy for him that just at this crisis an angel troubled the fountains of his being, and in the outflow of his after life there were cleansing and health.

"This good man did not hide his light under a bushel, but fed it into a flame that burned higher and brighter until the close of his life. His home became a house of prayer, and his very eccentricities, turned into the proper channel, were productive of good.

"Camp-meetings, fifty years ago, afforded many precious privileges throughout our sparsely settled State. These he loved to attend, and he took his whole family to the tented ground. Once upon a time, having brought home a wagonful of professedly converted negroes, and finding their lives by no means a practical comment upon the Scriptures which he daily read for their instruction, he watched the opportunity for sending them all to another camp-meeting to be converted over again.

"How beautiful the simplicity of this good man! How scrupulously exact in all the externals of religion! How diligent in seeking every means of grace, and yet not by these expecting to be saved! No, no! he sought to be approved of God, and was the recipient of his choicest gifts. His was an imperial nature — the world knew it, and acknowledged him the child of God." *

He lived to a good old age, blessing the Church by his great liberality, his pious exhortations, and godly walk. In 1837, after a long life of usefulness, "he bid adieu to this world, in full view of his heavenly inheritance."

---

* Letter to the author from Mrs. Julia A. Tevis, of Shelbyville, Kentucky.

We have already referred to Dr. Thomas Hinde. He "was born in Oxfordshire, England, in July, 1737. He studied regularly both branches of his profession—surgery and medicine—in London, under the direction of the celebrated Dr. Thomas Brookes, who superintended St. Thomas's Hospital. At the age of twenty, Dr. Brookes, from personal friendship to his pupil, and from an assurance that his indefatigable industry had qualified him for the examination, presented him before the Doctors' Commons, (a board of physicians and surgeons,) and would have him to pass an examination at an earlier period of life by one year than was usual on such occasions. He soon after obtained for him a commission as surgeon's mate on board the British navy. Dr. Hinde having entered the service of the government of his native country, he was ordered into foreign service, and the fleet to which he was attached arrived at New York on the 14th of June, 1757. He was with the squadron at Louisburg the same year, and 1757–58, wintered at Halifax, Nova Scotia. In 1758, he was at the reduction of Louisburg, under Amherst; in 1759, he was at the reduction of Quebec, under that distinguished general, Wolfe: he belonged to the vessel which Wolfe left to go on shore, to contend with Montcalm for the palm of victory on the plains of Abraham. Soon after the fall of Quebec, he returned to England. He was at the reduction of Bellisle, and afterward was promoted to surgeon. After peace was concluded with France in 1763, having formed an intimate acquaintance with a young Virginian who was his fellow-student under Dr. Brookes, he was induced through his young friend, who had returned home, and Dr. Brookes, to accept the invitation of an aged practicing physician in Essex county, Virginia, to assist him in practice, and about 1765, settled himself near a place called Hobb's Hole, in Essex county, Virginia. He afterward removed to King and Queen county, and settled at a place called Newtown, which he purchased, and commenced the practice of surgery and medicine with great success.

"In 1767, September 24, Dr. Hinde married Mary T. Hubbard, daughter of his countryman, Mr. Benjamin Hubbard, an English merchant; and some time after, disposing of his possessions at Newtown, removed to Hanover county, and settled in the neighborhood of that distinguished orator, statesman, and patriot, Patrick Henry, and became his family physician.

"In 1788 or 1789, the Methodists began to preach in the neighborhood. An elderly gentleman, a High-churchman, who resided four or five miles from the Doctor's, possessed a very fine cherry-orchard. It was usual with the old gentleman to give annually to the youth of both sexes a cherry-feast. Indeed, feasting and amusements constituted the grand round of employment with the youth of that day. He never failed, on all such occasions, to have some of the Doctor's family to attend. His eldest daughter had married and moved away; his second was then just grown up, and about this time she attended. Old Mr. David Richardson (the High-churchman) was a great opposer of the Methodists: two of his sons had attended their meeting, contrary to his express orders, and both of them had returned under serious awakenings. They were young and inexperienced, and did not know what to do or where to go, but they dreaded their father's wrath: however, they returned home, and the old man having learned that they had attended one of those meetings, seized the oldest by the collar, and while he was dealing out his blows with his staff in a most unmerciful manner, his son professed to get converted, and praised the Lord. The father soon after was seized with remorse of conscience, and in order to make some atonement for what he had done, caused his large barn to be removed to a beautiful grove, near an excellent spring of water, and fitted it up for a Methodist chapel. And although this old gentleman for a long time continued to be an opposer to vital piety, yet at his death, I am informed, he sought the Lord and found mercy. His eldest son at that early day was so filled with love and zeal in the good cause of the blessed Redeemer, (alas! since backslid,) that he turned upon the Doctor's daughter. He admonished her of the error of her ways, her sinful state by nature, of the necessity of a change of heart, and of the awful consequences of dying unprepared to meet God. It made a deep, and ultimately a lasting, impression upon her mind; and through the day, while she was reflecting on the subject, very serious convictions reached her heart. In the evening, she threw herself upon the bed, and in great agony began to pray to the Lord to have mercy upon her soul. But O how gloomy was her situation! She began not only to reflect upon her own case, but saw the situation in which her parents were also. She was induced afterward to attend a meeting, but it was a Methodist meeting! and now, how could she meet her parents? Her father a confirmed deist, her mother cheerful and lively, she herself brought up in the gayest circle of society—she could find no person with whom she could take counsel, the whole settlement being composed of a gay and fashionable people. The tempter pleaded hard with her, and argued, that if she did now seek the Lord, and would go to hear these people, that although she had the most tender and affectionate parents, they would disown her, and turn her out-of-doors; that she would bring a reproach upon them, and be forsaken by her companions. But however desperate her case might be made to appear, her resolution was fixed, and she was determined to abide the consequences.

"The deep awakenings of the daughter made a deep impression upon her mother's mind. The Doctor at length, through some channel, learning the result of the visit, and seeing the visible change in his daughter's appearance, all of a sudden on this occasion was at once roused to the highest pitch of desperation. The threatened storm begins now to gather round this new subject of awakening grace. He calls for a servant, directs him to prepare a horse and chaise to take his daughter to her aunt's, (Mrs. Harrison,) a widow then living in Caroline county, forty miles distant; and with the most vehement protestations, that unless his daughter relinquished her purpose, never to see his face again. How feeble are the efforts of man without grace! When Heaven designs to do the work, what is a human being's puny arm to resist, or to be raised to oppose it? How providential was this singular event: her aunt, unknown to the Doctor, had gone to hear these strange people, had embraced religion and joined society, and opened her house for preaching. He could not have sent her to a more convenient and suitable place. But to the Doctor's great annoyance, his wife became more and more sensibly affected; her awakenings were deep, and she desired to go and hear the Methodists for herself. In this the old Doctor opposed her. A quarterly meeting was to be held at Richardson's Chapel, (called the Barn,) to which she desired to go. Although on all occasions the Doctor perhaps was not excelled as a husband or parent for tenderness and affection for his family—indeed, he carried his indulgence to an extreme—on this occasion it was strange, it was really astonishing, to see how his feelings were wrought upon; they were aroused beyond control. He most positively denied his wife the privilege of going to this meeting: he became persuaded in his own mind that these people had set those persons thus affected crazy, and thus concluded that his wife and daughter were really deranged, and that without a proper remedy being immediately applied, the consequences would become very serious."*

---

*Methodist Magazine, Vol. X., pp. 260, 261, 263, 309, 310.

Opposed to Christianity, he availed himself of every opportunity to arrest the tide of religious emotion, that had swelled the hearts of his wife and daughter, until at length his madness culminated in the application of the blister, to which we referred in our sketch of Mrs. Hinde. We are indebted for the following sketch to Bishop Kavanaugh:

"After the blister-plaster was put on, she and her daughter went on to the meeting again. The next day, the Doctor asked how her blister was coming on. 'Did the plaster draw well?' She said, 'I know nothing about the plaster.' He exclaimed, 'What! did you not take it off?' She answered, 'No.' Of course he knew that it was in a bad condition. He stood astounded, until, she told me, he looked as if he were petrified, and doubted if he had the use of himself. She said she arose from her seat and purposely brushed by him, when he staggered and caught, showing the want of self-control, from the intensity of his feelings; for though he had thus treated his wife, he loved her with a warm devotion. Reflecting on this transaction, conviction seized on his mind, and troubled him for his sins. He dressed the blister as best he could, and taking a seat by his wife, he said, 'I expect if you were to join these people you would feel better.' With animation she exclaimed, 'Thank you, blister-plaster! thank you, blister-plaster!' believing that her blister had accomplished that much for her.

"She and her daughter now went to Church much elated. They thought their victory so grand, they invited the preacher home with them. This was rather too fast for the Doctor; but, as a matter of civility, he politely entertained the preacher, and asked him to have prayers at night. The preacher prayed with such mighty power, that one or two of the girls fell prostrate on the floor, and looked as though they were dead. The Doctor quietly crawled on his hands and knees to them, and felt their pulse, said he was satisfied that they could not die with that pulse, and so crawled back to his chair again.

"The meeting went on, and the Doctor would make it convenient, in visiting his patients, to go by the meeting and hear the sermon—would sit at the door and hear as much of the class-meeting as he could. He was very serious, and soon gave himself to prayer, and was converted to God. His particular exercises of mind at the time of his conversion, I do not remember to have heard detailed. This I regret. In detailing the circumstances that brought him to God, and the knowledge of his salvation, he often adverted to the blister-plaster. I once heard him say, I think it was in a love-feast, 'I put a blister-plaster on my wife to bring her to her senses, and lo and behold, it brought me to my senses!' On one occasion, going to love-feast, his wife remarked to him, 'Doctor, if you should have occasion to speak this morning, you need not say any thing about the blister-plaster, for everybody knows that.' I suppose he thought he would not, until he began to speak, and when he came to the part that brought in the plaster, he paused a moment, and looking over to his wife, said, 'Honey, I can't get along without that blister-plaster.' He then gave an account of it, and passed on.

"Few, I suppose, ever took more pleasure in the habit of prayer than did Dr. Hinde, or practiced devotions more frequently. On the place which he cultivated in Kentucky you might often see little houses built of sticks of wood, and covered, most usually, with bark, with a door for entrance. His grandchildren, (myself among the number,) who were accustomed to joyous gambols over his grounds, were rather perplexed as to the use of these singular structures. At length the old Doctor was overheard at his private prayers in one of these houses. After that we all called them 'Grandpa's prayer-houses.' He aimed to conceal his person, but did not pray very silently—he could often be heard a considerable distance. On one occasion, he went into what we termed there a 'sink-hole,' to pray. This was near the road. He became very much engaged, struggling for the blessing of God upon him. One of his neighbors, by the name of Lion, was passing by, and hearing the voice of prayer, but not seeing from whence it came, looked about to see if he could find its source. It seemed to him to be in the direction of the sink-hole. He approached it softly, and looking down into it, he saw the Doctor on his knees, who, just at that time, received his blessing, and, in a very earnest manner, gave glory to God, and shouted hosannas to his name. Lion passed on, awe-struck with the scene that came under his notice, having, as he told me himself, this train of reflections: 'Well, there was a man who could not be a hypocrite: he was alone and concealed, engaged in private prayer with God for a blessing on his soul. He wrestled with God, and prevailed. Without a consciousness that any eye was upon him, but that of God, he was happy under his blessing—a proof this, that Christianity is founded in the truth, and has a claim on every man.' His reflections fastened conviction on his soul, and he never rested until he too sought the God of all grace, until he realized peace with God through our Lord Jesus Christ.

"In his family devotions, the Doctor was very fervid and full of feeling. He would often pause in reading a chapter, with an expression of admiration, a word of exposition or application, sometimes exclaiming, 'This is a blessed chapter.'

"In his later days, he lived with his daughter, Mrs. Mary McKinney, of Newport, Kentucky, who had a little son, to whom he was greatly attached. He taught him, at the conclusion of prayer in the family, to say 'Amen.' The sound of the little boy's voice on that word would thrill him with peculiar pleasure. On rising from his knees, he would cry out, 'Where is he?' would run to him, and embrace and caress him very fondly.

"At his own table, he would require his grandchildren to come around the table, whether they could get seats or not, and hold their hands over the table until he would ask a blessing, when every little voice would say, 'Amen.' This afforded him a high sense of pleasure.

"His piety was not morose—any thing but a sour

godliness. It was a religion of love, joy, and peace. His reverence and affection for ministers of the gospel were very great. On their arrival at his house, he would run out to meet them, saying, 'Come in, thou blessed of the Lord, come in!' and he would embrace them in his arms. He esteemed them very highly for their work's sake.

"As might well be supposed, he had a high appreciation of class-meetings. Where he was well acquainted, and a preacher who was less acquainted might be leading the class, he would sometimes get before the preacher, and when he would come to a good case, he would say, 'Here, brother, here is an humble soul, whom God blesses.' Again: 'Here is a prayerful soul, and zealous for the Lord.' But when he had not so much confidence, he would merely announce his name, and after the leader had finished talking to him, he would stoop down and say to him, 'You must pray more.' On one of these occasions, he was conducting a preacher round the class, and came to his wife, and said, in an animated tone of voice, 'Here is my wife, my sister, and my mother,' alluding to the fact that his wife had been the instrument of his conversion, and was, therefore, his mother. The preacher paused, reflected a while, and then proceeded.

"A prominent trait in the Doctor's character was a carelessness of worldly goods. This was carried, perhaps, farther than might be commended. He had very little appreciation of them. I do not know that he ever called upon any persons for money they owed him; and if any one paid him money, it was likely that he would throw it into the lap of the first female member he passed in reaching home, and pass on. It was understood that he gave it to them. He had a military claim, for services rendered in the British Army, for four thousand acres of land. I think it was Patrick Henry who asked him why he did not locate it. He offered Mr. Henry one-half of the claim, if he would attend to that. It was accepted, and the claim was located on a splendid tract of land, lying between Lexington and Winchester, in Clarke county, about twelve miles from the former, and six miles from the latter place. For very trifling sums, he disposed of a large portion of his remaining two thousand acres. I suppose that a good deal of this was done before he removed to it; for some one asked him why he sold such valuable land for so small an amount, and he replied, 'I thought it was in the moon, and never expected to see it.'

"After giving up the practice of medicine, at the solicitation of his daughter, (then Mrs. Mary Taylor, but already alluded to as Mrs. Mary McKinney, which name she took by marrying Col. McKinney, of Newport,) the old Doctor and his wife lived with her until each one of them died. During this period, he gave himself up to reading, meditation, and prayer, and appeared utterly dead to all worldly cares and interests.

"The subject of religion seemed always present to his mind. In illustration of this, several characteristic anecdotes of him are told.

"He was one day standing on the bank of the

Ohio River, when a salt-boat came floating by, and a man on the boat hailed him, and asked, 'How is salt selling?' The Doctor replied, 'I know nothing about salt; I know that grace is free.'

"At another time, he was taking a morning walk, and met Gen. James Taylor, a relative by marriage, who said, 'Good-morning, Doctor; where are you going?' 'I am going to heaven; where are you going, General?' The General, at that time, had some doubts whether his road led to the same country, and made no reply; but it is hoped he found the way to everlasting life before he left the world.

"One of his grandsons, Wm. W. Southgate, was running for Congress, and the race was a close one. Some of the family urged the old Doctor to help out his relative with a vote, explaining the matter to him to his satisfaction, and he promised to go and vote. So he started off to the court-house. His memory was very frail at this time, and the court-house was the place at which he was accustomed to worship. He walked on slowly, humming a tune, and got quite in the spirit of devotion by the time he reached the court-house. He walked in, and the judges of the election, seeing so aged a man coming to the polls, cried out, 'Clear the way, gentlemen, and let Dr. Hinde vote. Whom do you vote for, Doctor?' The election had gone out of his mind entirely. He looked up with an air of surprise, and said, 'Whom do I vote for? Why, for the Lord Jesus Christ, for ever!' The judges said, 'That is the best vote cast here to-day, but we do not know that he is a candidate for the position now in question.' Meanwhile one of his grandsons said to him, 'Grandpa, you have not come to meeting, but to the election.' 'O yes,' he said, 'I understand it now.' He then voted as he had purposed. He returned home, full of holy thoughts and mellow feelings, and, it is said, some one asked him where he had been. He said, 'I have been to meeting. We had a glorious time.'

"Particularly in relation to recent events, his memory was very treacherous. I was once in his presence, in the second year of my itinerancy, when he looked at me with an inquiring look, and said, 'Brother Kavanaugh, where did you come from? Did you come from Virginia?' I told him, 'No; I am a native Kentuckian, but my ancestors were all from Virginia. My grandfather, Dr. Thomas Hinde, was an early immigrant to Kentucky, and settled in Clarke county.'* 'What,' said he, 'Hannah's son?' 'Yes, sir.' He rose from his chair, and, seizing me round the neck, exclaimed, 'Whom the Lord calls, he qualifies. Be faithful to your calling.' And yet, in this same interview, he told me when he was examined on his studies as a student of medicine, the questions that were asked him, and the answers he gave. In allusion to this failure of memory in his advanced age, he was once heard to say, 'I have forgotten my dear friends and my children; but, glory to God, I have never forgotten my Saviour.'

"Of the last days and dying exercises of my grandfather, I have never been particularly in-

---

* Dr. Hinde settled in Kentucky in 1797.

formed. The only item that I now distinctly remember being referred to was his desire that his wife, with whom he had spent so happy a life, should die with him. And one of the last things he did was to feel her pulse, when he said, 'Honey, you cannot go.' It is strange to myself that I am not better informed as to his dying exercises; but I have no anxiety as to the death of a man who, while living, rejoiced evermore, prayed without ceasing, and in all things gave thanks. His end must be peace. He died at the age of ninety-two years, and passed away to the country where there is no more death."

In the accounts we have given of the extraordinary revivals noted in this chapter, the reader has not failed to observe the exercises, such as jerks and dances, which occasionally occurred. We are not prepared to account for them. Various reasons have been assigned for those strange accompaniments by different writers, none of which are entirely satisfactory.

The influence upon the morals and sentiments of the communities in which these revivals occurred, and, indeed, the change they produced in the religious faith of the nation, is worthy of consideration. Infidelity was the profession of the times. Men in high position rejected revelation, and denied the truth of Christianity; but before these demonstrations of Divine power, infidelity stood trembling and abashed, and then retired from the field. From this period, but few persons have been found in Kentucky who even professed it, and scarcely one to advocate its claims—while the man who holds its sentiments in public and social life is avoided as a monster.

It is natural that we should look for a large increase in the membership in Kentucky during this year. Emigration from Kentucky, however, had set in to the North-western Territory with resistless tide, and whole communities were now seeking settlements within its bounds. Our net increase, however, was far larger than in any previous year. In the *white* membership we had an increase of *eight hundred and ten*, and in the colored *sixty-eight.* Total, *eight hundred and seventy-eight.*

CHAPTER XIII.

FROM THE CONFERENCE OF 1801 TO THE CONFERENCE OF 1803.

The Western Conference—The early centers of Methodism in Kentucky—Clarke's Station—Ferguson's Chapel—Level Woods—Chaplin—Brick Chapel—Ebenezer—Grassy Lick—Muddy Creek—Foxtown—Mount Gerizim—Thomas's Meeting-house—Sandusky Station—The Conference of 1801 held at Ebenezer—Bishop Asbury present—Nicholas Snethen—Lewis Garrett—Large increase in membership—The Conference of 1802 held at Strother's, in Tennessee—Bishop Asbury present—Samuel Douthet—William Crutchfield—Ralph Lotspeich—James Gwin—Jacob Young—Jesse Walker—Red River Circuit—Barren Circuit—Winn Malone—Wayne Circuit—Increase of membership.

At the Conference of 1801, the western division of the work bears, for the first time, the style of the "Western Conference." This Conference embraced two districts—the Kentucky, and the Holston. The Kentucky District, of which William McKendree was the Presiding Elder, included Natchez, in Mississippi; the Scioto and Miami Circuit, in the North-western Territory; the Cumberland Circuit, in Middle Tennessee, and all the State of Kentucky. The Holston District embraced the Green, Holston, Russell, and New River Circuits—the first lying in Tennessee, and the three latter in Virginia. At this period Methodism, notwithstanding the opposition with which it had met, began to assume a more commanding position. Under the labors of the pious men who had devoted their energies to the advancement of the Church, it had spread until societies were formed in almost every community in the northern and central portions of the State.

While it would be beyond the range of our present work to mention the name of every society that had been formed up to this date, it is proper to allude to those points that, at this early period, constituted the great centers of Methodism in Kentucky, and from which it was promulgated into the regions around.

The society at Clarke's Station, in Mercer county, the first formed in the District of Kentucky, and afterward known for many years as Durham's Chapel, was one of the most prosperous in the State. John Durham, the first class-leader in Kentucky, with his excellent and pious wife, held his membership here. He was a remarkable man; and, under his guidance, and the faithful instruction and godly example of Francis Clarke, the society prospered; and from it a holy influence was sent out into all the surrounding counties. Through many years, camp-meetings were regularly held at this point, at which hundreds were converted and saved.*

We have already referred to the society organized in Nelson county, at Ferguson's Chapel; also, to the organization in 1796, by John Watson, known as the Level-woods society. These were

* This society continued until about 1858, when, after the revival of that year in Perryville, under the labors of the Revs. J. C. C. Thompson, L. G. Hicks, and others, in consequence of its contiguity, it was merged into the society at Perryville.

blessings to the communities in which they were planted, and still continue as great religious lights through all the contiguous counties.

"The society, the descendants and successors of whom now worship at Chaplintown, is one of the oldest in the State. In fact, it is said that the first Methodist sermon ever preached in Nelson county, was delivered by the Rev. Mr. Ogden, upon the farm of Capt. Jesse Davis, of the Revolutionary army, which farm lay some half-mile from the present site of the village. The Captain had collected a quantity of logs for the raising of a house, and upon these, extemporized into seats, the 'forefathers of the hamlet' sat, listening to the gospel as proclaimed, for the first time, with that zeal and clearness for which the pioneers of Methodism were so distinguished. How long, after this sermon, before there was a class organized, and regular circuit-preaching instituted, cannot now be ascertained; but evidently it was no great length of time. The first church-building was an old-fashioned log edifice, and was erected for this society during the year 1792. Some of the oldest inhabitants have a recollection of attending Divine service in this building, when they were so small that, becoming weary of the exercises, they would climb from the gallery through a crack in the wall, and then descend to the ground by means of a walnut-sapling that grew thereby. In this building preached such men as Wilson Lee, Williamson Portis, (or Daddy Portis, as he was called,) and men of that day. In 1816, a brick church was erected at the same place, and regular circuit-preaching continued; but the prosperity of the Church did not continue. It gradually waned until, in 1822, a few old people, representing eight or a dozen families, constituted its sole membership. Some time during this year, Jesse Davis, Jr., son of the Captain before mentioned, a man of influence and position in society, came to his death by tetanus, resulting from the sticking of a corn-stalk in his foot. Before he died, he was converted, and preached Jesus to all who came to his bedside. So triumphant and glorious was his death, that it made a most wonderful impression upon the community. This, taken in connection with his funeral-sermon by Jònathan Stamper, and a protracted meeting conducted by the Rev. Messrs. Medley and Ferguson, resulted in the awakening, conversion, and accession to the Church of over a hundred souls. From that time, the Church has remained in a flourishing condition, a light and power in the community. In 1845, the house proving too small, the present commodious and elegant building was erected in the village, some mile and a half from where the former stood; and now the grass-grown grave and the marble slab, proclaiming the city of the dead, alone mark the spot first consecrated to God by the erection of the old log meeting-house."*

"Between the years 1795 and 1800, a society was formed in Shelby county, about four miles north-

*Letter to the author from the Rev. George T. Gould, of the Kentucky Conference.

east of Shelbyville. The members who composed it, when first organized, were George Cardwell, Sarah Cardwell, Moore Weaver, Drusilla Weaver, Edward Talbott, and Elizabeth Talbott. This church was known in after years as the Brick Chapel. This chapel, built in 1804, under the supervision of Bishop McKendree, was the first brick church-edifice erected in Kentucky under the auspices of Methodism, and the second of any denomination in the State. Previous to its erection, the preaching was in private houses, until a school-house was obtained, where the meetings were held.

"In 1801, during a quarterly meeting at the school-house, there was a most extraordinary revival. A vast number of persons, arrested by Divine power, fell down; a great many would start to run away, and fall in the attempt, some one hundred, some two hundred, and some three hundred yards, and others a quarter of a mile from the stand. The woods were literally strewn with them, and the most of them never arose until the good Lord converted their souls. Mr. Reuben Ross, a local preacher, who was at the meeting, gave me the facts I have written." *

Through a long succession of years, the Brick Chapel was one of the great centers of Methodism in the portion of the State in which it was located. In 1810, the session of the Western Conference convened there, and in its vicinity camp-meetings were

---

* Letter from J. H. Magruder, Esq., of Shelby county, Kentucky, dated August 4, 1867.

long held, which resulted in blessings to thousands. For many years, this society was associated with Shelbyville, both forming one station; but for several years past, preaching has been discontinued there altogether, the entire class having removed their membership to Shelbyville.

Ebenezer, situated on the Todd's road from Lexington to Winchester, twelve miles from the former, and six from the latter place, was also one of those centers from which there went out a great religious influence.

It was through the instrumentality chiefly of a single Christian lady—Mrs. Mary Todd Hinde—that Methodism was planted in this community.

"The first Methodist society at Ebenezer was organized in 1797, and consisted of eight persons, as follows, viz.: Dr. Thomas Hinde, Mary Todd Hinde, Martha Hinde, Williams Kavanaugh, Hannah Kavanaugh, John Martin, Mr. Summers, and Elizabeth Hieronymus.* In the year 1798, the first church was built upon the lands of John Martin and Dr. Thomas Hinde, of logs; and in the year 1810, it being found too small for the congregation who attended, it was enlarged. Seven camp-meetings were held in the neighborhood between 1820 and 1830, and were largely attended—this being a great central point for Methodism in those days. In the year 1826, the old log church gave way to a neat brick church, which, in 1843, was replaced with a

* Mrs. Hieronymus was the grandmother of Mrs. Julia A. Tevis, of Shelbyville, Kentucky.

still larger and more finished building, which was burned in 1853; since which time the society there has been connected with the Church at Winchester. Ebenezer has sent forth from its society thirteen preachers, among whom are Jonathan Stamper, H. H. Kavanaugh, B. T. Kavanaugh, W. B. Kavanaugh, and William Askins.* All the first preachers of the Connection have, at some time or other, preached at this point. Bishops George, Bascom, McKendree, and Kavanaugh, have all held forth the word of life to the people there. Maffitt, in 1841, held a protracted meeting there, and received many in the Church. The present membership in the neighborhood numbers twenty persons, all connected with the society at Winchester. An effort is now being made to rebuild Ebenezer, on the pike leading from Lexington to Winchester, about two miles from its former location. The enterprise will probably be a success, as about two-thirds of the money has already been subscribed. We expect to be in the new house by August, 1868."†

No one of the early societies in Kentucky was instrumental in accomplishing so much good for the Church as that at Ebenezer. Not to refer to the host of valuable members of the Church who embraced religion here, and have blessed the world by

*In addition to these names, a letter from the Rev. B. T. Kavanaugh, of Houston, Texas, gives us the following, as persons who started out from the Ebenezer society: Leroy H. Kavanaugh, Henry McDaniel, Stephen and Obadiah Harber, twin brothers.

† Letter to the author from the Rev. W. T. Poynter, of Winchester, Kentucky.

their holy lives, the simple mention of the names of the ministers sent forth from her altars in the days of her prosperity, to proclaim a Redeemer's love, identifies this Church with the history of Methodism in Kentucky during all the years that have passed since its organization.

"The measure of religious influence exerted by the society at Ebenezer is not to be confined to the number of her members, or the ministers she has sent out; but it is entitled to the credit of having given rise to other societies, and in greatly aiding such as had a previous existence. The Church at Winchester, for example, was wholly constituted by members from Ebenezer. The Church at Lexington received great aid from the camp-meetings held at or near Ebenezer. In 1819, the Church at Lexington was very small, and worshiped in a little ill-shaped house, far out in the east end of the town, which was afterward sold for a cabinet-shop. In the fall of 1819 and 1820, the revival influence was carried from the camp-meetings at Ebenezer into Lexington, by those who had attended it; and the society there thus received its first religious impulses toward a large and healthy growth. Previous to that time, there was not a young person in the society—none when I joined there. Old Father Chipley, Challen, Bryan, Gibbon, and a few others, were the fathers of the Church. In 1820 and 1821, the revival continued, and a great many young people were brought into the Church." *

---

* Letter to the author from Rev. B. T. Kavanaugh, of Houston, Texas.

The light of a Church that has accomplished so much for the cause of Christianity, should never be extinguished, nor its luster grow dim. We rejoice that steps are being taken for its resuscitation, and we hope that a brighter star—a star that never more shall set—may rise above it, and shedding its mellow light, may witness its greater prosperity and glory, until the end of time.

Grassy Lick, in Montgomery county, was also a prominent preaching-place before the commencement of the present century. It was a camp-ground on a creek bearing that name, about seven miles west of Mount Sterling. "It was a preaching-place in the Hinkstone Circuit, when that circuit was first formed, in 1793. Richard Bird was the first preacher who was appointed to it. I suppose Methodism was planted at Grassy Lick as early as that date, if not earlier. Among the first members at Grassy Lick, were the Wrens, Riggses, Sewells, Tauls, and Farrows. Their house of worship was a hewed-log building, standing on a beautiful hill or ridge; and near it was a camp-ground. But they now have an elegant frame church in the valley, or foot of the hill. It is connected with the Mount Sterling charge, and they have regular preaching the first Sabbath in each month." *

The Rev. D. B. Cooper, the pastor of the Methodist Episcopal Church, South, in Mount Sterling, says, in a letter we received from him, dated Mount Sterling, April 2, 1868:

---

* Letter to the author from the Rev. W. B. Landrum, of the Kentucky Conference.

"Grassy Lick was a preaching-place as far back as 1793. James Wren gave the ground, and a hewed-log house, twenty-four by thirty-four, was built about 1800. The church-building at present is part frame and part log, so arranged as to have the appearance of a frame church. The logs are the same that were in the original house. The membership at Grassy Lick in early times numbered about one hundred, but it gradually declined until a few years back, when it numbered about twelve. God revived his work there some years ago, and now there is a growing, flourishing membership.

"Susan Taul, familiarly called Mother Taul, is the oldest member of the Church there. She joined there in 1807. She is a relic of old Methodism; and perhaps she has done as much or more than any one person in these parts, to sustain and hold up the Church of God.

"She told me some time ago, that she used to attend as many as seven camp-meetings in one year. Said I, 'Mother Taul, how could you do that?' 'Why, when one was over, I would come by home, kill a mutton or two, cook five or six hams, and bake fifteen or twenty loaves of light-bread, put them on the cart, and drive to the next one,' was her reply. I am told that she used to send provisions to the preachers by the cart-load. She was born of Baptist parents, in Brunswick county, Virginia, March 1, 1787, came to Kentucky when a small child, and Burke was the first Methodist preacher she ever heard preach."

Among the later "members of the Church at

Grassy Lick, was Henry Fisk, two of whose sons were there converted, and became valuable members of the Kentucky Conference. John Fisk was converted in 1820, and joined the Conference in 1826. He was highly gifted as a preacher, and won for himself a fine reputation in the Conference for the short period in which he lived. From Grassy Lick there went out a salutary Methodist influence, which reached Mount Sterling, the Orear settlement, and other parts of the county. For a long time old Father Spratt was almost the only member of our Church in Mount Sterling, when the revival power reached that place first in 1825, and some of the principal families were converted, among them Dr. E. Jones. The Church grew rapidly until 1827, when Milton Jamison was stationed there, when it reached its full maturity of strength and power." *

We may also mention two points in Madison county, in which Methodism was early planted, and from which a saving influence went out. One was on Muddy Creek, in the north-western part of the county, and the other was near Foxtown, six miles from Richmond, in a westerly direction. The following letter we received from the Rev. E. L. Southgate, dated Richmond, Kentucky, February 11, 1868, will give us an account of their present condition:

"The first point you mention, on Muddy Creek, has for many years been known as Concord. The society was formed there some time in the first de-

* Letter from the Rev. B. T. Kavanaugh.

cade of this century, and for a long time was celebrated as a camp-ground. The ground still, I am told, belongs to the Church, but is not used. I believe the old building is still standing, but not used. There is no society immediately at this point; but there is one near by at a place called Pace's Chapel, where there is a respectable society, now included in Madison Circuit. Texas is not very far from it, and, I am told, is the strongest Methodist community in the county. They have two very nice churches—Northern and Southern—with about fifty members in each society.

"The second place, near Foxtown, is now called Providence. I went to see old Brother Harber, the oldest member of the Church; but his memory had failed a good deal, and he could tell me very little. He produced a Church-book, however, that was first used about 1811. The Minutes of the first Quarterly Conference recorded, fix the bounds of Madison Circuit, and, I believe, give it the name.

"Providence was formerly called Proctor's Chapel. It now has a large church-edifice. I should judge it to be about sixty by forty feet, and a society of about forty members. The Church is not very strong, but has an excellent membership—in need, like many others, of a revival of religion. This appointment is connected with Richmond, in my charge."

Methodism was also established at an early day in Harrison county, at Mount Gerizim. The Rev. Geo. S. Savage, of the Kentucky Conference, furnishes us with the following information in reference to it:

"Mount Gerizim, or Broadwell, in Harrison county, is a historic Church. It was built about the beginning of the present century. The ground where it stands was given jointly by Richard Timberlake and Samuel Broadwell, the former a Presbyterian, the latter a Methodist. The first house was built of blue-ash logs, so nicely and smoothly hewed that not a trace of the scoring could be seen. The logs were furnished by the neighbors; and when they were all collected on the ground, one of the neighbors, because his set of logs was not as nice as some others, hauled them away, and got out an entire new set, determining to excel all the rest. This house was burnt about 1825—accidental—when the brick house now standing was erected. Two Conferences were held here. This Church, which was the great center of Methodism for all of now interior Kentucky, was, at this early period, in the old Hinkstone Circuit, which circuit was traveled by William Burke, Dr. Cloud, Littleton Fowler, Samuel Parker, Learner Blackman, James Ward, William Patterson, George Askins, H. B. Bascom, William Holman, Jonathan Stamper, etc.

"More than a dozen camp-meetings were held here. The numbers attending were immense. At one of these camp-meetings, Bascom and Stribling preached on different days from the same text—being accidental; hence quite a discussion among the people which preached the greater sermon.

"This Church stood for many years as a great beacon-light, long before there was any Church at Cynthiana, Millersburg, or Paris. Mount Gerizim, or Broadwell, is hallowed on account of the great revivals of religion. Thousands of souls have been converted to God on its consecrated ground. It is about three miles from Cynthiana, on the turnpike leading from that place to Ruddell's Mills."

Thomas's Meeting-house, in Washington (now Marion) county, and Sandusky Station, (now Pleasant Run,) in Marion county, seven miles south-east of Springfield, deserve to be mentioned in this connection—the former for the piety and zeal of its early membership, as well as for the beneficial results that, in early times, extended from it, as a great religious center, in every direction. Among the first members of that society were Owen Thomas and his excellent wife. One of the first preaching-points established in Kentucky, it was visited by all the pioneer preachers; while the house of Mr. Thomas, amid their toils, and sufferings, and labors, afforded them always a place of welcome and rest. The old house still stands, though in a state of dilapidation. It is fast crumbling to decay, and the men who first sounded the tidings of mercy within its walls have ceased from their labors.

Sandusky Station has been the scene of many blessed revivals of religion. In a former chapter we referred to the first revival at that place in 1800. Now known as the Pleasant Run Church, it has sent into the ministry several useful and pious ministers,* and at present contains a large membership, and is

---

* John Sandusky, Elijah M. Bosley, Jonathan Thomas, and Thomas G. Bosley, all went out from this society.

in a prosperous condition. Col. John Hardin and his wife were members of this Church.

At this period there were many other points of interest where Methodism had been firmly planted, but those to which we have referred were the principal centers. As yet but few societies had been established in the towns—they were the last to foster the spirit of Methodism, until the country had led the way.

The Conference of 1801 was held at Ebenezer, commencing October 1st. Bishop Asbury was present, and presided over the body. The Bishop says:

"Our brethren in Kentucky did not attend: they pleaded the greatness of the work of God. Twelve of us sat in conference three days; and we had not an unpleasant countenance, nor did we hear an angry word. And why should it not always be thus? Are we not the ministers of the meek and lowly, the humble and holy Jesus?

"N. Snethen gave us two sermons. We ordained on *Friday*, *Saturday*, and *Sabbath-day*, and upon each day I improved a little on the duties of ministers. On the *Lord's-day* we assembled in the woods, and made a large congregation. My subject was Isaiah lxii. 1. On *Friday* and *Saturday evenings*, and on *Sabbath morning*, there was the noise of praise and shouting in the meeting-house. It is thought there are twenty-five souls who have found the Lord: they are chiefly the children of Methodists—the children of faith and of many prayers." *

---

* Asbury's Journal, Vol. III., pp. 36, 37.

In the list of Appointments for Kentucky this year, are the names of Henry Smith, Benjamin Lakin, William Burke, John Sale, and Lewis Garrett. Of the first four, previous mention has been made.

Although Lewis Garrett was brought up chiefly in Kentucky, and had entered the ministry in 1794, his labors up to this period had been bestowed upon other sections of the work. We are indebted for the following sketch to the Rev. J. B. McFerrin, D.D.:

"Lewis Garrett was one of the early preachers who bore a conspicuous part in planting Methodism, and establishing the cause of Christianity, in the West. His labors were not confined to this new and inviting field of toil, though some of the best days of his early life and ministry were spent in Kentucky.

"Mr. Garrett was a native of Pennsylvania; born April 24, 1772; but while he was yet a child, his parents removed to Virginia. There they continued only a few years before they set out for the fertile valley of the 'far West.' On the way, the father, Lewis Garrett, died, leaving a widow and eight children in the wilderness. They, however, pressed forward with sad hearts; and, accompanied by other immigrant families, reached Scott's Station, between Dix and the Kentucky Rivers, where they halted and erected temporary cabins. This was in the autumn of 1779. Here the family encountered sore difficulties. The winter was extremely cold, provisions were very scarce, and the

Indians hostile. Two of his brothers were captured by the savages, one of whom was a prisoner for eighteen months, and the other was never heard from.

"The family of Mr. Garrett became identified with the Methodists in 1786; but in 1790, a great revival prevailed in the settlements, under the ministry of Benjamin Ogden, James Haw, and Barnabas McHenry. It was in this revival that young Garrett was awakened and converted. In 1794, he entered the traveling connection. The Conference for the West was held that year at Lewis's, near the Kentucky River. Moses Speer and Williams Kavanaugh were admitted at the same Conference.

"For twelve consecutive years Mr. Garrett traveled and preached in Virginia, North Carolina, Tennessee, and Kentucky. In 1802, he was on the Lexington Circuit; 1803, Danville; 1804, Presiding Elder on the Cumberland District.

"His health having failed, he located for a season, and settled in Tennessee. He afterward returned to the itinerant work, and spent many days in the ministry, preaching on circuits, in towns, and on large districts. He was for many years a leading member of the Tennessee Conference, and filled many important appointments.

"He finally, in connection with the Rev. John N. Maffitt, commenced in Nashville the publication of the 'Western Methodist,' a popular weekly sheet, advocating the claims of the Methodist Episcopal Church. He also established a book-store, where he for years did an extensive business.

"He became somewhat involved in difficulties and serious strife with some of his brethren, which resulted in a severance from the Church for a few years. He, however, came back to the bosom of his mother, became a member of the Mississippi Conference, where he labored and preached with great success, till 'the wheels of nature stood still,' and he 'ceased at once to work and live.'

"He died at the home of his son, M. Garrett, Esq., near Vernon, Mississippi, April 28, 1857, in the eighty-sixth year of his age.

"Mr. Garrett was in person rather under size; slender, but well formed. His face was finely chiseled, and his features were indicative of strength and sprightliness of intellect. His eye was a dark brown, and very piercing. His voice was full and mellow; his accent and articulation superior; his manner very deliberate, and his sermons at times overpowering. Indeed, he was an extraordinary man, and accomplished much for the Church. He died in peace—yea, in triumph—and now rests from his labors, while his works do follow him."

During this year, Methodism took a firmer hold on the confidence and affections of the people than it had previously occupied. The controversies on the subjects and mode of baptism, as well as those on unconditional election and reprobation—the former with the Baptist, and the latter with the Presbyterian Church—had refuted the fallacious pretensions of the one and the heterodox views of the other, and emblazoned upon the pennon of Methodism, "For God so loved the world, that he gave his only begotten Son that whosoever believeth in him should not perish, but have everlasting life." Besides, the great revival was sweeping like a hurricane throughout the State; and while the ministers of other denominations, with but few exceptions, either denounced it, or refused to enter into its spirit, the Methodist ministry, taking the lead everywhere, rising with the excitement of each occasion, stood at the helm guarding the noble ship, on the one hand against a reckless fanaticism, and on the other against an Antinomian indifference and apathy. Success crowned their efforts.

We have already seen, from the Journal of Bishop Asbury, that "the greatness of the work of God" in the State was such that the preachers in Kentucky could not be present at the Conference, which was held this year in Tennessee. The increase in the membership was *one thousand and one.*

The Western Conference for 1802 was held at Strother's, in Sumner county, Tennessee, commencing October 2. Bishop Asbury was present. He says:

"*Saturday, October* 2. We rode forward to Station Camp, and found the Conference seated. By this time, my stomach and speech were pretty well gone. I applied to Mr. William Hodge and to Mr. William McGee, Presbyterian ministers, to supply my lack of public service, which they did with great fervency and fidelity: with great pleasure and in great pain I heard them both. I was able to ordain by employing Brother McKendree to examine those who were presented, and to station the preachers—

I hope for the glory of God, the benefit of the people, and the advantage of the preachers. The Conference adjourned on *Tuesday*." *

At this Conference, the names of Samuel Douthet, William Crutchfield, Ralph Lotspeich, James Gwin, Jacob Young, and Jesse Walker, are in the list of Appointments in Kentucky.

Samuel Douthet only labored one year in Kentucky. He entered the itinerant field in 1797, and was appointed to the Saluda Circuit, and the next year to the Little Pedee and Anson Circuit, both in the South Carolina Conference. In 1799, his field of labor was the Washington Circuit, in Georgia. He was then returned, at the ensuing Conference, held in the following spring, to the Little Pedee. In the fall of 1800, he was placed on the Green Circuit; in 1801, on the Holston. In 1802, he has charge of the Lexington Circuit, in Kentucky, and the next year he is sent to the Nollachuckie. "He was a hortatory and pathetic preacher."

William Crutchfield, a young man, "amiable, eloquent, and gifted, joined the Western Conference this year, and was appointed to the Danville Circuit; in 1803, to the Wayne; the following year, to the Nashville, where his health failed, and at the next Conference, he located. He "finished his course with joy."

Ralph Lotspeich was admitted on trial at the Conference of this year, and appointed to the Salt River and Shelby Circuit; in 1803, to the Red River; in

---

* Asbury's Journal, Vol. III., pp. 87, 88.

1804, to the Barren; in 1805, to the French Broad; in 1806, to the Holston. The remaining six years of his life, he labored in Ohio, on the Hockhocking, Fairfield, Deer Creek, and Scioto Circuits.

Ralph Lotspeich was of German descent, but was born in Culpepper county, Virginia. He removed with his father to Tennessee, in which State he entered the ministry. His intellectual endowments were by no means of a high order; but by close application and ardent devotion to his profession, he not only became a useful, but a sound gospel-preacher. In the several charges he filled, he was instrumental in the accomplishment of much good. The theme on which he chiefly dwelt in the pulpit, was experimental and practical Christianity; and he enforced the same by urgent appeals, accompanied with tears; which were made the more effectual by his godly deportment.

The Scioto Circuit, on which he labored two years, was the last on which he traveled. For several months previous to his death, his health steadily declined; but, anxious to devote his life to the great work to which he was pledged, he continued to travel and preach until a few weeks before his death. A few days before his decease his sufferings were great, but he endured them without a murmur. Contemplating the reward that awaited him, he frequently, during the last few days of his life, would sing:

> Great spoils I shall win from death, hell, and sin;
> 'Midst outward afflictions shall feel Christ within.

He called upon a friend to adjust his temporal

business, and, upon learning how much money he would leave, said: "That will keep my wife and children one year, and the Lord will provide."

He was asked, on the day on which he died, how he was: to which he replied: "I can only say I am sure of heaven; not a doubt or cloud has appeared since my sickness began." His last words were: "Tell my old friends all is well, all is well." *

The name of James Gwin† first appears in the General Minutes of this year, when he was admitted on trial, and appointed to the Barren Circuit, not then formed. He remained in the itinerant field but a short time, when the duties of home called him away. In 1808, we will meet him again in the itinerant ranks, laboring with energy and success.

Another name that stood with marked prominence before the Church for nearly sixty years, as a useful minister of the gospel, is that of Jacob Young.

In the early settlement of Kentucky, he removed to the State, soon after the treaty of peace with the Indians, and settled not far from where the village of Newcastle now stands. Engaging in the many sports so common to life on the frontier, he gave but little attention to the subject of religion, although deeply impressed from time to time. Brought up under an influence calculated to repress religious conviction, he was finally aroused from his apathy by the stirring appeals that were made by

* General Minutes M. E. Church, Vol. I., p. 238.

† He was the father of the Hon. W. M. Gwin, late United States Senator from California.

the Methodist preachers who came into the neighborhood in which his father resided. At a meeting where Daniel Woodfield was the preacher, he became more powerfully convicted than on any previous occasion, and, under deep religious feeling, he says: "My tears flowed freely; my knees became feeble, and I trembled like Belshazzar; my strength failed, and I fell upon the floor; the great deep of my heart appeared to be broken up." The following night he was converted. He soon became impressed with the conviction that he ought to preach the gospel, but, without the advantages of education, and naturally timid, and feeling the great responsibility of the work, he shrank from the performance of the duty. Losing, in a great degree, his religious enjoyment, he became fully aroused to a sense of the obligation, and, through the persuasions of his brethren, he at length accepted the sacred trust, and in 1802 entered the Conference.

His first appointment was to the Barren Circuit, with James Gwin; his second, to the "Wilderness," which "lay in the mountainous country lying north and west of the valley of East Tennessee."* In 1804, he was sent to the Muskingum and Kanawha; in 1805, to the Limestone, which was the last circuit he traveled in Kentucky. From this period until within a few years of his death—when he sustained a superannuated relation—in Tennessee, in Mississippi, in Pennsylvania, and Ohio—

*Life and Times of Samuel Patton, by the Rev. D. R. McAnally, p. 131.

whether in charge of circuits and stations, or presiding over a District—he proved himself worthy of the trust committed to him by the Church.

The memoir presented by the Ohio Conference, at the session immediately following his death, is so accurate a portrait of this good man, that we copy it entire:

"The Rev. Jacob Young, D.D., was born in Alleghany county, Pennsylvania, on the 19th day of March, 1776. His father was of the Church of England, and his mother of the Presbyterian Church, though both were strangers to the converting power of God until brought in after days to the feet of the Saviour through the labors of their own son. It has been often said, that the circumstances under which a man is born and reared have much to do in the formation of his future character, and that one coming into life amid great and stirring scenes, the offspring of parents deeply interested in the great questions of human life and human liberty, would more probably be marked in his mental character with the influences of those struggles, and stamped through life with the spirit of the age. The subject of our memoir was ushered into life amid the struggles of a nation for the boon of freedom, and the parents who rejoiced in the birth of a son were permitted in four months more to rejoice in the birth of a nation by the Declaration of Independence. The first years of the life of our brother were passed amid the wildest scenes of frontier peril, and the objects of early familiarity were sites of renowned conflict and the port-holes of his father's cabin. The high hopes of his parents, based upon his physical and mental activity, and his uncommon natural courage, were suddenly overcast by malignant disease, followed by confirmed asthma, which lasted until his fifteenth year; but his active mind struggled through the disabilities of bodily affliction, and, under the care of an affectionate mother, he grappled in childhood with many of those great thoughts which afterward swelled his mature and manly heart. The simple grandeur of the New Testament made its impress upon his heart, and love kindled for the Saviour as he read the history and design of his sufferings. He looked by faith, and heard the Saviour say: 'Be of good comfort, thy sins are all forgiven.' For a while he was joyful and happy, but improper association stole the treasure from his heart. His health having recovered, and his father removing to the State of Kentucky, he for a while divided his time between the hard labor to which duty and honor bound him for the maintenance of his family, and the wild sports of thoughtless frontier men. While thus engaged, he became alarmed at the extent of his own wickedness, and resolved to seek again the path of life. After a severe struggle with the old doctrines of the Westminster Confession of Faith, he turned to the word of God alone. Under bitter anguish of spirit, and against the wishes of his friends, he attended the preaching of the word by the Methodist ministry, and was guided through his dark and painful struggle into the peace of God which passeth all understanding. His conversion was as strongly marked as his agony had been deep and unutterable. He united soon with the Methodist Episcopal Church, but felt all the power of the tempter, and learned painful and bitter lessons, which were of service to thousands in after days. Holy men in the Church began to point to his future path, and the prayer of faith offered by many claimed gospel qualification from the Holy Spirit for the future minister of Christ. He felt within him an irrepressible thirst for knowledge, and seized with avidity the means of improvement. The fire of the Lord was shut up within his soul, and, under an impression which he dared not farther resist, at the close of a day of fasting and prayer, and without formal authority from the Church, he preached his first sermon, saw a congregation bathed in tears, and felt in his own spirit the anointing from the Holy One. In September, 1801, he was licensed as a local preacher, and on the 17th of February, 1802, under the direction of that great master-spirit, William McKendree, he was thrust out into the active work of the ministry, to fill the place of Gabriel Woodfield, on a large frontier circuit. As an ably written life of this distinguished man of God, with the facts furnished by himself, and revised by Dr. E. Thomson and D. W. Clark, is already before the Christian public, embracing fifty-five years' connection with the itinerant ministry, and affording a rich feast to his personal friends, and the friends of true piety and self-developed greatness, we forbear to refer to the especial fields of his labor, or dwell upon the success which attended the work of this faithful man. It seems to us almost a useless attempt, even to bear a truthful and sincere testimony to his rare abilities, ripe Christianity, and unwearied labors, for the name of Jacob Young, bringing with it an association of excellences, is burned in imperishable characters, and over so wide a territory, that the kindling of our feeble lamp would be obscured by the already ever-burning light in the mind and memory of his numerous friends. Permit us to say, that as helper on the circuit, in charge of the work, presiding over important Districts, in the great councils of the Church, he was ever marked as one chosen of God, and the heart of the Church ever thrilled with gratitude at the thought that God had favored her with his labor and his counsel. We would speak more particularly of that portion of his life from the close of his biography to his happy departure from time. He had fully taught his junior brethren the great lesson, how to battle with all the difficulties which can surround the days of manhood, and which call forth the strength of maturity. It was his to teach us another lesson: how to be truly great, and exhibit the ripe fruits of Christian experience, and the fresh treasures of active old age, amid the shades which often surround the decline of life, and the felt decay of once vigorous and giant power. He was then great in the beautiful symmetry of his Christian character, his sweet submission to the will of God, his deep interest in all the improvements of the Church, and the more than martial fire he infused into the hearts of his junior brethren. His voice fell on the ear of the junior as that of an oracle, and the full expression of his countenance kindled battle within the depth of their soul. He had long enjoyed the blessing of perfect love, and in his last days that light was clear, and that power was full. One year ago, during the sitting of our Conference in the city of Columbus, he made his last public address in the college campus, at the Ohio Wesleyan University. His survey of early struggle and early privation was full of interest; his rehearsal of desires long pent up within the laboring mind, finding vent, and realizing full satisfaction in the noble provision which there met the eye for the cultivation of the youthful mind of the Church and of the community, was a rich feast to the vast concourse which hung upon his lips. In the love-feast on the next morning, he delivered his last testimony, like Moses about to be gathered to his fathers, while his countenance beamed with the reflection of heaven. In the homelike sick-room, in the house of our Brother Towler, in the city of Columbus, he still spoke such lessons as only fall from the lips of the great and the good; and when removed to the house of his oldest son, surrounded by the loved members of his own family, and a few friends whom strong attraction had drawn to the place, being ready for his departure, on the 16th of September, 1859, he breathed his blessings upon those around him, audibly pronounced the words, 'Sweet heaven! sweet heaven!' and then passed upward at the call of his Master. On the following Sabbath, the Rev. Joseph Casper preached an appropriate funeral discourse in Town-street Chapel, in the city of Columbus, which fell like a message from eternity upon the hearts of a vast and weeping audience. Devout men bore his remains to his burial, and his body sleeps in the calm quiet of Greenlawn Cemetery. The sigh of the Church responds that a 'prince and a great man has fallen in Israel.'" *

Jesse Walker was admitted this year into the Western Conference, on trial. His first appointment was to the Red River Circuit,† which had previously been embraced in the Cumberland, and lay partly in Kentucky. In 1803, he was appointed to the Livingston, and in 1804 and 1805, to the Hartford. His labors on the Hartford Circuit closed his work in Kentucky. From this period, as long as he was able to travel and preach, he occupied the most dangerous and difficult posts on the frontier. In 1806, his circuit was the Illinois, embracing all of what is now that flourishing State, where he could find a community that would hear the gospel. In 1807, he was sent to the Missouri Circuit, to occupy the country embraced in that vast territory. On the following year he was returned to the Illinois Circuit; in 1809 and 1810, to Cape Girardeau; and in 1811, we find him again in Illinois, prosecuting with apostolic zeal his high and holy calling. In 1812, he was placed in charge of the Illinois Dis-

---

*General Minutes M. E. Church, for 1860, pp. 273, 274.

†On the Sulphur Fork of Red River, the first attempt was made by Benjamin Ogden to form a society, the first that was made by the Methodists in Cumberland circuit. Some few joined.

trict—then included in the Tennessee Conference, and embracing the Missouri, Coldwater, Maramack, Cape Girardeau, New Madrid, and Illinois Circuits—where he remained for four years. In 1816, we find him in the Missouri Conference, in charge of the Missouri District, over which he presides for three years. In 1819 and 1820, his appointments are: Jesse Walker, missionary, investing him with authority to extend his labors to the farthest borders of civilization, and to plant the standard of the cross upon its very verge.

In 1821, he was appointed missionary to St. Louis, and in 1822, he was the Conference missionary in the State of Missouri. In 1823, his appointment reads: "Jesse Walker, missionary to the Missouri Conference, whose attention is particularly directed to the Indians within the bounds of said Conference;" and in 1824: "Jesse Walker, missionary to the settlements between the Illinois and the Mississippi Rivers, and to the Indians in the vicinity of Fort Clark." In 1825, he is in the Illinois Conference, and missionary to the Pottawatomie Indians. In 1826 and 1827, his appointment is to the Pottawatomie Mission; in 1828, to the Peoria, and in 1829, to the Fox River Mission. In the year 1830, he has charge of the Chicago Mission, and the following year he is Presiding Elder on Mission District, embracing five separate charges, and also missionary to Deplain. His appointment for 1832 is to the Chicago District, and missionary to Chicago, and the following year to the Chicago Mission. This was his last charge. From the Conference of

1834 until his death, he sustained a superannuated relation.

Amongst the preachers of his day, for sacrifice, labor, and suffering, Jesse Walker stands without a peer.

The following sketch, from the pen of the Rev. A. L. P. Green, D.D., of the Tennessee Conference, will be read with interest:

"The Rev. Jesse Walker was a character perfectly unique: he had no duplicate. He was to the Church what Daniel Boone was to the early settler—always first, always ahead of everybody else, preceding all others long enough to be the pilot of the new-comer. Brother Walker is found first in Davidson county, Tennessee. He lived within about three miles of the then village of Nashville; and was at that time a man of family, poor, and to a considerable extent without education. He was admitted on trial in 1802, and appointed to the Red River Circuit. But the Minutes, in his case, are no guide, from the fact that he was sent by the Bishops and Presiding Elders in every direction where new work was to be cut out. His natural vigor was almost superhuman. He did not seem to require food and rest as other men; no day's journey was long enough to tire him; no fare too poor for him to live upon; *to him*, in traveling, roads and paths were useless things—he blazed out his own course; no way was too bad for him to travel—if his horse could not carry him, he led him, and when his horse could not follow, he would leave him, and take it on foot; and if night and a cabin did not come together, he would pass the night alone in the wilderness, which with him was no uncommon occurrence. Looking up the frontier settler was his chief delight; and he found his way through hill and brake as by instinct—he was never lost; and, as Bishop McKendree once said of him, in addressing an Annual Conference, he never complained; and as the Church moved West and North, it seemed to bear Walker before it. Every time you would hear from him, he was still farther on; and when the settlements of the white man seemed to take shape and form, he was next heard of among the Indian tribes of the North-west.

"In 1807, he was sent to Missouri, and at once bent his way to St. Louis, which was at that time as destitute of true piety as any point in America. On reaching the town, he passed through it in various directions in search of a Methodist, but found no one who could inform him where such a character could be found. At length he passed out, and was making his way into the country beyond; but when he had gone quite out of the town, he drew up his horse, and looked back upon the place for a few minutes, and at length said, in the name of that Saviour who said to his disciples, 'Go ye into all the world, and preach the gospel to every creature,' I will not give you up; I will try again! So he turned about, rode again into the town, and renewed his inquiry. At length he was told that there was a man down on Front street who was a Methodist. Taking the name and directions, he went in search of his man, whom he soon found. Calling him brother, telling his own name and business, he asked such countenance and coöperation as the circumstances of the case required. The man gave him the *wink*, and beckoned him into a back-room, several persons being present, and said to him about as follows: '*Look here:* I was a Methodist where I came from, but it is not generally known here, and I do not wish it to be. You cannot do any thing in this town, and it is useless to try.' Brother Walker soon after learned that the man was keeping what would be called in these days a 'doggery,' and could not be relied on in Church matters. He went at once to a public-house, and put up. He made inquiry where he could rent a room. An old shell of a house was soon found and rented, and in a few days Walker had set up housekeeping on a scale of economy which would astonish the present generation, and took measures to have preaching in his own room; so that his little establishment was kitchen, chamber, dining-room, parlor, and meeting-house; and, gloomy as the prospects were, he soon gathered together a little handful of serious, well-disposed persons, some three or four of whom had been members of the Church before. But not much could be done, for the want of a house of worship. He could not rent a suitable building, and would not have been able to pay for one if it could have been found. At length he was told by an individual that he would give him timber to build him a church, but it was across the Mississippi, on the Illinois shore, growing in the forest. But notwithstanding, light began to break upon the mind of Walker. Next, he had the offer of a lot to build upon. So his plan was at once laid. He hired a man to aid him, took his tools, cheese and crackers, crossed over the river, and went to work, *cutting*, *hewing*, and *sawing*, and in a few months had his frame and plank all gotten out: his plank was put into a kiln to dry, and by the time he had put up his frame, the plank was sufficiently seasoned to work. The result was, that at the end of the year he reported to Conference a church in St. Louis—house, congregation, and all—the labor of his own hands. Such was Jesse Walker. His education, as we have before stated, was poor, with but little opportunity for reading, though he studied nature closely, was wonderfully gifted in prayer and exhortation, while his faith was uncompromising; and being well acquainted with human nature, he became a powerful instrument, in the hands of God, of spreading the gospel in the Valley of the Mississippi. . . . . . . And it may be said of Walker, that he knew what books were made out of: he understood how to use the raw material. He took lessons from rocks and trees, mountains and rivers; he held Nature's keys, and forced her, secretive as she is, to divulge her secrets. He lived in the ante-chamber of Wisdom's storehouse. He slaked his thirst from the mountain-brook at its source, plucked flowers from stalks that had never been transplanted, and read the volume of nature in the first edition, without note or comment. He was one of nature's great men."

Previous to the admission of Jesse Walker into the Conference, he resided in Davidson county,

Tennessee. Deprived of the advantages of education, yet possessing a soul burning with a desire for the salvation of the people, he offered himself to the Conference, and was accepted. With a wife and several children, he was not deterred by the difficulties that must meet him in the support of the loved ones intrusted to his care. Of moderate preaching abilities, he was unable to discuss those doctrines of the Bible involved in controversy, but, with "thoughts that breathe, and words that burn," he would tell the simple story of the cross in such a manner as to melt the hardest heart. Success crowned his labors wherever he went, and through his instrumentality thousands were awakened and brought to Christ, and the wilderness and solitary places were made glad, and deserts rejoiced and blossomed as the rose.

Superannuated! how hard the stroke on such a spirit as Walker's! His labors for the Church closed, he bows in sweet and calm submission to the Master's will, and patiently waits until his end comes. Nor did he wait long. On the 5th of October, 1835, while the Illinois Conference, of which he was a member, was in session, at his own home, in Clark county, Illinois, and in the bosom of his family, he passed to the inheritance of the blessed. "The last moments of our deceased brother were such as might be expected from his long and laborious life in the way of doing good. To a ministerial brother, who visited him shortly before his demise, he said, God had been with him from the time of his conversion, and was still with him. His last moments were tranquil, and he died in full and confident hope of a blessed immortality."*

Methodism was now extending its borders in the southern portion of the State. The Red River Circuit, which lay partly in Kentucky, and to which Jesse Walker had been appointed, had previously belonged to the Cumberland Circuit, but this year was enlarged by the labors of Mr. Walker. We will hereafter include a portion of the membership of this circuit in our statistics. The Barren Circuit, to which James Gwin and Jacob Young were appointed, was also formed this year. A small membership of *one hundred and fifteen*, made up of societies formed chiefly through the ministry of the Rev. Richard Pope, a local preacher from Virginia, who had removed to Kentucky, and settled in Barren county, was reported to the Conference of 1802, as the nucleus around which the Barren Circuit was to be formed. The Buck Creek Church, in (now) Allen county, was the principal society. An interview between the two preachers appointed to the Barren Circuit impressed them both with the belief that the territory designed to be embraced in the Barren Circuit, and through which the Big and Little Barren, Green, and Cumberland Rivers flowed, beginning at the line that divided Kentucky from Tennessee, extending eastwardly to near the Crab Orchard, was too large to be embraced in one circuit. They agreed upon a division of the work, Mr. Gwin taking the western, to be called Barren

*General Minutes, Vol. II., p. 487.

Circuit, and Mr. Young the eastern, to be called Wayne.

One of the first societies formed in Barren county by Mr. Gwin was at the house of Winn Malone. He had removed from Virginia in 1788, and settled nine miles north of Glasgow, on the Greensburg road. His wife, Mrs. Jane Malone, had joined the Methodist Church in Brunswick county, Virginia, about the year 1785; and Mr. Malone, though at that time not a member of the Church, offered his house, so soon as an opportunity was presented, as a place for preaching,* and a home for the weary itinerant. For more than thirty years his neighbors assembled beneath his roof to hear the word of life. There many quarterly meetings were held, and many revival seasons blessed the labors of the ministers of Christ. Among those converted to God were four of his sons—Benjamin, Green, Isaac, and Thomas R Malone, all of whom became useful itinerant ministers. The first, Benjamin, died in great peace, in Indianapolis, Indiana, in 1856. Green Malone, after having filled many important positions in the Church, breathed his last in great triumph, near Eufaula, Alabama, in the autumn of 1860. Isaac Malone resides in Muhlenberg county, Kentucky, where he preaches as his health permits, having been compelled to retire from the itinerant work in consequence of physical inability. Thomas R. Malone, the youngest of the four brothers, re-

* Preaching was continued at the house of Winn Malone until 1835, when Concord Church was built.—*Letter to the author from Mr. Malone's grandson, the Rev. J. S. Malone, of the Louisville Conference.*

sides with his son, the Rev. Joseph S. Malone, of the Louisville Conference—at present (1868) the pastor of the Methodist Church in Russellville—and is confined with a rheumatic affection, from which he has suffered through long years, exhibiting that patience which Christianity alone can bestow.

In 1814, Winn Malone joined the Church; and in 1841, after twenty-seven years of devotion to its interest, he died in the triumph of Christian faith.

His excellent wife survived him for a few years. In 1847, after a connection with the Church of sixty-two years, in holy triumph she entered upon eternal rest. They both died in Barren county, Kentucky.

In the Barren Circuit, as organized by Mr. Gwin, he was greatly aided in his work by the Rev. Richard Pope,* a local preacher, who, a short time before, had emigrated from Virginia. In fact, several of the societies were formed by Mr. Pope previous to the visit of Mr. Gwin to Barren county. He had been a traveling preacher in Virginia, but after three years in the itinerant work, his constitution gave way, and he was compelled to "circumscribe his labors."

"In his public ministrations, he was plain, pointed, and energetic, and, while an itinerant, had many seals to his ministry. As a local preacher, he labored much, and was useful," so long as his health permitted him to preach. Many of the first societies in Southern Kentucky were formed by him.

---

*He was the father of the Rev. Solomon Pope, formerly of the Kentucky Conference.

His whole life was characterized by strict conformity to the teachings of the Bible; so that, during his last illness, he often said: "I have nothing to do but to die."

On the 1st of July, 1820, he passed away. "But a short time before his ransomed soul forsook its earthly tenement, he comforted his weeping companion with his prospects of heaven, and exhorted his children, and all about him, to prepare to meet him at the right hand of God, and his last and dying words were, 'Glory, glory!'" *

In that division of the circuit confided to Jacob Young, he labored with tireless energy. Entering upon his journey, he says: "In two days I arrived at Manoah Lasley's, where I spent a few days, rested my horse, and recruited my wardrobe. I found myself at a very great loss to know how to form a circuit in that vast wilderness, and had no one to instruct me. I preached on Sabbath-day in Father Lasley's house, and set off on Monday on my great and important enterprise. I concluded to travel five miles, as nearly as I could guess, then stop, reconnoiter the neighborhood, and find some kind person who would let me preach in his log-cabin, and so on till I had performed the entire round.

"I set out early, but had to travel ten miles before I found a preaching-place. I was directed to call on an old gentleman by the name of Step. I found him cribbing his corn; two large negroes were doing the work, and he was keeping count. I

* Methodist Magazine, Vol. IV., p. 80.

spoke to him, but he gave me a very cold reception. I told him my business, but he was more intent on measuring his corn than talking about preaching. I felt determined not to be discouraged till I had pushed things to the bottom. I then said to him, 'I am a Methodist preacher, sent into this country to try to form a new circuit.' He rose up, looked me full in the face, exclaiming, 'You are a Methodist preacher?' I responded, 'Yes.' 'Come into the house,' said he. I walked in, and found a very neat log-house, pretty well furnished. 'Now,' said the old gentleman, 'this is your home.' He then went on to say, 'I thought, when you first spoke to me, you were a Baptist preacher.' He then informed me that he had no fellowship with the Baptist Church, nor did he believe the doctrine they preached; neither did he think they were doing any good. I stayed all night, and enjoyed the brother's society well.

"The next day he sent out his servants, and gathered in a good congregation. I preached, and had a delightful meeting. A Presbyterian Elder attended the meeting; his family were converted, and he caught the spirit of revival. I went home with him, and spent the evening at his fireside, much to my own satisfaction. This gentleman's name was Kelsey. He was an intelligent man, a devoted Christian, and was a great advantage to me through the year.

"The next day I traveled five miles, and stopped at the house of Mr. Guthrie. Here I found a congregation waiting for me. The most prominent man in that neighborhood was George Taylor. With his assistance, I immediately formed a society there, which flourished all the time I remained on the circuit.

"Next day I had a long ride through a dreary country. Late in the evening I came to a little log-cabin, standing in the woods, with no stable or out-buildings of any kind. Seeing a woman in the door, I rode up and asked if I could stay all night. She seemed to think not. I paused a few moments, thinking what to do. I was afraid to go any farther, lest I should have to lie out all night. That I was afraid to do, as the weather was very cold, and there were always a great many ravenous wolves in the barrens. My life would be in danger, and there was nothing to encourage me to stay at this place. I knew I would have to tie my hungry, tired horse to a tree, without any shelter or food. The cabin looked very dreary, and the woman was unwilling to let me stay. She was not entirely alone, but had several children, and one daughter partly grown, which inclined me to think I could stay with safety. I finally concluded to let her know who I was, and what business I was on. I said to her, 'I am a Methodist preacher, sent by Bishop Asbury to try to form a circuit.'

"This information appeared to electrify her. Her countenance changed, and her eyes fairly sparkled. She stood for some time without speaking, and then exclaimed, 'La, me! has a Methodist preacher come at last? Yes, brother, you shall stay all night. Mr. Carson is not at home, but we will do the best we can for you with a glad heart.'"

Thus he passed on from place to place, occasionally finding small classes that had been formed by pious local preachers who had settled in the country—sometimes receiving a cordial welcome, at others meeting with repulses—until he had formed a full four-weeks' circuit.

During the year, his labors were greatly blessed. Revivals of religion, under his ministry, animated his heart, and made him say, "These are great and glorious days."

Not yet an ordained minister, Lewis Garrett, who had charge of the Danville Circuit, exchanged a round of appointments with him, "regulated the classes that had been formed, baptized all who wished to be baptized—adults and children—preached many sermons on baptism, and answered all the Baptist arguments to the general satisfaction." Having closed his year's labors, he says: "I was now leaving my new circuit, while, as yet, I had given it no name; and, as I would have to report it at Conference, it must, of necessity, have a name. I called it Wayne Circuit, after Gen. Anthony Wayne. I had taken three hundred and one members into Church this year."

Up to this period, Methodism had not extended its influence into the counties in the western portion of the State. In these counties were to be found "a good many scattering members" of the Church, but without any organization. Amongst those who had professed religion in the Red River Circuit, was

Peter Cartwright, whose father, about this time, removed from Logan to Livingston county. Previous to his leaving Logan county, Mr. Cartwright was licensed by Jesse Walker to exhort, and invested by John Page, the Presiding Elder, with authority "to travel through all that destitute region, hold meetings, organize classes, and, in a word, to form a circuit, and meet him the next fall, at the fourth quarterly meeting of the Red River Circuit, with a plan of the new circuit, number of members, names of preachers, if any, exhorters, class-leaders, etc." *

Mr. Cartwright was successful, and in the fall of 1803, reported to Messrs. Page and Walker the Livingston Circuit, with about one hundred members, to which Mr. Walker was appointed the following year.

At the close of the year, we find an increase of *five hundred and eighty-four* members.

---

* Autobiography of Peter Cartwright, p. 59.

CHAPTER XIV.

FROM THE CONFERENCE OF 1803 TO THE CONFERENCE OF 1808.

Conference meets at Mount Gerizim — Bishop Asbury present— Anthony Houston — John McClure — Adjet McGuire — Fletcher Sullivan — Louther Taylor — John A. Granade — Learner Blackman — Increase of membership — The Conference of 1804 — Abdel Coleman — Joshua Barnes — Joshua Riggin — William J. Thompson—Edmund Wilcox—James Axley—Peter Cartwright —Asa Shinn—Benjamin Edge—Miles Harper—George Askins— Samuel Parker—Death of Wilson Lee—Livingston and Hartford Circuit—Churches organized in Ohio county—Church organized at Thomas Stith's, in Breckinridge county—Thomas Taylor—Margaret Taylor—Licking Circuit—Increase of membership—The Conference of 1805 — Bishop Asbury present — Thomas Hellums — Henry Fisher—Samuel Sellers—David Young—Moses Ashworth— William Ellington — Richard Browning — William Houston — Joshua Oglesby—A small class in Louisville—Increase in membership—Conference of 1806—Bishop Asbury present—Abbot Goddard—Hector Sandford—Joseph Bennett—Frederick Hood—Zadoc B. Thaxton—Abraham Amos—Joseph Williams—John Thompson —William Hitt — Joseph Oglesby — The first deed of ground, on which to build a church, in Mason county—Increase of membership — The Conference of 1807 — Bishop Asbury present — Thomas Stillwell — Mynus Layton —Josiah Crawford —John Craig —William Lewis—Jacob Turman—Henry Mallory—James King—Sela Paine — Milton Ladd — Joseph Hays — Elisha W. Bowman — The Silver Creek Circuit, in Indiana Territory, formed — Kennerly Chapel — Pond Meeting-house — Increase in membership — Causes of locations—Our Review.

The Western Conference for 1803, met at Mount

Gerizim, in Harrison county, on the 2d of October. Bishop Asbury presided. On his way to the Conference, he passed through Ohio, to look after the interests of the Church in that Territory; and on the 28th of September, "crossed the Ohio River into the State of Kentucky, Fleming county, stopping at Salathiel Fitch's."

On the following day, he passed "through Bourbon county," and "rode thirty-three miles to Benjamin Coleman's, at Mount Gerizim, the place appointed for the Conference." On the Sabbath preceding the Conference, he "had to preach from a stand in the woods to about two thousand people." On Monday, he says, "We entered fully upon our Conference work; but I had to preach, nevertheless. We had preaching every day; and the people continued singing and prayer, night and day, with little intermission. On *Wednesday* the meeting closed. We hope there were twenty souls converted to God, besides five who are reported to have been converted at a family meeting. Our Conference ended on *Thursday*, the 6th. I had taken cold, but rode twelve miles to Smith's, and was driven by illness early to bed. Next day I rose unwell, and continued my route through Paris. The day was excessively warm, but I made twenty miles to Dr. Hinde's, in Clarke county. Brothers McKendree, Garrett, Douthet, and Granade were with me." *

Anthony Houston, John McClure, Adjet McGuire, and Fletcher Sullivan, were admitted on trial, and

---

* Asbury's Journal, Vol. III., pp. 130, 131.

Louther Taylor, John A. Granade, and Learner Blackman, who had previously entered the itinerant field, received appointments for the first time in Kentucky.

Of the early life and conversion of Anthony Houston we have no information. He entered the Conference this year, and was appointed to the Barren Circuit, where, "by his piety and zeal," he was remarkably useful. In 1804, he was sent to New River, in Virginia; the following year, he was appointed to Holston; in 1806, he was sent beyond the Ohio to the Scioto Circuit; in 1807, to the Wachita; and in 1808, to the Claiborne, in Mississippi. In 1809, he was returned to Kentucky, and appointed to Limestone and Fleming Circuit, and, at the close of that year, located.

During the seven years of his connection with the Conference, he was excelled by none of his colleagues in his devotion to the Church. Whether he preached in Virginia, in Ohio, in the lowlands of Mississippi, or in Kentucky, he made "good proof of his ministry," everywhere laboring to the utmost of his strength. Unable longer to endure the toils incident to the life of a traveling preacher, in 1810, he asked for a location. He settled in Flemingsburg, where he engaged in the practice of medicine.

The Rev. Jonathan Stamper thus speaks of him in his "Autumn Leaves:"

"Dr. Houston was a man of more than ordinary preaching talents. He was fond of investigation, and often went into such fine-spun metaphysical disquisitions as to be sometimes suspected of heterodoxy; but he always insisted that he was a Methodist of the Wesleyan school. He was possessed of a serious mind, and his manners were grave and dignified. Great afflictions had befallen him in his family relations. He lost his wife, and every child but two, in the course of a single week, by cholera, during the prevalence of that disease in 1833; but he submitted without a murmur. He was finally called away by apoplexy, without a moment's warning, and I trust rests in peace."

John McClure, who entered the Conference this year, was appointed to the Limestone Circuit. In 1804, he was sent, with Asa Shinn, to the Wayne, and in 1805, to the Clinch Circuit, which "included Russell, Scott, and part of Lee counties, Virginia, and a part of Tennessee, lying north of the Holston River." In 1806, his appointment was to Powell's Valley, which "embraced all the settled counties lying between Clinch River and the Cumberland Mountains, from about Lee Court-house in Virginia, on as far west as the settlements extended." The following year, he had charge of the Cumberland Circuit. In 1808 and 1809, he presided over the Mississippi District, as successor to Jacob Young. The three following years, he sustained a superannuated relation. In 1813, he was sent to the Flint Circuit, in the Nashville District, and, at the close of the year, located.

Adjet McGuire was also admitted this year, and appointed to the Salt River Circuit; in 1804, to the Danville; and the following year, to the Licking. In

1806, he was sent to the Mad River Circuit, in the North-western Territory; and, at the close of the year, was returned to Kentucky, and traveled again on the Salt River Circuit, on which he finished his labors as an itinerant. At the Conference of 1808, he located.

The name of Fletcher Sullivan appears on the Minutes for only two years. In 1803, he has charge of the Shelby Circuit; and in 1804, he is the colleague of William Crutchfield, on the Nashville; after which his name disappears from the roll of the Conference.

Louther Taylor became an itinerant in the spring of 1800, and was appointed to the Dover Circuit, and in the autumn of the same year, to the Cecil—the former in Delaware, and the latter in Maryland. In 1801, he was transferred to the Western Conference, and appointed to New River, and in 1802, to the French Broad Circuit, both in the Holston District. In 1803, he enters Kentucky, where he continues but one year, having charge of the Limestone Circuit. The remaining two years of his connection with the itinerancy, he spends in Ohio, on the Scioto and Muskingum Circuits, and locates at the Conference of 1806.

Among the early itinerants in the West, no one, perhaps, attracted more attention, considering the brief period of his connection with the Conference, than did John A. Granade. He was a remarkable man. He came to Tennessee about the year 1798. In the State of North Carolina, where he had previously lived, he had made a profession of religion;

and believing it his duty to preach the gospel, yet rejecting the Divine call, he lost his religious enjoyment, while deep despair settled over all his hopes.

The deep anguish of heart evinced in his melancholy countenance excited the sympathy of the Church, and the commiseration of all who knew him. By the community in which he resided, he was termed "the wild man." His "agony was so intense that he scarcely took food enough to support nature," while his abstinence was fast wearing him away. By many he was thought to be deranged. "Days, and weeks, and months together, he slept in the woods, crying for mercy." The Bible was his constant companion. He attended preaching when within his reach; and "on his way to church, sitting on his horse, he would lift his hands toward heaven, and pray to God to have mercy upon him."

Endowed with a poetic talent, during his depression he would give vent to his feelings of anguish in strains of melancholy poetry, that would touch any heart. He continued in this state of mind until the extraordinary meeting held at Desha's Creek, in 1799, by John McGee, at which time he was reclaimed from his backslidden state.

His conversion presented a "scene that was awful and solemn beyond description. It drew the attention of hundreds of people on the ground; and the clergy as well as the laity were struck with wonder, while they witnessed a change, the like of which had never before come under their notice. Heaven was pictured upon the face of the happy man, and his language, as though learned in a new world, was apparently superhuman. He spoke of angels and archangels, cherubim and seraphim, and dwelt with rapture upon the fullness and freeness of the gospel of Christ for the salvation of a lost world." *

In a poem written by himself, commemorative of this event, are the following stanzas:

> One evening, pensive as I lay
> Alone upon the ground,
> As I to God began to pray,
> A light shone all around.
>
> Glory to God! I loudly cried,
> My sins are all forgiven;
> For me, for me the Saviour died—
> My peace is made with Heaven.†

From the time of his conversion, he went forth as a herald of the cross. Of commanding appearance, of a vivid imagination, and familiar with the Bible, everywhere he preached, listening and anxious multitudes crowded around him, eager to catch the words of life as they fell from his lips. Success attended his ministry; and hundreds, through his instrumentality, were brought to Christ.

In his exuberant zeal, he indulged in some views that caused the arrest of his official character by the Quarterly Conference over which Mr. McKendree presided, and his suspension from the ministry for three months, yet giving him permission to hold religious meetings and exhort. When the secretary of the Conference read to him the decision of the

* John Carr, in Christian Advocate, February 19, 1857.

† Finley's Sketches of Western Methodism, p. 291.

Conference, he exclaimed, with emphasis: "*What! not preach for three months?* Stop the devil," he said, "for three months, and I will submit to your decision." He at first refused to give up his license, but being told that he might exhort during this parenthesis, he yielded to the decision.

He went forth from that Quarterly Conference, and during the three months of his suspension from the ministry, as an exhorter he labored with an energy and success that, tireless and useful as he had previously been, had not distinguished his earlier efforts. At the end of three months, his license was returned to him; and in the autumn of 1801, he was admitted on trial into the Western Conference, and appointed to the Green Circuit, in East Tennessee; in 1802, to the Holston. In 1803, he came to Kentucky, and labored on the Hinkstone Circuit.

During the short period of his connection with the Conference, he discharged his ministerial obligations in a manner that defied criticism. Eloquent, bold, energetic, deeply pious, he passed through the various charges to which he was appointed like a flaming meteor; and in the highways, in private families, as well as in the pulpit, he proclaimed the Redeemer's love. If he portrayed the glories of heaven, his audience seemed to gaze upon the blessed reality. If he described the horrors of the lost, one seemed to stand upon the fire-crested battlements of hell, and hear the groans of the damned. Revivals blessed his labors everywhere; so that his memory and his name became dear to the hearts of thousands.

In the revivals of religion so common at this period, the Church was indebted to his poetic genius for many of the spiritual songs that fanned the sacred flame.

Entirely broken down in health, at the close of the third year in the ministry, he located, and returned to Middle Tennessee, only able to speak in a low tone of voice. As often as he could, he preached, though only in a whisper, yet his preaching was attended with power. He settled in Wilson county, and devoted himself to the practice of medicine. He only lived a few years, when he peacefully passed away.

Although the labors of Learner Blackman were bestowed chiefly on other fields, yet, during the few years he traveled in Kentucky, he won a warm place in the affections, not only of his brethren in the ministry, but of the communities in which he preached the gospel of Christ. Among the early itinerants, the name of Learner Blackman will always be cherished for his abundant labor, and for the sacrifices he made and met, as well as for his deep devotion to the Church, for the sweetness of his temper, the purity of his life, and the success that crowned his ministry.

He was the son of David Blackman, and was born in Great Egg Harbor township, Gloucester county, in the State of New Jersey, on the 19th day of June, 1781. His grandfather, who originally emigrated from one of the New England States to New Jersey, "had a great partiality for the Presbyterian Church, and was probably a member of that Communion.'

His father, though not a member of any Church, until a late period in life, when he joined the Methodist, threw around his children the restraints of morality. The neighborhood in which David Blackman resided was visited, in the spring of 1797, by his son-in-law, the Rev. John Collins, a young Methodist preacher. From "a wicked and gay young man," Mr. Collins had, a short time previous, been converted to God, and "with his soul flaming with religion, came into the neighborhood in which his father-in-law resided." He at once became the chief instrument in the commencement of the great revival with which that portion of New Jersey was blessed at this period. Among the many who were brought to Christ through his instrumentality, was the family into which he had married, including Learner Blackman, then in the sixteenth year of his age. In referring to his conversion, he says: "I was blind, but now I see; now I feel the love of God; now I know God is my God, Christ is my Saviour, and the Holy Ghost is my Comforter, and that I love God. I love his people, his worship, his ordinances, and his word. O glorious change, never to be forgotten!"

In the Blackman family, among those who resided at home, the wife and mother was the first to become connected with the Church. She was, however, immediately followed by her eldest unmarried daughter, and, in a few weeks, by her husband and five other children. Around the family altar, David Blackman, "while leading in the devotions the third night after he joined the Church, and the first time he attempted to pray in his family, was powerfully converted."

The family, occupying a high social position, and so deeply imbued with the spirit of religion, sent out in the community in which they lived a sacred influence that was felt to its utmost limits.

Before his conversion to God, and even from his childhood, young Blackman had a strong presentiment in reference to the ministry, and "felt a desire to become a preacher, when arrived at manhood." Now, however, divinely called to assume its responsibilities, "more timid than any other member of the family," he shrank from the duty, until, though strictly observing the forms of religion, he lost much of its enjoyment. Faithfully watched over by Mr. Collins, who discovered in him the buddings of promise and future usefulness, he advised him "to take up his cross and speak to the people." In the eighteenth year of his age, he was licensed to exhort, and before he was nineteen, to preach, and recommended to the Philadelphia Conference, held the 1st day of June, 1800, at Duck Cross Roads, "and was admitted on trial."*

In his earlier efforts to preach the gospel, Mr. Collins gave no signs of promise. His wife, the first of her father's family who was converted, and had joined the Church at the same time with her husband, feeling a deep solicitude for his reputation, advised him to desist, stating at the same time that he could never succeed. "I think it likely, Sarah,"

---

* From a manuscript of Learner Blackman in possession of the author.

was his candid reply; "but though I may never become a respectable preacher myself, it is my purpose to continue trying until I am instrumental in the conversion of some one who will make a preacher." In the evening of his life, he related this incident to Bishop H. H. Kavanaugh, and added, with much satisfaction, "It was not long before I was instrumental in the conversion of Learner Blackman, who became an eminent and useful minister of Jesus Christ."

Mr. Blackman's first appointment was to the Kent Circuit, in Maryland. In the spring of 1801, he was appointed to the Dover Circuit, in the State of Delaware; but in the autumn of that year, he was transferred to the Western Conference, and appointed to the Russell Circuit, and the following year to the New River, both in Virginia. At the session of the Western Conference for 1803, he first enters Kentucky, and is appointed alone to the Lexington Circuit. In Kentucky, however, he remains but one year, when, "in compliance with the request of the Bishops, he went on a mission to Natchez. Here a new scene of things presented itself to his view. He is now to face uncivilized natives, and a wilderness of four or five hundred miles. After a journey of ten or eleven days, and lying out as many nights, making his saddle-bags his pillow, his blanket and cloak his bed, the heavens his covering, the God of Israel his defense, he arrived safe in the Territory."*

---

*General Minutes M. E. Church, Vol. I., p. 274.

In 1805 and 1806, he presided over the Mississippi District, having for his associates such men as Lasley and Bowman. From that field of labor, so unfriendly to the constitution, he was removed, in 1807, to the Holston District, where he remained for two years.

In 1809, he is the Presiding Elder on the Cumberland District, embracing all of West Tennessee, Madison county in the Mississippi Territory, all Kentucky below the mouth of Green River, and the counties of Ohio and Breckinridge above Green River, extending into Tennessee on the waters of Elk and Duck Rivers. In 1810, he was reäppointed to this District, which this year was so enlarged as to "include the St. Vincennes Circuit, in the Territory of Indiana."

During his connection with this District, he passes through Louisville, and stops with "Brother Biscourt, and preaches to one hundred persons on a very cold night with but little liberty." And then again we see him at the "Red Banks, (Henderson,) preaching to fifty persons, at the court-house," and the following day crossing the Ohio and penetrating the Territory of Indiana as far as Vincennes: he attended his quarterly meeting at Westfall's, for Vincennes Circuit, where, under his preaching, the "awful power of God came down, sinners felt a tremendous shock, and cried for mercy as" he had "seldom seen." He visits, by invitation, the Hon. William Henry Harrison, then Governor of Indiana Territory, preaches at the seminary, receives every courtesy at the hands of the Governor, and pronounces him the best unconverted man with whom he had met. He frequently mentions in his journal, as persons to whose fraternal hospitality and kindness he was greatly indebted, the names of Browder, Wall, Phipps, Stateler, Vantress, Stephens, Groves, Bayley, White, Tunstall, Bibb, Ament, Newton, Dixon, and Taylor.

His entire diary breathes the sentiments of one wholly consecrated to God. He says: "This morning I entered into the following resolution: to ask myself twelve times in the course of each day this important question, Am I prepared to die? First, when I awake in the morn; second, third, and fourth, in private retirement that number of times before private devotion; fifth, at family worship; sixth, when I arise on my horse to travel to appointments; seventh, when I alight off my horse at meeting; eighth, when I begin to preach; ninth, in class-meeting; tenth, in private devotion; eleventh, at family prayer; twelfth, when I lie down to rest at night." His diary indicates the faithful observance of his vow.

Whenever he preached, he expected immediate results; and he was but seldom disappointed. "I am alarmed," said he, "when sinners are not converted." No danger daunted him, no privations were shunned. In the pulpit, in the altar, in the social and family circle, everywhere, he was the faithful embassador of Jesus Christ, and "counted not his life dear," if he could be instrumental in the accomplishment of good.

Among the preachers of this period, there was no

one who showed a more profound devotion to the Church than Mr. Blackman. From the time when, a mere youth, he entered upon his ministerial career on the Kent Circuit, until his eventful and useful life was closed, he labored with untiring zeal, and with uncommon success. We regret that he has left us no journal of his travels previous to 1809; but from that period until he passed away, his diary presents to us evidences of ardent piety, unyielding energy, and unreserved consecration to God.

As we pass over his journal, we pause to wonder at the extent of his travels, the severity of his sufferings, and the immenseness of his labors.

From the time he was appointed to the Cumberland District to the close of the first year, he tells us in his journal that he had "rode more than five thousand miles, preached three hundred and forty-one sermons, and to ninety-five thousand and seventy-one persons, though to some of this number over and over again."

During this year, not forgetful of his filial obligations, he visits the home of his childhood, and freely mingles again in the old familiar household. On his way to New Jersey, he preaches at Scarborough, beyond the Cumberland Mountains, at Blacksburg, in Winchester, Georgetown, at Washington City, at the Navy-yard, at Baltimore, at Wilmington, and Philadelphia—making the journey on horseback, amid the snows of winter, preaching all along his route to congregations varying in number from fifteen to two thousand persons, and witnessing almost everywhere rich displays of Divine power.

On the 26th of October, 1809, we find him in Russellville, "dining at a tavern" where he "could scarcely have any peace" for the profanity of persons at the table; and the following day we see him "lost in the swamps of Muddy River," while on his "way to the quarterly meeting on the Hartford Circuit." The quarterly meeting was one of thrilling interest, "a sweet time." In the bounds of this circuit he stops with a Mr. Owen, who "is a remarkable man, professes no religion, but great attachment to the Methodists, and does as much for the Church as any member in the settlement;" and he asks, "Shall he lose his reward?" Laboring side by side with Cartwright, Kennerly, Valentine Cook, McGee, and others, he travels through the country, over roads almost impassable, from thirty to forty miles per day, and preaches to listening hundreds "the unsearchable riches of Christ." The day he was twenty-nine years old, he preached at Russellville—"the nursery of wickedness—in the court-house, to sixteen persons, some of whose hearts were touched."

In 1811, he was appointed to the Nashville District, over which he presided for three years. On the 28th of December, 1812, having just held his quarterly meeting in Franklin, he was invited to enter the army as a chaplain to the Tennessee Volunteers, ordered to the lower country, under the command of Gen. Jackson. After prayerful deliberation, he accepted the responsible position.

He "embarked with Gen. Jackson on the 10th of January, 1813, on board a flat-bottom boat, and in it descended the Cumberland River." During the first night, he "preached on the boat to a few officers and soldiers." Speaking of Gen. Jackson, he says, "He appeared to exert all his power to promote the welfare of the detachment. In very many respects he is well qualified to make a great general. He treats religious characters with respect, and religion with veneration." *

In less than three months, the volunteers were dismissed by order of the Secretary of War, and he was permitted to return to his District, which he reached on the 1st day of April.

During the brief period of his connection with the army, he "learned many lessons of usefulness," besides having the privilege of preaching to the soldiers, and watching over their comfort, as became a minister of Jesus Christ.

On the 22d of the following June, he was married to Mrs. Elizabeth Elliott, of Sumner county, Tennessee, a young widow of fine intelligence and fervent piety.

His last appointment was at the Conference of 1814, to the Cumberland District, which embraced portions of Tennessee and Kentucky.

On the 11th day of November, he entered upon his round of quarterly meetings, and passing through his District like "a flame of fire," success crowned his ministry everywhere. In Kentucky and Tennessee, his quarterly meetings were places of religious feasts, to which thousands came to worship

* Blackman's manuscript.

God. With the same zeal that had distinguished him in the earlier years of his ministry, he prosecuted his "high and holy calling," until throughout his District he was hailed as a harbinger of mercy. The winter had passed away beneath the balmy air of spring, and spring, too, was just fading into summer, when, worn down by constant and unremitting toil, he, accompanied by his wife, made a visit to his brother-in-law and sister, the Rev. John Collins and his wife. He never returned to his work.

The following letter, which we received from the Rev. J. F. Wright, of the Cincinnati Conference, gives the sad termination of his useful life:

"Learner Blackman was drowned in the Ohio River, on June 6th, 1815, about 10 o'clock in the forenoon. He was returning from a visit to the Rev. John Collins and wife (his sister) to his work in Tennessee, having an appointment to preach in Cincinnati on Sunday, June 4th. He tarried in the city over Sunday and Monday, and on Tuesday, in company with Mrs. Blackman, he resumed his journey on horseback, intending to return to Nashville by way of Lexington. He entered the ferry-boat on the Ohio River, about the foot of Main street, Cincinnati. Mr. and Mrs. Blackman dismounted from their horses, and he held them securely by their bridles. On putting off from shore, as the boat was not propelled by steam-power, the managers of the vessel hoisted sail; and the turning of the canvas, and the flapping of the folds with the wind, so frightened the horses that they suddenly leaped overboard, dragging Mr. Blackman with them. In their struggling in the water, they dragged him under; and before any assistance could be rendered, he sank to the bottom. Mrs. Blackman, distracted and beside herself with grief, could with difficulty be prevented from plunging in after him. Alarm was instantly given, and efforts made to recover the body; but it was not till after the lapse of some hours that it was drawn from the water.

"The funeral obsequies were attended to at the 'Old Stone Church,' now Wesley Chapel, in Cincinnati. A sermon was preached by the Rev. Oliver M. Spencer, a local preacher; after which, the remains were interred in the little burying-ground in the rear of the chapel. Here the dust now reposes. A simple sandstone slab was erected at the head of the grave, but the frosts and heat of fifty years have effaced the inscription, leaving only the name barely legible."

From a letter received from Mr. Edward Sargent, of Cincinnati, dated March 24, 1868, we take the following extract:

"There is one circumstance connected with Mr. Blackman's death which I heard from my father-in-law, who resided here at that time, and which my mother-in-law, who is still living, (aged eighty-six,) distinctly recollects. It is this: That after Brother Blackman had been in the water a short time, at two different times he rose to the surface, two boats went out from this shore to his assistance, but an oar of each boat was broken before they reached him, rendering them powerless for aid. It would seem he was not to be saved in that way. *This item is reliable.*"

To us, the Providence is mysterious that deprives the Church of the labors of so devoted and useful a minister as was Learner Blackman.

At the early age of twenty-four, he was elevated to the responsible office of Presiding Elder. Endowed with executive talents of a high order, he discharged the duties of the office not only with ability, but to the satisfaction of both the ministry and the laity in the several Districts over which he presided.

Enjoying in the highest degree the confidence of his brethren in the Conference, he stood at the head* of the list of the representatives of the Western Conference in the General Conference of 1812, the first delegated General Conference held by the Methodist Episcopal Church.

In personal appearance "he was commanding and attractive—nearly six feet high, and remarkably straight. In the pulpit he stood erect, while his address was most pleasing. His voice was soft and agreeable, and its modulations in exact accordance with nature." In every department of his work he excelled. If he preached upon the duties of Christianity, he impressed upon his hearers the paramount importance of a holy life. If he presented the great doctrines of the Bible, he handled error with a giant grasp. Frequently he bore down every thing before him. Inspired often with the grandeur of his

---

*Journal General Conference, Vol. I., p. 97.

theme, he arose to the loftiest heights of oratory, and in words of burning eloquence portrayed the "exceeding sinfulness of sin," and the fearful doom of the ungodly; and then "dipping his pencil in living light," he would "paint the agonies that Jesus bore" on Calvary, while the hundreds who sat before him would be melted to tenderness and tears.

The increase in the membership for this year was *eleven hundred and thirty-five*, which greatly exceeded that of any year before.

In 1804, commencing October 2d, the Western Conference again met at Mount Gerizim, the same place at which it was held the previous year. No Bishop being present, the Rev. William McKendree, the Presiding Elder of the Kentucky District, was elected to preside over the deliberations of the body.

Joshua Riggin, Edmund Wilcox, Abdel Coleman, William J. Thompson, Joshua Barnes, James Axley, Peter Cartwright, Benjamin Edge, Miles Harper, and Samuel Parker, were this year admitted on trial. The names, also, of George Askins and Asa Shinn appear in the Appointments in Kentucky.

Abdel Coleman and Joshua Barnes traveled only one year; Joshua Riggin and William J. Thompson located at the close of their second year's labor. At a later period, however, we find William J. Thompson in the Ohio Conference; but he located in 1831. Edmund Wilcox also retired at the close of the first year, but was reädmitted in 1807, and traveled successively the Maramack and Fleming Circuits, and located at the Conference of 1809.

James Axley, "droll, witty, argumentative, and sometimes powerful," and Peter Cartwright, bold, fearless, and eccentric, entered the itinerant ministry this year. Their labors, however, more properly identify them with the history of Methodism in Kentucky at a later period, where we shall find them.

Asa Shinn traveled four years before he came to Kentucky. He was admitted on trial in 1800, and appointed to the Red Stone, and in 1801, to Shenango Circuit, in the Baltimore Conference; in 1802, to the Hockhocking, and in 1803, to the Guyandotte in the Western Conference. In 1804, he had charge of the Wayne, and in 1805, of the Salt River Circuits. With this year, his labors as an itinerant closed in Kentucky. During the two years in which he had charge of the Wayne and Salt River Circuits, he was distinguished for his ardent zeal, his great success, and his fervent piety. We part with him here for the present, but shall meet him again, when in the full strength of a matured intellect, he occupies prominent positions in the Church.

Benjamin Edge was among the most zealous and indefatigable preachers to be found in the West at this period. We, however, take leave of him for the present, but will meet him again in 1810.

Miles Harper was also admitted this year. He labored in Kentucky only two years, the first on the Red River, and the second on the Lexington Circuit; after which, he was absent from the State for two years; but in the autumn of 1808, he presides over the Cumberland District, embracing within its territory the Red River, Barren, Livingston, and Hartford Circuits. In this field we shall again see him, lifting "the consecrated cross," as a successful evangelist.

George Askins came to the West in 1804. For four years he had been an itinerant, preaching on the Montgomery, Ohio, Shenango, and Muskingum and Little Kanawha Circuits. His first appointment in Kentucky was to the Limestone Circuit; his second, the Hinkstone. In 1806, he was sent to the Lexington, and the following year, to the Danville; and in 1808, he had charge of the Shelby, on which he closed his labors in Kentucky.

In 1809, he was appointed to the Scioto Circuit; and in the spring of 1810, transferred to the Baltimore Conference, where he continued a faithful evangelist the remainder of his life.

The Rev. Jonathan Stamper, in his "Autumn Leaves," in speaking of Mr. Askins, says:

"George Askins was another one of the early preachers in this country, although he was a native of Ireland. I am not able to say when he came to the United States, but he joined our traveling connection in 1801,* and spent the greater part of his ministerial life in the West. He was a man of small stature, and a cripple, one of his legs being withered up to the hip; yet he was more active on foot than any cripple I ever saw. Notwithstanding this bodily infirmity, he was full of spirit, and a

---

* Mr. Stamper follows the General Minutes; but Mr. Askins joined the traveling connection in 1800.

stranger to fear. No threats could deter him from speaking his sentiments, no matter who might hear them, and he would reprove sin wherever or by whomsoever committed. In doing this, he often gave great offense, and on one or two occasions suffered personal injury. He was a great stickler for the peculiarities of Methodism, and used to say that class and love-feast meetings were green pastures beside the still waters. I remember when I was a boy to have gone with my mother to class-meetings held by him, and received impressions under his admonitions which were never erased from my mind, and, I have no doubt, had a salutary influence on my after life.

"Askins was a good preacher because he preached a pure gospel in the power and demonstration of the Spirit. He was fond of combating the various doctrines opposed to Methodism, and managed his subjects with considerable adroitness, although he was sometimes a little too severe, especially when pursued by an opponent. He was an impassioned and often eloquent orator, and I have seen whole congregations stand aghast while he was descanting upon the punishment of the wicked. A certain man, after hearing him upon one occasion, said, 'I do not like to hear Askins: he makes me feel as if I was in the very suburbs of hell; and that is a position I do not like to occupy.' From those harrowing descriptions of torment, he often passed to an eloquent discourse on the joys and triumphs of heaven, growing more and more rapt until he and his audience together broke forth into the joyous exclamation, 'Hallelujah! The Lord God Omnipotent reigneth!'"*

During the five years of his connection with the work in Kentucky, by his constant and assiduous labors, he made good proof of his ministry. Regardless of the toil and sacrifice incident to his "high and holy calling," he cultivated the fields assigned him with the utmost care, and saw, wherever he labored, the most happy results.

In the Baltimore Conference he traveled the Bottetourt, Staunton, Berkeley, Chambersburg, and Frederick Circuits. The Frederick was the last to which he was appointed.

"His last discourse was delivered on Sabbath evening, the 18th of February, 1816, in Fredericktown, to a large congregation, with more than usual zeal and acceptability, when an inflammatory fever immediately ensued, which he bore with great patience and resignation to the will of Heaven.

"On the evening of the 26th, he had a severe conflict with the enemy of his soul; but was enabled to declare that God had delivered him, and immediately commenced singing, Glory! glory! glory! hallelujah!

"The evening preceding his death, his afflicted companion asked him, 'My dear, are you going to leave us?' To which he replied, 'Leave that to the Lord—if I go, I shall go happy.' A few minutes before his departure, he saw his affectionate wife kneeling by the bed, and asked her if she was will-

*Rev. Jonathan Stamper, in Home Circle, Vol. III., pp. 213, 214.

ing to let him go: she replied, 'That is hard to say, but I desire to be resigned to the will of God.' He answered, 'That is right,' and took his leave of her. During his illness, he continually gave himself up to his God in prayer, frequently calling upon the surrounding friends to sing and pray, expressing an unshaken confidence in God, and a desire to depart and be with Christ, and even to his last moments would raise his hands and praise God.

"He retained his senses to the last, and about ten minutes before his exit, asked his Christian friends to sing, 'O glorious hope of perfect love.' Some of his last words were, 'The Lord our God is *my* God;' 'O what a beautiful prospect lies before me!' 'Holiness is the way to heaven;' 'Be ye clean that bear the vessels of the Lord—get all you can in the way to heaven—my God is mine and I am his—I have been in the dark mountains, but King Jesus has given me complete victory—glory, honor, praise, and power be to God!'

"He died on Wednesday morning, about four o'clock, the 28th of February, 1816, in the triumphs of faith, and with a hope full of glorious immortality." *

Samuel Parker, who was this year admitted on trial in the Western Conference, and appointed to the Hinkstone Circuit, was among the most devoted and useful of the preachers of his day, and soon rose to eminence in the Church. His labors in Kentucky, however, belong more properly to a later

---

* General Minutes M. E. Church, Vol. I., pp. 277, 278.

period. In 1814, we shall meet him on the Kentucky District, "a burning and a shining light."

We record this year the death of Wilson Lee. Prostrated in health, he had left Kentucky in 1793, after contributing so largely to the planting and the formation of the character of the infant Church in the West. He returned to the Baltimore Conference, with which he had previously been identified, and remained to the close of his useful life. With the exception of two years—one of which he was supernumerary on the Montgomery Circuit, and the other, which was his last, superannuated—he had been an effective laborer. Worn down in health, to the very last, "his zeal for the Lord would urge him on to surprising constancy and great labors." The labors on the Baltimore District, on which he performed his last work as an effective preacher, while not more than equal to his zeal, far surpassed his strength, and did much to hasten his death.

In April, 1804, he was taken, while in prayer with a sick person, with a heavy discharge of blood from his lungs. At his death, a blood-vessel of some magnitude was supposed to break; so that he was in a manner suffocated with his own blood in a few minutes. He died at Walter Worthington's, Anne Arundel county, Maryland, October 4, 1804." *

However gratifying to catch the last words of such a man, as he enters the river, or to listen to the notes of triumph falling from his dying lips as he obtains a glimpse, for the first time, of his heav-

* General Minutes, Vol. I., p. 128.

enly inheritance, yet we need not these to assure us of his entrance into rest.

The Livingston Circuit, which had been formed in 1803, under the indefatigable labors of Jesse Walker, had so extended its boundaries previous to the Conference of 1804 as to embrace the counties of Henderson and Ohio.

In the Minutes of 1804, the work in this department is recognized under the style of "Livingston and Hartford," to which Jesse Walker and Joshua Barnes were appointed.

Previous to the Conference of 1804, a quarterly meeting was held at Isham Browder's, in Hopkins (then Henderson) county, embracing the 17th and 18th days of August, at which the following official members were present: Lewis Garrett, Presiding Elder; Jesse Walker, Assistant Preacher; Miles Harper, Joshua Barnes, Thomas Taylor, James Axley, Wiley Ledbetter, Josiah Moors, John Travis, Benjamin Parker, Taylor White, Isham Browder, Pleasant Axley, Moses Shelby.

At this Quarterly Conference, James Axley and Joshua Barnes were "recommended to travel."

Before Mr. Walker had embraced Ohio county in the Livingston Circuit, under the efficient labors of a few local preachers, societies had been formed at Goshen, Bethel, and No Creek, in that county.

"The first Church organized in Ohio county was at Goshen, two miles south of Hartford, in the year 1804. Very shortly after this, in the same year, another Church was organized at Bethel, seven miles north-east of Hartford. Next, and about the same time, in the same year, No Creek Church was organized.

"These Churches were established as the result of a great revival which took place in December, 1803, commenced by the Presbyterians, in connection with two or three local preachers, who had settled in this part of the country.

"The first and leading local preacher connected with this work was Thomas Taylor, a man of more than ordinary ability and decisive character; and, through his influence, the masses of the converts were led into the Methodist Episcopal Church.

"Associated with him was Lodwick Davis, also a man of good preaching ability; also Joshua Barnes, of ordinary talents.

"During the Conference-year commencing in the fall of 1804, this circuit was blessed with extensive revivals of religion. They swept, like fire in dry stubble, all over the country. The people went from far and near to attend them—were awakened, and converted to God." *

These early societies were a nucleus, from which went out a fine religious influence into all the surrounding country. From the time of their first organization to the present, they have prospered, being the scenes of many revivals of religion.†

---

* Letter from the Rev. H. C. McQuown, of Hartford, Kentucky.

† The society at Goshen now worships in a neat and commodious frame church, numbers nearly *eighty* members, and enjoys an average degree of spirituality. The society at Bethel enjoyed a fine revival of religion last spring, in which *thirty-five* were converted, and *thirty-eight* added to the Church. Class-meetings are kept up by them.

During this year, Mr. Walker entered Breckinridge county, and organized a society at Thomas Stith's, on the road from Hardinsburg to Louisville, sixteen miles from the former place. The names of the members who composed this society were: Thomas and Rhoda Stith, William and Nancy Stith, Richard and Betsey Stith, Matthew Sanders, Mrs. Jordan and her two daughters, (Lucy and Katy,) Little Dick Stith and his wife, and Betsey Hardaway—*thirteen* members.

"A few years afterward, Stith's Meeting-house, a log church, was built, at an obscure point, four miles west of Big Spring. The first camp-meeting in this county was held on Sugar-tree Run, sixty years ago, under the supervision of John Craig." *

In this community Methodism has always prospered, and at the present period presents one of the most interesting fields in the State.

They have a neat frame house of worship. The society at No Creek, three miles north of Hartford, had a good revival in January. Its fruits were *thirteen* conversions and *twenty-one* additions. It numbers now about *ninety*. They have a new, large, frame church—the best in the country—and keep up class-meetings. There is also a society ten miles north-east of Hartford, (time organized not known.) They have a large frame church, *one hundred and sixteen* members, and enjoy an average degree of spirituality. A society, seven miles east of Hartford, with *twenty-nine* members, in good condition. They have a new frame church. Six miles north-east of Hartford is the Union society, numbering *twenty-eight*. They worship in a log house. In Hartford the society numbers *sixty-five*.—*Letter to the author from the Rev. H. C. McQuown, dated Hartford, Kentucky, January* 23, 1867.

* Letter from the Rev. H. C. Settle to the author, dated Big Spring, Kentucky, June 11, 1867.

The original thirteen members were burning and shining lights. Without a single exception, they all died in holy triumph. The last of the number, Katy Jordan, (first the wife of the Rev. W. F. King, and, after his death, of the Rev. Pleasant Alverson, both itinerant ministers in the Methodist Episcopal Church,) survived the others, having died in hope of eternal life, in Breckinridge county, in 1867.

The most of them were remarkable for their zeal, but none more so than William and Nancy Stith. Mrs. Stith, before her conversion, had been fond of the gayeties and amusements of the world; and when she embraced religion, she was equally zealous as a Christian. At home, in the family circle, as well as in her private devotions, she frequently praised God aloud. In the house of God her feelings often overcame her, and she shouted his praises.

On one occasion, the minister, interrupted by her shouts, requested her, in a private interview, to restrain her feelings until he should close his sermon. Unwilling to be a source of annoyance to any one, the old saint readily promised, and requested him, if he should observe any signs on her part of an intention to shout, to wink at her, and she would repress her feelings. At the first meeting after this interview, he thought he discovered indications of her purpose to shout, and he gave the promised wink. In a moment she was calm, but it was only for a moment. He winked again, and again her feelings were subdued. Once more her countenance, beaming with joy, told too plainly of the ent-up emotions struggling to be free; and once more the preacher winked, but it was in vain. She arose from her seat, exclaiming, "Brother, you may wink, and you may blink, as much as you please, but I must shout!" Her end was joyous and triumphant.

We have already referred to Thomas Taylor,* a local preacher, to whose influence and labors the Church in Ohio and the surrounding counties was so much indebted for the organization of the early societies. He was born in Frederick county, Virginia, February 26, 1763. His parents were poor, but of high respectability, and bequeathed to him the legacy of a pure and unsullied character. His father and mother were reared in the Church of England, and endeavored to instill into their children the principles of Christianity. Independent in thought from early childhood, he became impressed with the excellency of Methodism, and at twelve years of age he was a member of the Church, and when quite young became a local preacher.

In 1802, with his small family, he came to the West, and was among the first to raise the standard of Methodism in the Green River country.

Among the early local preachers in Kentucky, for his untiring devotion to the Church, he was not surpassed. The opposition to Christianity, so common among the early settlers in the State, so far from arresting his efforts to accomplish good, was

---

* He was the father of the Hon. Harrison J. Taylor, of Hartford, Kentucky.

to him only an incentive to extraordinary exertion. The country being destitute of ministers, Mr. Taylor traveled extensively, having appointments at distances remote from his home, in the territory now embraced in Henderson, Hopkins, Muhlenburg, Butler, Grayson, Hardin, Larue, Hancock, Daviess, and McLean counties.

To promote the welfare of the Church, and to advance its interests, was one of the highest aims of his noble life. Without the advantages of early education, by close application to study he so far improved his mind as to become one of the most popular and influential preachers in the Green River country.

Thoroughly versed in the Holy Scriptures, his vindication of the doctrines of Methodism was resistless, while, "with words that burn," he impressed the practical duties of religion on the minds of the hundreds who heard the gospel from his lips. Without appealing to the passions of the people, he stirred the depths of their hearts. Usually plain, yet argumentative, he sometimes "arose with his subject, and, giving utterance to his own feelings, he would dwell on the beauties of religion, the sublimity of the Divine attributes, the deep and dying love of the Saviour, and the horrors of the day of retribution, when justice shall be meted out. On occasions of this kind, his language would flow with that deep, intense, native sublimity, which no art or study can equal." *

* Letter to the author from Mr. H. J. Taylor.

Inflexible in his purposes, and uncompromisingly opposed to sin, he exposed its hideousness, in whatever shape it assumed, and in whatever circle it moved. Influenced only by the purest motives, and possessing sterling integrity, he made no allowance for the aberrations of others, but, unmasking vice in the varied walks of life, he administered the most scathing rebukes, taking the Bible as the great stand-point from whence he defended the doctrines of his Church; as, in his life, he aimed to be governed by its holy precepts.

When more than seventy years of age, and only two years before his death, he changed his Church-relations, entering as a minister the Methodist Protestant Church. This involved no change in doctrines, yet it would be gratifying to us, if he had remained to the close of life in the Church he had labored so faithfully to plant and build up.

On the 25th day of April, 1836, he departed this life, at his own home, in Ohio county, Kentucky, in full assurance of a blessed immortality.

To no one man is Ohio county so much indebted for the moral and religious influence they now enjoy, as to Thomas Taylor.

His wife, Margaret Taylor, who had borne with her husband the privations and sacrifices of pioneer life, and had stood side by side with him in the great battle for religious truth, survived him nearly twenty years. She belonged to the representative women of Methodism in Kentucky. After a long life of usefulness, on the 25th of October, 1855, she closed her eyes in death.

We make the following extract from a letter we received from her son, Judge Taylor, of Hartford, Kentucky:

"My mother retained her membership in the old Church until her death. I well recollect her consulting with me as to her course, and after she had summed up, I was more than ever convinced of the propriety of her course, and so was every other person, even my father.

"From that day, however, she might have been classed as a member of each. Her house, her heart, and her purse were alike open to all. The members of the old Church loved her more than ever for remaining with them, while the Protestant Methodist revered and respected her for her firmness and decision of character."

The Licking Circuit appears on the Minutes this year, for the first time. It had been detached from the Limestone Circuit, and embraced in its territory the village of Newport, and had for its first preacher Benjamin Edge. On the 10th of September, 1805, we have the following record in Bishop Asbury's Journal: "Next day I called on Elijah Sparks, at Newport, and baptized two of his children. We dined with the widow Stephens. I rejoiced to find that a new circuit had been formed, and there were several growing societies. Much of this has been effected by the faithful labors of Benjamin Edge."

Although the increase, as reported in the Minutes for this year, was considerably less than the year previous, yet all the circuits had been blessed with precious revivals of religion, and in every charge there was an increase, except the Hartford, the Limestone, and the Salt River and Shelby Circuits. The decrease in the Limestone may be accounted for by the formation of the Licking Circuit. The total increase was *three hundred and sixty-three.*

The Western Conference for 1805 was held at Griffith's, in Scott county, Kentucky, commencing October 2. Bishop Asbury was present, accompanied by Bishop Whatcoat. He says:

"*Wednesday, October* 2. We opened our Conference in great peace. There were about twenty-five members present. Six hours a day were steadily occupied with business. The Committee of Claims and of Addresses did much work, and it was done well. I completed my plan for the coming year, and submitted it to the Presiding Elders, who suggested but two alterations—may they be for the best! On the *Sabbath-day,* I preached to about three thousand souls. On *Tuesday,* after the rise of Conference, I rode to Lexington; and on Wednesday, to J. P. Hoard's, Jessamine county. I was under affliction of body, but perfect love, peace within, and harmony without, healed every malady."*

Thomas Hellums, Henry Fisher, Samuel Sellers, David Young, and Moses Ashworth were admitted on trial.

The names, also, of Joshua Oglesby, William Ellington, William Houston, and Richard Browning appear for the first time in the list of the Appointments for Kentucky.

---

* Asbury's Journal, Vol. III., pp. 203, 204.

The name of Thomas Hellums gathers around it a melancholy interest. His uniform piety, his fervent zeal, and his commanding talents as a preacher, together with his tragic end, at once awaken our anxiety.

His parents were pious, and they instructed him in religion from an early age. He was awakened under the ministry of the Methodist Church, and soon after his conversion became a preacher.

From the time he was admitted into the itinerant ranks until the Conference of 1813, he labored without intermission in Kentucky, Ohio, Tennessee, and Mississippi. Worn down by constant toil and exposure, he was compelled to seek for rest, and in 1813 asked for a location.

In a local sphere, he first engaged in teaching school as a means of support; but, compelled to relinquish this for want of health, he entered upon "the practice of law, having previously studied that profession." Impressed, however, with the belief that it embarrassed his ministerial and Christian standing, he abandoned it.

Subsequent to his location, his labors for the Church, so far as he had strength, were characterized by the same untiring zeal that had distinguished him as an evangelist.

Under protracted "affliction of body, his mind became a ruin, and the remainder of his life was spent in a state of partial insanity. During this period he traveled extensively, and preached often; and it is remarkable, that no trace of derangement could be seen in his discourses. He investigated subjects with clearness and force, but immediately after leaving the pulpit exhibited signs of his malady. He was fearful of all who came near, imagining them to be enemies who were trying to injure him, and often exhibited defensive weapons as a means of deterring them.

"The end of this good brother was melancholy. While traveling in what was then the Territory of Arkansas, he fell in with some acquaintances, who induced him to attend a camp-meeting. But he seemed to be greatly harassed by fear from the time he reached the camp-ground, and could not be persuaded to preach until some time of the day on Sunday, when he took the stand, and preached one of the most lucid and powerful sermons those present had ever heard. On leaving the pulpit, he became deeply deranged, manifesting alarm at the approach of his best friends, whom he forbade to come near him, at the same time showing in his hand a large knife. He at length got his horse, and started from the meeting, (which was held on the border of an immense prairie,) out into the trackless waste, and has never been heard of since. Whatever became of him, none are able to tell. Some imagine that he was murdered by highwaymen, who were known to infest that region. He rode an uncommonly fine gelding, and the presumption was, that they destroyed him for the sake of getting his horse. What strengthens this supposition is, that his horse and accouterments have never been heard of either. It is said that, some months afterward, the skeleton of a man was found, away out in the prairie, but there was nothing left to form a clue to his identity. So it was: Thomas Hellums must have perished in that far-off solitude, without any to minister to his wants, or to bury him. He is lost to the world; but we have no doubt that God has taken him to himself, and that he now stands among those who have gone up through great tribulation. He was an able and useful preacher, greatly beloved by those who knew him, and much lamented in his death." *

Henry Fisher remained in the Conference but a single year, when his name disappears from the Minutes.

Samuel Sellers and David Young, who entered the Western Conference this year, became useful and eminent ministers of Jesus Christ. In another volume we shall trace them in the various fields they occupied, and witness their labors in the cause of truth.

Moses Ashworth entered the Conference this year, and located in 1809. His first appointment was to the Salt River Circuit, after which he was sent successively to the Wayne, Silver Creek, and Holston. We, however, find him again in 1817, a member of the Tennessee Conference, and in charge of the Lebanon Circuit. At the close of this year he again located.

William Ellington and Richard Browning had entered the Western Conference the previous year, but each spent only one year in Kentucky—the

* Rev. Jonathan Stamper, in Home Circle, Vol. III., pp. 214, 215.

former on the Wayne, and the latter on the Hinkstone Circuit. After traveling four years, the two latter in Ohio, Mr. Ellington located.

The labors of Mr. Browning were more extensive. He remained in the itinerant field until 1810, during which time his name stands connected with the Roaring River, Hinkstone, Clinch, Natchez, and Cumberland Circuits. He traveled on the Cumberland Circuit two years.

Extensive as were the labors of William Houston, from 1804, the time of his entrance into the Conference, until his location in 1817, they were bestowed almost entirely on other and distant fields. In 1805, he was appointed to the Livingston, and in 1807, to the Limestone Circuit; after which, we find him no more in Kentucky. In Tennessee, Ohio, Mississippi, Maryland, and Virginia, he nobly prosecutes his glorious work. At the Conference of 1817, he located.

The labors of Joshua Oglesby belong more properly to a subsequent period.

It was also during this year that the first society was organized in Louisville, at that time a small village, embraced in the Salt River and Shelby Circuit.

We regret that the names of the members composing it have not all been preserved. Among them, however, are the names of Mrs. Morrison, William Farquar, Thomas Biscourt, and Messrs. Catlin and Mosely. They worshiped in a small schoolhouse that stood on the ground now occupied by the court-house, and prayer and class-meetings were held at Thomas Biscourt's, who lived on Jefferson street, between Seventh and Eighth.

In a subsequent volume we propose to give a succinct history of Methodism in Louisville, and hence take leave of it for the present.

The increase for this year was only *four hundred and thirteen.*

In 1806, the Western Conference was appointed to meet at "Ebenezer, Nollichuckie, in Tennessee, September 15th." The session, however, did not begin until the 20th.* Bishop Asbury presided.

At this Conference Abbot Goddard, Hector Sandford, Joseph Bennett, and Frederick Hood, were admitted on trial.

The only field of ministerial labor occupied by Abbot Goddard in Kentucky was the Barren Circuit, to which he was appointed this year. In Ohio he preached for many years. He located in 1810, but in 1814, we again find him a member of the Conference. In 1822, he again locates, but in 1829, we find him on the list of superannuated members of the Ohio Conference, on which he remains until 1841, when he again located.

Hector Sandford was admitted this year, and after traveling the Limestone, Miami, White River, and Mad River Circuits, located.

Joseph Bennett traveled successively the Danville, Scioto, Barren, and Guyandotte Circuits, after which his name disappears from the Minutes.

Frederick Hood was this year appointed to the

---

*Asbury's Journal, Vol. III., p. 236.

Salt River Circuit, and in 1807, to the Guyandotte, after which no mention is made of him.

Zadoc B. Thaxton, a name familiar to the Methodists of Kentucky for half a century, was admitted on trial in 1805, and appointed to the Nashville Circuit. The following year, he enters Kentucky as an itinerant, in charge of the Red River. In 1807, we find him, with untiring energy, prosecuting his labors on the Duck River Circuit. Failing in health, at the Conference of 1808, he is placed on the *supernumerary* list, and appointed to the Roaring River Circuit, having for his colleague that excellent man, John Travis. In 1809, somewhat restored in health, he travels the Barren Circuit, and located at the close of that year. We here take leave of Mr. Thaxton for the present. In a future volume we shall meet him again, in the itinerant field, a faithful minister of Jesus Christ.

Abraham Amos, who entered the Conference in 1803, was appointed that year to Natchez, with Moses Floyd, Hezekiah Harriman, and Tobias Gibson. In 1804, he was sent to the Miami and Mad River Circuit, and in 1805, to the Guyandotte, in Virginia. He appears, for the first time, in 1806, in Kentucky, and is placed on the Licking Circuit, and the following year on the Livingston. His next appointment is to the Missouri Circuit, and in 1809, he is appointed to the Illinois. At the Conference of 1810, he located.

Joseph Williams was admitted on trial in 1804, and appointed to the Hockhocking Circuit; in 1805, to New River. In 1806, he came to Kentucky, and was appointed to the Hinkstone; in 1807, to the Whitewater; and in 1808, to the Scioto; and located in 1809.

The name of John Thompson only appears in the Minutes for the years 1805 and 1806; the former year he was appointed to the Mad River, in Ohio, and the latter, to the Hinkstone Circuit, in Kentucky.

William Hitt was admitted in 1805, and appointed to Powell's Valley, and in 1806, to the Danville Circuit; and then his name disappears from the Minutes.

Joseph Oglesby had been an itinerant for three years before he entered Kentucky as a preacher. His appointment for 1806 is to the Shelby Circuit. At the next Conference, he removed from Kentucky, but we shall meet him again, in 1811, on the Salt River Circuit, faithfully discharging his duties as a minister of Christ.

But little attention had as yet been paid to the erection of church-edifices in Kentucky. "The first deed for ground on which to build a church, on record in Mason county, is dated 1806. The lot contained an acre, and was located about two miles above Maysville, where a road came to the Ohio River, and a town called Rittersville was at an early date laid out. Harry Martin, for the sum of one shilling, sold an acre of land to build a house of worship for the Methodist Episcopal Church. Samuel Shrouck, Benjamin Pollard, John Shepherd, John Pollard, Leonard Simms, Richard Ritter, and James Miles, were the trustees." *

* Letter to the author from Dr. M. F. Adamson, of Maysville, Kentucky.

The religious excitement, that had prevailed in Kentucky since 1799, had somewhat abated. Besides, the Territories beyond the Ohio River were inviting emigration from Kentucky, and hundreds of families, influenced by the cheapness of the lands, had accepted the invitation, and were leaving the State; yet, with all these disadvantages, the Methodist Church continued to increase in membership. At the close of this year, we are able to report an increase of *two hundred and sixteen members.* This year is distinguished for the extension of Methodism into the far West. The name of Missouri Circuit appears in the Minutes for the first time.

The Western Conference for 1807, was held at Chillicothe, Ohio, September 14. Bishop Asbury again presided. He says: "On *Monday*, we opened our Conference in great peace and love, and continued sitting, day by day, until Friday noon. A delegation of seven members was chosen to the General Conference. There were thirteen preachers added, and we found an addition of two thousand two hundred members to the society in these bounds; seven deacons were elected and ordained, and ten elders; two preachers only located; sixty-six preachers were stationed." *

After the adjournment of the Conference, Bishop Asbury visited Kentucky, passing through Cynthiana, attending "the Camp-meeting at Mount Gerizim," and preaching at several points.

At this session of the Conference, Thomas Still-

* Asbury's Journal, Vol. III., p. 268.

well, John Craig, William Lewis, Jacob Turman, Mynus Layton, Henry Mallory, and Josiah Crawford, were admitted on trial.

Thomas Stillwell, Mynus Layton, and Josiah Crawford traveled each in Kentucky only one year. In 1807, Thomas Stillwell was appointed to the Livingston Circuit, Mynus Layton to the Limestone, and Josiah Crawford to the Shelby.

John Craig, who was admitted this year as an itinerant preacher, was appointed to the Hartford Circuit. Plain, eccentric, and faithful in the discharge of his ministerial duties, he labored assiduously in the effective ranks, until the Conference of 1835, when he was appointed to Kingston Circuit, (Holston Conference,) as supernumerary. At the next Conference, he was placed on the list of superannuates, where he remained until he was released by death. In a subsequent volume we shall give some account of his labors and his life.

William Lewis traveled only three years. His appointments were to the Hartford, Dixon, and Henderson Circuits. He located at the Conference of 1810.

Jacob Turman spent the first two years of his itinerant ministry in Kentucky, on the Limestone and Hartford Circuits. In 1809, he was appointed to the Roaring River, in 1810, to the Guyandotte, and in 1811, to the St. Vincennes Circuit. In 1812, he was returned to Kentucky, and placed in charge of the Christian Circuit, then in the Wabash District, in the Tennessee Conference. At the Conference of 1813, he located.

Henry Mallory was connected with the Conference for four years, all of which were spent in Kentucky, on the Lexington, Shelby, and Hinkstone Circuits.

James King, who was this year appointed to the Wayne Circuit, had entered the ranks as an itinerant at the previous Conference, and traveled on the Hockhocking Circuit. In 1807, his name appears on the roll for Kentucky. He remained in Kentucky two years, having spent the second on the Limestone Circuit. In 1809, he was appointed to the Saltville Circuit, and located in 1810.

Sela Paine had also joined the Conference in 1806, and after traveling the White River Circuit in Ohio, was appointed in 1807 to the Wayne Circuit, in Kentucky, where he remained for two years. In 1809, his appointment was to Silver Creek, in Indiana. The following year, he is sent to the Natchez Circuit, and in 1811, to the Wilkinson, both in Mississippi. In 1812, we find him prosecuting his labors on the Holston Circuit, and the following two years, on the Nollichuckie and Abingdon. He located at the Conference of 1815.

Milton Ladd entered the Conference in 1806, and was appointed to the Scioto Circuit. In 1807, he enters Kentucky, and is placed in charge of the Licking Circuit. In 1808, he is appointed to the Tennessee Valley Circuit, and in 1809, he labors on the Lexington Circuit, and locates at the close of the year.

Joseph Hays, whose name stands this year in connection with the Lexington Circuit, became an itinerant preacher in 1802. He first appeared on the Stafford Circuit, and then traveled successively the Fairfax, Pendleton, Littleton, and Tioga, all in the Baltimore Conference. He spent but six months on the Tioga Circuit, when he was transferred to the Western Conference, and appointed to the Hock-hocking, in Ohio, and the following year, which closes his labors as an itinerant, he preaches in Kentucky, on the Lexington Circuit. In 1808 he located.

Among the men who gained a merited distinction in the Church, we mention with pleasure the name of Elisha W. Bowman. The sacrifices he made, the privations he suffered, and the labors he performed, as one of the pioneer preachers, entitle him to the gratitude of the whole Church in the South and West; and his great usefulness embalms his memory in the hearts of thousands. In our next volume we will make a record of his faithful labors.

The rapid progress that Methodism was now making in the West, was an occasion of devout gratitude to God. The Silver Creek Circuit, in the Indiana Territory,* was formed this year, and placed upon the Minutes in the Kentucky District, and Moses Ashworth appointed in charge of it. In Southern Kentucky, our work was enlarging. A small society this year "was organized, about ten

*As early as 1793, there was a preaching-place about one mile from Utica, which is a few miles above Louisville, on the Indiana shore, where Judge Prather, William Farquar, and John Bate held their membership. This place was included in the Salt River Circuit.

miles north of Russellville, consisting of Philip Kennerly, Jane Kennerly, John Hanner and his wife, and John Groves and his wife. This little band of six members worshiped for a few years, in a private house, when they built a neat log house in 1811, and called it Kennerly's Chapel." * It "was also during this year that the Rev. Richard Pope, mentioned in a previous chapter, passed through Logan county, and preached at the residence of John Price, about seven miles north-east of Russellville. In that neighborhood, soon after, a society was organized, of which Maxey Price, Thomas and Mary Johnson were members." †

About the same time a society was organized at the Pond Meeting-house, about two miles north-west of Franklin, in Logan (now Simpson) county. A few Methodists had settled in this county, among whom were Messrs. Slocum, Wright Taylor, and Edward Hall. Under the labors of these pious laymen, a meeting was held at Mr. Hall's,‡ which resulted in a blessed revival of religion. Shortly afterward, a flourishing society was organized, and the Church known as the Pond Meeting-house, erected.§

These organizations became centers of Methodism in their respective localities, and sent out a healthful religious influence into all the country around.

---

* Letter to the author from the Rev. A. C. Dewitt, of Logan county, Kentucky.

† Letter from the Rev. A. C. Dewitt.

‡ Edward Hall became a preacher.

§ Letter from the Rev. J. F. Redford.

They have been the scenes of many revivals, and at the present period enjoy prosperity.

The increase in the membership in Kentucky for this year was *five hundred and forty-three.*

We have not failed to observe the large number of the preachers, whose names disappear from the roll of the Conference, after they had traveled a few years. Indeed, many of them only remained for a single year in the itinerant field. This cannot be attributed either to any want of stability, or of devotion to the Church. The privations, the sacrifices, and the exposures, incident to the life of a traveling preacher, at this period, as well as the great amount of labor to be performed, exceeded the strength of the majority of men.

It is gratifying, however, to know that these men, when, with impaired health, they were compelled to dissolve their connection with the Conference, carried with them into their retirement, hearts devoted to the great work in which they had been engaged, and in a sphere more circumscribed, they contributed their influence and their energy to the welfare and prosperity of the Church. In them the itinerant preacher always found wise counselors, and the Church, in the communities in which they located, patterns of patience and of piety.

We think this an opportune period at which to close our first volume.

Only twenty-two years had elapsed since the name of the "Kentucky" Circuit first appeared in the General Minutes of the Church. Two men, influenced by the highest motive—the salvation of souls—had left the comforts of home, to preach the gospel of Christ to the early settlers in the District. In the prosecution of their glorious work, with their lives in their hands, they encountered perils at every step. Their successors, too, have passed in review before us. During this period some had gone from labor to reward. We are not only permitted to recount the privations, sacrifices, and toils of these noble men, but the remarkable success with which their ministry was rewarded. Instead of a single circuit in Kentucky, we have twelve pastoral charges, in which twenty-two preachers are employed, and comprising a membership of *six thousand three hundred and eighteen.*

Since the Conference held in the spring of 1800, the population of Kentucky had increased less than *one hundred per cent.*, while, during the same period, the membership of the Methodist Episcopal Church had increased nearly *three hundred per cent.*

Nor were the beneficial results of the labors of our fathers confined to Kentucky. While embodying, as Methodism does, the true spirit of apostolic Christianity, it continually increased in strength, so that it became incorporated by degrees into the various religious systems in the State, imparting to them its vitality and energy. At the same time, it looked beyond its own limits, upon each rising State, on our borders in the West, and became the center from which the whole West has been evangelized.

As early as 1799, the Miami Circuit, in the North-western Territory, appears in the Minutes; in

1803, the Illinois; in 1806, the Missouri, and in 1807, the Silver Creek, in Indiana, and at an earlier period, in Middle and East Tennessee, Circuits had been formed, and flourishing societies organized, and to "the lowlands of Mississippi" the message of salvation had been sent, and the tidings of mercy proclaimed. As at this time we look upon the vast field embraced in this Western Conference, of which the Kentucky Circuit, formed in 1786, was the nucleus, with its *five districts, forty-one circuits, sixty-six traveling preachers, and fifteen thousand two hundred and two white* and *seven hundred and ninety-five colored members,* extending from the Lakes in the North to the Gulf of Mexico, and from the Alleghany Mountains in the East as far toward the setting sun as civilization had made its impress, we stand amazed, and with hearts filled with gratitude, exclaim, "What hath God wrought!"

THE END.

www.ingramcontent.com/pod-product-compliance
Lightning Source LLC
LaVergne TN
LVHW020924110826
845150LV00004B/763